Meister Eckhart on Divine Knowledge

MEISTER ECKHART
ON
DIVINE KNOWLEDGE

C. F. Kelley

DHARMACAFÉ BOOKS
COBB, CALIFORNIA

NORTH ATLANTIC BOOKS
BERKELEY, CALIFORNIA

Published by DharmaCafé Books
P. O. Box 1289
Cobb, California 95426

and

North Atlantic Books
Berkeley, California

Cover and book design by Matt Barna
Printed in the United States of America

Meister Eckhart on Divine Knowledge is sponsored and published by the Society for the Study of Native Arts and Sciences (dba North Atlantic Books), an educational non-profit based in Berkeley, California, that collaborates with partners to develop cross-cultural perspectives, nurture holistic views of art, science, the humanities, and healing, and seed personal and global transformation by publishing work on the relationship of body, spirit, and nature.

DharmaCafé Books' publications are available through most bookstores. For further information, visit our Web site at www.dharmacafe.com.

North Atlantic Books' publications are available through most bookstores. For further information, visit our Web site at www.northatlanticbooks.com or call 800-733-3000.

Library of Congress Cataloging-in-Publication Data

Kelley, C. F. (Carl Franklin), 1914-?
  Meister Eckhart on divine knowledge / by C.F. Kelley.
    p. cm.
  Originally published: New Haven : Yale University Press, 1977.
  Includes bibliographical references and index.
  Summary: "Explicates the mystical teachings of Dominican theologian Meister Eckhart"—Provided by publisher.
  ISBN 978-1-58394-252-9
  1. Eckhart, Meister, d. 1327. 2. Mysticism—Germany—History—Middle Ages, 600-1500. I. Title.
  BV5095.E3K44 2008
  248.2'2092—dc22
                                2008035598

3 4 5 6 7 8 9 OPM 20 19 18 17
North Atlantic Books is committed to the protection of our environment.
We partner with FSC-certified printers using soy-based inks
and print on recycled paper whenever possible.

To
J.L.K.

When I stood in the Principle, the ground of Godhead, no one asked me where I was going or what I was doing: there was no one to ask me. . . . When I go back into the Principle, the ground of Godhead, no one will ask me whence I came or whither I went. There no one misses me, there God-as-other passes away.

—Meister Eckhart

Contents

Foreword

Although it is only in the past few decades that the late medieval German Dominican spiritual master Meister Eckhart has come to be regarded as the greatest of all Western Christian mystics, in the nearly seven centuries since his death he has exerted an extraordinary, if largely unacknowledged, influence upon Western culture. Besides Johannes Tauler and Henry Suso, direct disciples who themselves became eminent theologians, the list of those who have come under Eckhart's enduring spell includes such spiritual and philosophical luminaries as Jan van Ruysbroeck, Nicholas of Cusa, Jakob Boehme, G. W. F. Hegel, Friedrich Schelling, Arthur Schopenhauer, Rudolf Steiner, C. G. Jung, Martin Heidegger, and Thomas Merton. Their company was swelled by the post World War II wave of scholar-practitioners of Asian religions, including D. T. Suzuki, Ananda Coomarsaswamy, Aldous Huxley, and Alan Watts. Given Eckhart's extraordinary East-West appeal, unprecedented for a Christian mystic, it is surprising that even today there are only a mere handful of truly worthy English language studies of his writings. While this is at least partly due to the fact that it was only relatively recently, in the 1980s, that we were provided with reliable English translations of both Eckhart's principal German and Latin works,[1] it surely also reflects the ongoing ambivalence with which the Western church has regarded Eckhart's underlying non-dualism. (Despite the current scholarly consensus that Pope John XXII's condemnation of portions of Eckhart teaching, in the infamous *In agro dominico,* issued in 1329, but two years after Eckhart's death, relied upon a mistaken interpretation of his teachings, the condemnation has yet to be revoked by the Church.)

Among the leading studies of Meister Eckhart, three books stand out as indispensable. Bernard McGinn, the great contemporary historian of Western Christian mysticism, wrote two of them. *The Mystical Thought of Meister*

Eckhart: The Man from Whom God Hid Nothing and *The Harvest of Mysticism in Medieval Germany* give us the widest possible view of Eckhart's life, work, and philosophical and theological context. The third, Carl Franklin Kelley's *Meister Eckhart on Divine Knowledge,* is their perfect complement, adding an incomparable depth to McGinn's capacious breadth. In my view, no other study of Meister Eckhart has so well penetrated to the marrow of the great Dominican teacher and preacher's philosophical and theological achievement. In the process of exploring what he has called the "axial theme" in Eckhart's teaching—his insistence that we learn to "think principially...*in divinis*", which is to say, from the point of view of Divinity Itself, Kelley has also managed to produce the greatest philosophical and theological exegesis on non-dualism to come out of the Christian tradition.

*   *   *

Like many of my generation, I first read Meister Eckhart at the behest of scholars who recognized the unique affinity between his writings and Eastern non-dual wisdom. Although deeply impressed by him, as a secularized, would-be ego-fulfilling Westerner, I could neither accede to Eckhart's insistence upon the necessity of Divine Grace (to be received and known through "the birth of the Word") nor respond to his call to a pious life of demonstrated "detachment," which I read as a life-long sentence to ascetical renunciation. The world beckoned large and it was not difficult to put Eckhart, necessary Grace, and unwelcome self-discipline aside in favor of the more amenable popularizations of Taoism and Zen Buddhism delivered by Orientalists who, after all, admired him as much as I did.

Several years later, well after I took refuge at the feet of the Divine Avataric Master, Adi Da Samraj, justly regarded to be a uniquely great non-dual Realizer,[2] I came across *Meister Eckhart on Divine Knowledge.* Having by now greatly benefited from intensive study and practice of my own Master's Teachings while receiving a small ocean or two of His Divine Grace, I was far better prepared to take Kelley's master class in the profundities of late medieval mysticism.

Although the text is rigorous and demanding, I was riveted by his exposition of Eckhart's doctrine of "unknowing knowledge" and his companion teaching of "naked," "structureless," or "pure" *isness*. I had just been through an amazing season of Adi Da Samraj's revelatory instruction on just those themes. For days and nights on end, I had heard Adi Da discourse plainly, truly to "everyman," on what He called "Divine Ignorance," all the while employing seemingly every ordinary and extraordinary means to simplify us down to the Realization that "all there is is *Is*." While Eckhart employed the apparatus of Scholastic theology, Adi Da Samraj's own teachings are entirely *sui generis*. Besides sharing common themes, however, both men dared preach "in the vernacular" to the lowborn of their times. Although I was well aware of Eckhart's ultimate limitations—his teaching's absence of a functional psycho-physical esotericism and, despite his insistence that the true path is without mode or structure, his advocacy of the universal human tradition of what Adi Da Samraj terms "the great path of return" (to God, Self, or Reality) via dissociative introversion—Kelley's book nevertheless left me in wonder at Eckhart's instinct for the philosophical marrow of non-dual Realization.

* * *

Meister Eckhart (1260–1328 C.E.) was a singularly extraordinary man living at the apogee of one of the most creative periods of cultural change the Western world has ever known—the High and Late Middle Ages. Despite its pogroms, inquisitions, and the Crusades, historians rightly see the twelfth century as the beginning of a "medieval renaissance." The fervent devotional mysticism of Bernard of Clairvaux and St. Francis of Assisi softened the ascetical world-denial so characteristic of Augustinian spirituality, releasing an evangelizing ideal into a rapidly urbanizing Western Europe. Charged with a zeal to "teach and preach," and patronized by a rising bourgeoisie, the new mendicant orders—especially the Franciscans and the Dominicans— brought both scriptural education and spirituality out of the

monasteries and into the laity. The reconquest of Spain
infused a vigorous, absorptive Scholasticism with the riches
of Islamic science, philosophy, and theology, helping
Europe's proliferating cathedral schools and great new universities to gather students and teachers from across Europe.
Both within and without the academy, the teachings of the
Schoolmen may have jostled with both monastic and vernacular theologies, but all were united by the fact that the life
devoted to contemplation yet remained the public ideal. A
sensus spiritualis, the instinct to identify the animating sacred
principle in all things, informed all forms of learning. Thus,
although the social structure of the High and Late Middle
Ages was rigidly hierarchical, the cultural separation between
popular culture and the academy that we take for granted
today was far less in force at that time. This is why, in the esti-
mation of Bernard McGinn, "the period 1200–1350 was
arguably the richest era for the production of mystical literature in the whole history of Christianity."[3]

Meister Eckhart's daring vernacular sermons were widely
celebrated in his own day. Shadowed by the heretic-hunting
archbishop of Cologne, Henry II of Virneburg, the coura-
geous Dominican *lebemeister's* stunningly original biblical
exegeses, homilies, and theological arguments were
recorded by nuns and no doubt repeated by monks, nuns,
and throughout the hundreds of households of celibate,
quasi-cloistered women, the famous beguins, who were
determined to pursue the apostolic life in towns and cities
throughout France, Germany, and the Netherlands. Many of
these beguin households associated themselves with
Dominican priories, not least to avoid inquisitorial scrutiny,
and Eckhart surely served some of them as well. Therefore,
his non-dual teachings appeared within a vigorous religious
and spiritual environment. The thirteenth century was witness to a veritable explosion of female spirituality led by, but
not limited to, the beguins, and much that Eckhart had to
say was clearly meant to help them transcend the visionary
and absorptive mystical paths that epitomized spiritual life
in his time.

* * *

It is precisely in regard to his non-dualism that Meister Eckhart has so often been subject to confusions and misunderstandings, the principal expression of which has been the controversy over whether he should be regarded as a "mystic" or as a "philosopher." Of course, the short answer is that Eckhart was both. Why in this book, then, does Kelley takes such great care to deny that Eckhart was a "mystic"? And, if he was not a mystic—indeed a surpassingly great mystic, what is the word we should use to describe what kind of spiritual figure he actually was?

Adi Da Samraj has spoken to this. In His description of the great path of return, He makes a fundamental distinction between the mystical search for *salvation* via participatory "union" with God and the transcendental search for *liberation* via awakening to the certainty of "Divine Knowledge" of one's "identity" to the Divine Reality. The latter is the characteristic goal of the Oriental quest for Enlightenment, epitomized by the ancient Vedic expression "Tat Tvam Asi" ("You Are That"). Spiritual union with the Creator-God, however, is the highest reach of the Semitic religions. In the words of Jeanne Ancelete-Hustace, one of Eckhart's biographers, "The mystical life of the Christian is a life of union with God given to the soul by Grace."[4]

Even so, there is a reason why sainthood is most often a posthumous acknowledgement. The medieval church was only grudgingly tolerant of mystics who confessed to achieving great intimacy with God. When doing so, they were expected to acknowledge that their experience of union was only temporary, positively describe God's Attributes via analogy with human virtues, affirm an unbridgeable difference between creature and Creator, and otherwise endorse the ultimacy of Papal authority. Eckhart never challenged that authority, but his doctrine of Divine Knowledge was a fundamental critique of all forms of experience and knowledge via union with God because these always presuppose a relational distinction between the devotee and the Divine. Once we become capable of the participatory disposition, we must go beyond it.

[P]articipatory knowledge, even at its mystical heights
and no matter how extensive, is well short of and
never to be confused with pure knowledge, from
which all-inclusive standpoint every limited mode of
knowledge is relationally naught. It is the relational
ignorance of those who confound participatory knowledge with pure knowledge, as well as the total ignorance of those who think they know by adopting a
stance of "looking at" reality, that the doctrine of
Divine Knowledge is ordained to destroy.[5]

To transcend this "stance of 'looking at' reality" is to move
beyond the root egoic conceit that Adi Da Samraj calls "the
illusion of relatedness," the subject-object distinction itself.
This is what appears to take place in the event of Eckhart's
famous "breaking-through" (*durchbrechen*):

In the breaking-through, when I come to be free of
will of myself and of God's will and of all his works and
of God himself, then I am above all created things,
and I am neither God nor creature, but I am what I
was and what I shall remain, now and eternally.[6]

It is the moment celebrated in the *Lankavatara Sutra*, one
of the core texts of Mahayana Buddhism, as "a 'turning
about' in the deepest seat of consciousness."[7] Adi Da Samraj
explains that the "breaking-through" is occasioned by a
"revulsion to all possibility," which, in its ultimate form, he
describes as "the Realization of 'positive disillusionment' relative to the causal (or root-egoic, and, therefore, fundamental or original) subject-object division in Consciousness
(or Conscious Light) Itself."[8] In that event, Kelley tells us, we
move beyond the *exstasis* of mystical exaltation known via
union *with* God to the post-mystical *instasis* of identification
as the Divine Self. Such a development does not make a person a philosopher. It makes him or her a sage.

Meister Eckhart's great and salutary genius was to
unabashedly advocate this great leap—this "breaking-
through"—to "knowledge through identity." Kelley's bril-
liant exposition of Scholastic theology convincingly demon-
strates that Eckhart's radical turn nevertheless remained

within the bounds of Christian theology. Although he is by no means the first scholar to make the case for his orthodoxy, Kelley makes a crucial distinction between Eckhart's teaching and the rest of the Western mystical tradition that I believe all other scholars have missed.

Immediately after acknowledging that Eckhart appeared "to bring the medieval theological development to a conclusion not far removed from the pure monism of Vedanta," the cultural historian Christopher Dawson goes on to affirm his orthodoxy in this way:

> [W]hen Eckhart asserts that God is all, that creatures are a sheer nothing and that it is a fallacy to speak of God as good, he is merely expressing in paradoxical and unguarded language the commonplaces of Dionysian theology which are to be found in a more balanced but no less complete form in the standard works of Ulrich of Strasburg and of St. Thomas himself.[9]

By "Dionysian theology" Dawson means the *apophatic* mysticism of the Pseudo-Dionysius (also known as Dionysius the Aeropagite), the name given to an unknown fifth-century monk who was heavily influenced by Neoplatonic philosophy and whose impact upon the entire Christian tradition can hardly be overstated. Both Eastern Orthodox and Western Christian mysticism trace their origins to his writings. The word "apophatic" literally means "saying away," and instead of cataloging and affirming God's positive attributes (by analogy to human virtues) via so-called *cataphatic* mysticism, the *apophatic* mystics practice a *via negativa* in which they assert God's ultimate unknowability. In so doing, they seek to strip the aspirant of the comforts and consolations of every kind of presumptive assertion about both self and Divinity. St. Augustine, the Scholastic mystics, the anonymous English author of *The Cloud of Unknowing*, and many other mystics were enormously influenced by the Pseudo-Dionysius' insistence upon God's ultimate unknowability.

Few mystics can safely be relegated to any single philosophical category. One of Eckhart's most influential contemporaries, the French beguin mystic Margaret Porete, who was burned at the stake in 1309, strongly demonstrated both *apophatic* and *cataphatic* elements. But Kelley is eager for us to understand that her notion of the "annihilation" of the ego-soul (which, by the way, could well have been influenced by the Sufi doctrine of *fana,* or "extinction") falls short of Divine Knowledge. "Annihilation" of the will and intense, even rapturous absorption in the Divine may well temporarily suspend the sense of egoic selfhood. However, unless the "unlimited will to know" is fully satisfied in Divine Knowledge, the shadow of individuality yet remains. He writes:

> Thus it is that while "negative theology" closely approximates Divine Knowledge insofar as it indicates Godhead as its Principle, it falls short of finally constituting us wholly within the supreme Principle. That there are further considerations in Divine Knowledge that lie beyond the content of "negative theology" is clear, inasmuch as this content is restricted to the simple denials of certain multiple possibilities of individual determination. But the content of Divine Knowledge is manifest and unmanifest All-possibility, as already explained. It is the person who, by uncreated grace, realizes "I know God, yet I do not know him" that Eckhart refers to as being blessed with "unknowing knowledge," and who is truly saved by being liberated from all that is not in function of Divine Knowledge.[10]

From this perspective, even Bernard McGinn's description of Divine Knowledge as a "radical apophaticism" in which we realize our "fused identity" with the Godhead might be a hedge—for, in the Realized Simplicity of the indistinct Unity or Isness of Being, how can there be any separate anyones to be fused or joined together?

* * *

That being said, it is extremely important to understand that we cannot simply choose to be identified with God—a will-less event that by definition no ego can willfully accomplish. Although Eckhart calls us to "think principially," his non-dual teachings do not relieve us of the necessity of the profound moral, religious, and, eventually, spiritual preparatory disciplines required of all true aspirants, however apparently dualistic such a submission might appear to be. C. F. Kelley's own career as a Christian scholar and practitioner (he spent years in England's Downside Abbey under the demanding Rule of St. Benedict) is itself testimony to this process.

C. F. Kelley published only four books in his life, three of them in the early 1950s. Of the latter, one was a translation, accompanied by his extensive introduction, of *The Book of the Poor in Spirit by a Friend of God,* a perhaps spurious early history of Rhineland mysticism that obviously speaks to Kelley's lifelong preoccupation with Meister Eckhart and his milieu. The other two were on St. Francois de Sales, the Reformation era French Catholic apostle of "the Way of Divine Love." One of these was his pocket-sized selection of de Sales' "spiritual maxims." Kelley wrote its companion volume, *The Spirit of Love: Based on the Teachings of St. Francois de Sales,* in a beautiful devotional style. In that book, he brings an advanced religious practitioner's sympathies and sensibilities to bear on de Sales's deep reflections on the role of love in "the devout life," the *via affectiva,* all the while displaying great psychological acuity regarding the tasks and trials that love demands of all serious spiritual practitioners. While unfailingly orthodox, Kelley is not afraid to offer his very genuine and heartfelt ecumenical appreciation of other devotional traditions. (A subchapter of the book titled "Bhakti Religion' unabashedly celebrates Hinduism's great devotional schools.) It is the kind of book found in all enduring religious and spiritual traditions where a mature practitioner organizes his or her hard-won wisdom in a manner that will illuminate the path for generations of those who will follow.

Having celebrated the great virtues of dualistic religious devotion in the first half of his career, Kelley took nearly two decades to do the research and writing that became *Meister*

Eckhart on Divine Knowledge—ample time to understand the
dualistic limitations that tend to characterize the *via affec-*
tiva. Not that love and wisdom are in any way mutually
exclusive. Although the Dominicans were renowned for
their insistence upon the primacy of the *Intellectus,* the intuitive faculty whereby we apprehend Divine Oneness, none
of them, including Eckhart, ever failed to acknowledge and
affirm that Divine Knowledge is always accompanied by
deeply felt devotional love, and that the Love that accom-
panies Divine Knowledge fully encompasses and ultimately
transcends both creature and Creator. For in Divine
Knowledge the ego-self and the God that is the ego-self's
other vanish in the Godhead (*Gottheit*) that is also the Divine
Ground (*Grund*).

* * *

There is a serving genius behind C. F. Kelley's *Meister Eckhart*
on Divine Knowledge, the fruit of a lifetime spent in homage
to and emulation of Meister Eckhart. Although this is a
demanding book, it abundantly rewards our deepest intuitive intelligence. I believe that anyone with a serious interest in spiritual Realization, whatever the tradition he or she
might favor, will find that it is absolutely worth his or her
time.

William Stranger
September 7, 2008

Preface

This book on the essential teaching of Meister Eckhart is the result of many years of personal study. My introduction to Eckhart's writings came about through the suggestion of one of my professors at the University of Berlin in the mid-1930s. At that time, however, there was still much confusion in the minds of scholars as to the genuineness of the published texts. Not only were many of the German Sermons and Tractates of the famous Pfeiffer edition held in question, but only a fraction of the extensive and vital Latin works were in the process of being made known through the publications of the Sancta Sabina series in Rome.

Word was out, however, that the Research Commission of the German government was sponsoring professors Josef Quint, Josef Koch, and their colleagues in a new and promising project of Eckhartian research and scholarship. The genuine Latin and German works of the Meister began slowly (interrupted by World War II) to be published in the excellent ten-volume Kohlhammer quarto edition, which, although a few portions and the indexes still remain to be published, is a critical and definitive production that far surpasses all previous editions. Despite the fact that the Meister never completed certain parts of the *Opus Tripartitum* and some other writings are known to have been lost, the student is at last in a position to arrive at an objective understanding of his teaching.

It was not until the early 1950s, when I was a Benedictine and a member of Downside Abbey in England, that my comprehensive study of Eckhart began in earnest. I was aided in my work by Dom Raymond Webster, the Abbey librarian, and members of the Thomas-Institute at the University of Cologne, where the major research work on Eckhart was in progress, and where I participated in medieval conferences. Then came two years of further research at the Grabmann-Institute of Medieval Studies at the University of Munich, for whose Archives I wrote a lengthy two-volume investigation of Eckhart's insights into "Principial Knowledge." A few of my articles also appeared in the *Downside Review* and suggested the need of an understanding and exposition of Eckhart's teaching that was completely different from those which had previously dominated the field of Eckhartian scholarship. The doctrine in question definitely called for a mode of study that transcended all philosophical and theological approaches, including that of "mysticism."

In other words, in writing this book I have made a concerted effort to follow Eckhart's counsel and adopt the standpoint of understanding and exposition that he himself adopted. The comprehension in my work is constituted as it were within God in his Godhead and not externally in terms of approach toward God. For Eckhart clearly states that the doctrine he expounds must always be considered from that *in divinis* standpoint.

What is here presented to the reader supersedes all former interpretations of Eckhart's teaching. It refuses to ignore what he precisely and repeatedly says cannot be ignored, that is, his exposition of the doctrine of Divine Knowledge in terms of the highest and most essential of all possible considerations. Certain previous studies of Eckhart's teaching are valid as far as they go—but they confine themselves to understandings which he denotes as externalizations to the basis of the doctrine. By that very fact they restrict and hence tend to distort that knowledge which is, in principle, wholly within Godhead and therefore pure and strictly divine.

Josef Quint, Jacques Maritain, and Aldous Huxley, who as friends were familiar with my studies and papers, urged me some fifteen years ago to write and publish what they considered a much needed book on this axial theme in Eckhart's teaching, but I regarded such a project as premature. The Kohlhammer publications were then only half completed, but I had access to Eckhart's genuine works in unpublished form through the Thomas and Grabmann institutes. Nevertheless much further study was needed on my part in order to present an exposition of a doctrine which, if not grounded in reflective metaphysical study, as well as in authentic sources, would otherwise run the danger of misleading the reader. For the same reasons I then felt obliged to turn down requests to write special articles on Eckhart's teaching for the *Dictionnaire Spiritualite* and the *Encyclopaedia Britannica.*

As a result of an ignorance of Eckhart's Latin writings and hence a great, though understandable, overemphasis on his German works, including several that are spurious, the interested public has been too long misled. What has for the most part, especially in English-speaking countries, been acknowledged as the teaching of the Meister can only be considered as a travesty of the doctrine in the name of which he speaks—the doctrine of Divine Knowledge. What is needed, of course, is an insightful English translation of all the works of Eckhart. To date the most reliable translation into English is that published by James Clark in England (about one-fourth of the German and a few excerpts of the Latin works), though his introductory interpretations of Eckhart's teaching are largely from the point of view of a philologist and deficient in metaphysical understanding. And such understanding is of prime importance, especially in the case of Eckhart.

Understanding, not erudition, is the concern in presenting this book, and it is the truth of Eckhart's profound insights that demand reflective consideration. While it has seemed appropriate to supply references, this has been done simply to show that the statements and insights attributed to Eckhart are derived from reliable sources. In any attempt to convey the true meaning of Eckhart's words as we have them in medieval Latin and German, however, literal translation into modern English would be unprofitable, if not an impossibility. Hence in working directly from the medieval Latin and German texts of Eckhart and by relying in part on the direction of Quint's scholarship and translations into modern German from the *Mittelhochdeutsch,* which he published separately, *explicatio interclusa* has been necessary when dealing with certain words, phrases, and even whole sentences. Moreover, I do not, and

I trust the reader will not, consider the use of the word *isness* pedantic, for any other way of rendering into English that which Eckhart means by *esse,* as a noun, promotes confusion.

One could quote extensively from either the Latin or the German works on nearly every important point in this presentation. Not always have the most inciting or eloquent passages been selected for exposition, but those which, I think, best serve the purpose of this meditative study. Unfortunately very little of Eckhart's humor, especially the deliberate, yet frequent, play on words and the subtle digs at stuffy rationalists and pious romanticists, can be conveyed in English. Even so, the reader should be aware that Eckhart is in no sense "heavy" in the typical Kantian mode, nor has his teaching anything in common with any modern or heterodox school of thought. Being wholly traditional in the truest sense, and therefore perennial, the doctrine he expounds will never cease to be contemporary and always accessible to those who, naturally unsatisfied with mere living, desire to know how to live, regardless of time or place.

This book, then, is not likely to appeal to those who, through some frustration of intelligence and a misdirection of the will to know, are self-determined subjectivists, mystics, or pious pretenders to a knowledge that is not divine in origin, and who present us with little more than caricatures of wisdom. It is meant, rather, for those who are dissatisfied with any teaching restricted by the mental horizon of mere human thought, who are disturbed by the closed systematizations of neotheologies, who are not seduced by the supposition that the grass is greener on the oriental side of the fence. It is likewise meant for those who continue, despite the pervasion of the socially irrational, to seek an abiding ground beneath the quicksand of relative values—in other words, all who somehow manage to retain a sense of intelligent inquiry and a trace of their innate and detached will to know. The evidence seems to indicate that such persons, especially among the young, are countless, and perhaps are ready to welcome a guide and teacher such as Meister Eckhart. There is, however, a great difference between contemporary modes of study and knowing how to study, particularly the writings of a great contemplative metaphysician who lived seven centuries ago. This book, then, may serve at once as a guide for learning how the doctrine that Eckhart expounds should be studied and as a means toward gaining insights into that doctrine, since both are inseparable in his exposition.

A special debt of gratitude must here be expressed to the editors and publishers of the Kohlhammer edition; to the Hanser publishers in Munich for Josef Quint's *Meister Eckhart;* and to all present and former colleagues in Germany and England, especially Christopher Butler, the former Abbot of Downside and now Bishop in the archdiocese of Westminster, without whose direction my study of Eckhart would have been overexposed and hence thwarted at a crucial point of development.

C.F.K.
August 1976

Introduction

Meister Eckhart has represented one of the most fascinating and frustrating puzzles ever to preoccupy the interests of research scholars. Until a hundred and fifty years ago the name of Eckhart had remained clouded in suspicion and almost total mystery. Then the Sherlock Holmeses of medieval history, particularly in Germany, began to apply their newly acquired skills to this enigma, deducing here and dusting off there. Though their investigative work fostered many misleading theories, as might be expected, it has finally removed much of the mystery and practically all of the suspicion. Still, it seems quite likely that some parts of the puzzle will never be solved.

Be that as it may, we now know that Eckhart von Hochheim (b. 1260-d. 1328) must be ranked on a par with the most profound intellects and spiritual guides of Christendom and, indeed, of our whole Western civilization. His authentic writings, together with his sermons as recorded by devoted students, unfold a traditional doctrine the sublimity of which can hardly be matched by any other human exposition.

The essential doctrine, in the name of which Eckhart speaks and which determines all particular aspects of his teaching, is the doctrine of Divine Knowledge.[1] It is the doctrine of "unrestricted knowledge itself" which, being unconditioned and beyond distinctions, transcends all manifest acts of intellection, just as it transcends every possible mode of experience.

Thus, contrary to widely accepted opinion, the doctrine expounded by Eckhart is not to be found in the study of mystical experience or even in what is normally understood as mysticism.[2] Nor is it to be found in the disciplines of theology or philosophy. To regard the doctrine under any of these aspects is to miss the mark and assure one's failure to gain insight into its axial content. Indeed one thereby desig-

1

nates oneself as an alien to a true apprehension of knowledge *in divinis,* the mode of which is strictly transcendent to and hence inversely different from any of these other modes of knowledge, valid as they may be within their own province. And to emphasize this difference Eckhart will call it "unknowing knowledge," which characterizes the meaning of the term "Divine Knowledge," constituted as it necessarily is within *Divinitas,* or Godhead.

In relation to Divine Knowledge even genuine religious mysticism is already an externalization. This is so by the very fact that it presupposes and maintains throughout a correlation between God and the self and emphasizes the experience, inexpressible as it may be, of sensing contact with God, of perceiving his presence in the soul and in individual manifestation. But it is not unrestricted knowledge itself, not God in his undifferentiated Godhead, with which Eckhart is pre-eminently concerned. "Undifferentiation," he says, "is proper to Godhead, differentiation to the creature."[3] Mysticism always retains a certain, though subtle, degree of differentiation.

Though mystical or negative theology closely approximates Divine Knowledge it is nevertheless to be distinguished from it, inasmuch as it implies an intellective state still grounded in the manifestation of that unrestricted and unmanifested knowledge itself. Though true as far as it goes, it is not situated as it were wholly within that purely transcendent order.[4] It is this latter consideration which constitutes the standpoint of the doctrine Eckhart expounds. While he does at times speak in terms of negative theology, which likewise far transcends his limitation as a writer and teacher, only confusion results if we recognize him primarily as a mystic, even in the genuine sense of the term.

Moreover, the proper limit of that genuine sense of "mysticism" has in modern times been stretched beyond the possibility of intelligent definition. It has fallen into the absurdities of being identified with esoteric occultism, the use of Allegory and symbol, mysteriousness, ideology, psychophysical phenomena such as visions and ecstacies: usages that have added to the difficulties of a complex subject and brought that higher intellection and moral decision which it expresses into disrepute. This is another, though secondary, reason for saying that the doctrine expounded by Eckhart is not to be found in mysticism.

Theology is even more external than genuine religious mysticism by reason of its formal or cataphatic knowledge of God, that is, knowledge of God established in structure and individuality. Rooted though it should be, but rarely is, in structureless or negative knowledge of God, theology is at best only an approximation to unconditioned Godhead. As for philosophy, it designates a standpoint of knowledge that is much more external than theology and hence is still further removed from the subject that Eckhart invites us to study and insists that we *must* study if we would understand reality as it truly is.

The purely transcendent knowledge with which Eckhart is fundamentally concerned does not partake of any of these higher or lower modes of individualized knowledge. But in order to be genuine *they* must somehow partake of *it,* at least in the sense of acknowledging it as the Principle of which they are but mere reflections. Thus the particular studies that go to make up these manifold and therefore restricted modes of knowledge cannot be regarded as containing Divine Knowledge, which in itself is unmanifested. Being all-inclusive, it cannot be contained in any distinctive mode of knowledge—in fact, the modes may turn out to be stumbling blocks by reason of the all too frequent mental oversights that result from a secularized kind of education.

In order to apprehend the doctrine that Eckhart expounds a special inquiry undertaken externally is of little use. It is not primarily a question of social science, philology, or psychology, or, as already noted, of philosophy, theology, or mysticism, inasmuch as all these studies, in one degree or another, pertain to that order of knowledge which Eckhart clearly considers as external. His consideration of them as external is not from disdain, but simply because that is the nature of their modes. His understanding of philosophy, theology, and also the mystical theology of Pseudo-Dionysius the Areopagite was very profound, and he was one of the great language masters of all time. But he regarded such understandings as really distinct from and reducible to the ultimate objective of the unlimited will to know.

The saintly John Tauler, who as the foremost student of Eckhart undoubtedly knew and understood the Meister better than any of his contemporaries, said in one of his sermons: "This wonderful Master spoke of that pure knowledge that knows no form or creaturely way. . . . He spoke in terms of eternity and you (regrettably) understood in terms of time."

Eckhart himself is quite clear concerning that "purely transcendent mode," wholly grounded as it is within unrestricted knowledge itself which infinitely and eternally is. The unassailable consideration of that mode he calls "pure metaphysics," or "detached intellection," and for good reason. After all, the order of knowledge thus signified as really transcending universal manifestation in every respect must involve an intellective standpoint that is supraindividual, supranature, beyond distinctions and situated as it were within the all-inclusive Principle. What is paramount throughout the writings of Eckhart is his recognition that it is only insofar as any question whatsoever is related to principles that it can be said to be treated in truth and therefore metaphysically. Since, however, all questions for intelligence must ultimately be related to the supreme Principle, which is unrestricted knowledge itself, then it is *pure* metaphysics that must be the fundamental intention.

If our notion of metaphysics is restricted to ontology and epistemology, which are respectively inquiries into "being" and "the course of human knowing," and drawn by abstraction from the world of our unregenerate, ungraced daily experience, Eckhart will rightly say that our notion of metaphysics is relatively impure. Though lit by the light of reason, though true and necessary as far as it goes *in via,* such a consideration, according to Eckhart, obviously limits itself by a certain insufficiency of means implied in an overvaluation of the conceptul graspings of the rational faculty of the intellect. It also limits itself by not drawing its intellection directly from within the formless light of divine revelation, from not first of all establishing itself *in divinis, in* Christ the Word, the unrestricted act of knowledge itself.[6] It is this truth that must always be kept central so long as the intention is to treat of *pure* metaphysics and not that of philosophical metaphysics, which is limited by its standpoint in universal manifestation.

Thus the doctrine of Divine Knowledge is properly to be acknowledged as a purely metaphysical doctrine, transcending all experience, all abstractions or conceptual graspings of the mind and, indeed, all individual manifestation and determined mystical states. Hence it opens up truly unlimited possibilities of insight. As such it can in no way be enclosed in any experience, mystical or otherwise, or in any system whatsoever.

Philosophy, like theology, cannot do without system. And the test of its ongoing value is whether or not it is a truly open system or, better, a method or course of questioning wholly constituted in the detached and unlimited will to know. If it is grounded in a participation in reality, points the unlimited will to know in the direction of the unlimited act of comprehension, and implies its own transcendence by supplying the requisite springboards, it may be regarded as open and also of great assistance to the human intellect. If, on the contrary, as is the case with most modern philosophy, it aborts the unlimited will to know by stopping to take a mental gaze at reality as though it were something "out there" separate from the knowing subject, thus shutting off any possibility of transcendence, it merits no further consideration. For then it is nothing but a closed conception, the more or less restricted limits of which are determined by the mental outlook of its author.

Already we can recognize a profound and irreducible difference, a difference in principle, distinguishing the doctrine of Divine Knowledge from anything that is included under the name of "open" or "participative" philosophy, rare and deserving of respect as that is. For in pure metaphysics, or in the detached intellectual consideration of unrestricted knowledge itself, even an open systematization is strictly impossible. Why? Because in pure metaphysics, as understood by Eckhart, the eternal Word is the "author" and everything pertaining to individual and structural order is absent.

In other words, Divine Knowledge is totally detached from all contingencies and from every manifestation of the unconditioned Principle, whether philosophical or otherwise. This is necessarily so because unrestricted knowledge itself is, in principle, that which God is in his Godhead, and such knowledge can in no way be enclosed within any structure, or even in any individual mystical state, however comprehensive it may be. This explains why, as Eckhart points out, there is no question of the individual intellect ever attaining a direct comprehension of the substantial essence of God when pure metaphysics is correctly considered. If this is so it is for the simple reason that in pure metaphysics God is not, in principle, apprehended in terms of individuality or in terms of the distinctions necessarily implied in the substantial essence of an intellective objective.

Though the terms "theology" and "Divine Knowledge" are in a sense etymologically equivalent, it must always be remembered that theology, when genuine, designates the formal and distinctive understanding of God and the supernatural order. Thus it is an understanding veiled in and therefore qualified by the structural manifestation of the ultimate Principle. Though it may reach beyond structure toward pure Spirit or infinite Personality, theology nonetheless cannot, of its very nature, transcend distinctive determination. Nor is it in its province ordained to do so.

On the other hand, *That* which Eckhart renders indicatively as Godhead or Divine Knowledge (for the want of any better term unless it be "unknowing knowledge") is the supradeterminate and indistinguishable Principle in itself, the unrestricted knowledge which God in his Godhead is. For the purely transcendent standpoint basically implies the consideration of God wholly as it were within the Principle. That means the consideration of God neither as *an* essence nor as a person, but of that which transcends all notions both of essence and of person; it is of God in his undifferentiated and indistinguishable Godhead. The infinite Personality in itself is indeed God's Self-affirmation as identically Knowledge and the Principle, but inasmuch as theology distinctly determines that Personality in relation to all manifestation, it by that very fact already indicates a relational understanding and hence a consideration from without.

Genuine theology, then, is the highest of the relational considerations and comprises the most profound of all determinations and distinctions. Still it must be acknowledged as constituted in qualified and distinctive knowledge. That which God intrinsically is in the undifferentiated Godhead is unqualified, strictly unconditioned, beyond distinctions and determinations, and in relation to it the entire order of manifestation as such is nothing.

Metaphysically, understood, manifestation can only be apprehended from the standpoint of its participation in and dependence upon the supreme Principle and in the quality of a support for the vault into that pure transcendent knowledge. As such, and therefore when considered in the inverse order, the participatory ontology and theology inherent in Eckhart's exposition of the doctrine, both in their positive and negative aspects, is an application of truth as in the supreme Principle. In any case, nothing more should be expected from all that pertains to participatory understanding—that is to say, nothing more than an indispensable support or springboard primarily designed to facilitate an openness to the uncreated grace requisite for a sustained insight into the unmanifested and unrestricted knowledge which God is.

It goes without question for Eckhart that the doctrine of Divine Knowledge is signified especially and directly by the Word, both revealed in Holy Scripture and incarnate in Christ.[7] Thus it is the sacred and traditional doctrine in its integrality, for this precisely is the significance of the Word considered as God's unique communication to man. It discloses the supreme Principle and also the common basis of the more or less secondary and derivative aspects that comprise those diverse conceptions in which certain people have affirmed so many rival and opposed systems.

Insofar as these conceptions are in accord with their transcendent ground they obviously cannot in truth contradict one another. On the contrary, they are bound mutually to complement and elucidate each other. But this in no way implies a syncretism, for the essential doctrine must be understood as integrally comprised in principle within the Word, beyond dialectic and from its primal source. Moreover, in its integrality sacred tradition, or that which is transmitted by the Word, forms a perfectly coherent whole; which however does not mean to say an enclosed systematic whole. And since all the genuine interpretations that it contains can as well be considered simultaneously as in succession, there is nothing really to be gained by inquiring into the historical order in which they may actually have been developed and rendered explicit.

This is why "Eckhartianism" is out of the question. Indeed, to study Eckhart is not primarily to study the early fourteenth-century teacher, but to meditate on the formless light of transcendent knowledge with which the intellect is coincident and in which this innermost contemplative metaphysics always takes its stand. It is for this reason that we are not here primarily concerned with the life and times of Eckhart the man. The reader who for some reason regards biographical understanding as helpful may easily consult other books on Eckhart for what little there is to be known.[8] True, Eckhart's expounding of the perennial doctrine actually began only a generation after the death of St. Thomas Aquinas and mainly in the schools of Paris and the Rhineland. Nevertheless he fully acknowledged that while exposition may be modified to a certain degree externally in order to adapt itself to this or that personal situation, the basis of the tradition always remains unchanged, and any outward modifications in no sense affect the essence of the doctrine.

The fundamental harmony of a conception with the essential principles of the tradition is the necessary and sufficient condition of its genuineness. Since these principles are wholly comprised within the Word, which is identical with the all-inclusive Godhead, it follows that it is agreement with the Word that constitutes the criterion of unassailable truth. In this sense it is, of course, the New Testament that unfolds the doctrine of Divine Knowledge strictly speaking inasmuch as it is directly inspired of Jesus Christ the incarnate Word himself and, as effected by the Holy Spirit, is a faithful recording of God's communication.

The New Testament not only forms the latter portion of Holy Scripture, but what is taught therein, so far at least as it can be taught, is the final and supreme aim of traditional and sacred knowledge in its entirety. In this sense it is detached from all the more or less particular and contingent applications derivable from it. And if the fourth or last Gospel ranks as supreme it is because, being the final Gospel, it pre-eminently sets forth in direct manner the very Divine Knowledge with which Eckhart is above all concerned. Thus one cannot insist too strongly that it is the New Testament which here discloses the primordial and fundamental tradition and consequently constitutes, in figures of speech and thought, pure knowledge in principle. From this it follows that in a case of doubt as to the interpretation of the doctrine, it is always to the primary and unconditioned meaning of Holy Scripture, and not to philosophers and theologians, formal or mystical, that it is necessary for the authority of the Christian Church to appeal in the last resort.

What the Scriptures and the sacred tradition essentially teach goes beyond all humanistic dimensions. What is not to be resisted is the call to vault beyond the limits of social science, philology, anthropology, and psychology, and also the limits of experience, conceptualization, and individuality. Not by denying their forms from without, but by transcending them within, and that can only be within the all-inclusive Principle itself.

No manner of scientific research can clearly and distinctly establish the communication of God which reveals the mode and reality of Divine Knowledge. This is not a miracle, not a "gnostic idea," and it requires from the critic who hopes to gain insight into it something far more than secular comprehension, ontological understanding, or mystical experience. The miraculous can be demythologized, reality analysed, and the wondrous explained, though little of real worth is gained thereby. But the persistent communication of the Scriptures will not go away. From the standpoint of individual manifestation the communication is irreducible: God intervenes in time, the infinite shatters the finite whereby the Word becomes known to man, and the course of human knowledge is interrupted and is never again the same. For the communication of the Word unfolds the intrinsic nature of Divine Knowledge. In other words, the unique possibility is granted man to understand all things in principle from the standpoint as it were of the unconditioned Godhead, the actual realization of which is strictly contemplative and wholly transcendent in mode.

Eckhart makes his purpose very clear: "It is the intention of the writer (Eckhart himself)—as it has been in all his works—to expound by means of the natural demonstrations of the philosophers, the doctrines taught by the holy Christian faith and the Scriptures of the Old and New Testaments."[9] In other words, well-grounded belief is seeking knowledge. Not merely the knowledge which justifies the belief, but pre-eminently that knowledge which transcends experience, human reason, and universal manifestation. Moreover, the means of expounding it to other knowing beings must not, of course, be repugnant to philosophical intelligence. It is in this sense that the Meister's Latin and German Expositions, Treatises, Tractates, and Sermons must be studied in their integrality, for they are essentially metaphysical commentaries on scriptural texts.

It should never be forgotten that Eckhart was wholly committed to the reasonable belief that Holy Scripture, "the testimony of God's unconditioned meaning for man and the world through Jesus Christ," is the direct result of divine inspiration. Thus it is in its own right that Holy Scripture maintains its unique authority, and in order to do so it must be independent of all other authority. In the same stroke,

however, Eckhart believed that in order to extol and preserve that authority, as well as to teach the doctrine of
Divine Knowledge that it contains, the Christian Church was
established by the incarnate Word himself. With the divine
promise of indestructibility, the Church is the ongoing community of men and women cooperating in the development
and diffusion of that doctrine.

Now insightful commentaries on the Scriptures play a
fundamental part in the development and diffusion of the
divine doctrine. As such they are analogous to induction in
that they derive their authority outside themselves. But to
avoid any misunderstanding as to the force of the analogy
indicated between indirect and direct knowledge, it is necessary to add, says Eckhart, that like every true analogy it
must be applied inversely. In other words, that which is finite, inasmuch as it is like that which is infinite, must be
considered as it were from the standpoint of the infinite in
which there are no real distinctions. Thus while induction
rises above sensible perception and permits one to pass on
to a higher level, it is on the contrary direct insight alone
which, by a transposition effected by uncreated grace, attains to the Principle itself. In so doing it attains to that
which is first and supreme, after which nothing remains but
to draw the consequences and determine the manifold implications.

There is no disputing the profundity of the interpretations of Holy Scripture expounded by the early Greek and
Latin Fathers. Moreover, the abiding import of the intellections disclosed in the writings of the medieval metaphysicians, especially Aquinas, should never be understated. But
when it is a question of expounding the doctrine as it were
from the standpoint of unrestricted knowledge itself, no
commentary unfolds deeper insight and greater single-
minded consideration of that transcendent mode of knowledge than that of Eckhart. Since all these esteemed commentaries on Holy Scripture, including Eckhart's, are traditional in the true sense of the term, we should not exag-
gerate the importance of their apparent differences of adap-
tation. Eckhart's exposition distinguishes itself simply

by its persistent consideration of all things from the stand-point as it were of pure, infinite Intellect. So far as partici-pative philosophy and theology go he stands squarely on the shoulders of Aquinas. But it is not on the *Summa Theologica* that his intellect is focused. Rather it is directly on and indeed as it were *within* that at which Aquinas and his tradi-tional predecessors point: the Word, Intellect-as-such, with which the manifest intellect is, in principle, identical—as the author of the *Summa* reminds us.

It is clearly incorrect to apply the term "liberal" to Eck-hart's exposition of Holy Scripture, as some persons have done. The inadmissibility of this expression arises especially from the fact that here the term "liberalism" is a compara-tive and necessarily implies the correlative existence of a "conservatism." But such a division cannot be applied to a consideration of the doctrine of Divine Knowledge. Liberalism and conservatism are not to be regarded as two divorced and more or less opposed doctrines but as two aspects of the same formal and systematic dogma, and as such have existed throughout the sacred tradition. This, however, does not apply in the case of the consideration of formless and unrestricted knowledge itself. In this case one can only speak of the mode of knowledge that inevitably pertains to the purely transcendent order where it is neces-sary always to take into account the incommensurable or noncorrelative, which is indeed what is most important.

Words and symbols, like concepts, ideas, and images, serve only by supplying supports for a course of knowing that must necessarily begin in each person, and by acting as requisite springboards to the apprehension of that un-manifested and unconditioned Principle. In this regard the only appropriate distinction to be made in Eckhart's expo-sition is no more than one between the letter and the spirit. It goes without saying that the true spirit and principle of the letter is not that meaning which is most divorced from the letter, but that which is innermost in it in the sense that only the purely transcendent can be truly innermost.

Eckhart recognizes that the doctrine of Divine Knowledge is accessible to all those who are intellectually and spiritually qualified—in other words, to all who are capable of sustaining a metaphysical insight. It is understood, however, only by those who through grace actually do sustain that insight, and who, in true humility, derive a real advantage from it for the expansion of awareness and the enactment of charity.

If it thus appears from a humanistic standpoint that there is a transcendent doctrine reserved for a chosen few, it is because it cannot be otherwise when one takes into consideration the actual capacities of human beings in their willingness to know. There is no trace here of the nontraditional "gnostic" sects of earlier time. Instead of extolling pure knowledge and the reflected higher intellect, which the designation "gnostic" should imply, the members of those sects lived in the conviction that they possessed a secret and mysterious revelation specially granted to them in conceptualizable form and inaccessible to others regardless of their intellectual capacities. Nothing is more abhorrent to Eckhart. Yet the doctrine in the name of which he speaks is indoctrinary by means of initiation, nonformal instruction, and an intellectual and moral discipline open to grace. Thus it differs greatly in all its methods from the secular education which is overrated in modern times, since there is no way in which the doctrine can be popularized.

In fact Eckhart makes it very clear that the intention in teaching the doctrine of Divine Knowledge is not to implant that knowledge in, or reduce it to the conceptual levels of, the minds of the populace or even the minds of a few men and women. This is an impossibility, inasmuch as that "unknowing knowledge" transcends mental activity and conceptualization. Rather, the very doctrine and its teaching denotes that it is ordained essentially to destroy ignorance, and it does this by designating that whereby a vault into purely transcendent knowledge is possible.

If it is primarily a question of an intellectual vault, that is because transcendent knowledge is in itself strictly incommunicable in human terms and not subject to formalization. Indeed, no person can attain it save by his own unlimited will to know effected and sustained by the grace of the Word. Original sin, according to Eckhart, is an inescapable

fact so far as the human process is considered in individual
manifestation. No original sin, no evil; no evil, no moral
choice; no moral choice and human freedom is meaningless
and man becomes a nonknower. But original sin does not
annihilate the will to know, rather it "wounds" it in such a
way that in order to remain detached and unlimited regen-
eration by the Word is indispensable.

Yet it was precisely because Eckhart insisted on teaching
the destruction of ignorance in the Dominican church in
Cologne and similar centers where people from every walk
of life gathered that he personally came under the attack of
certain systematic theologians. Indeed, there is a sense in
which we can understand why his students John Tauler and
Henry Suso later hinted that Eckhart's language was possibly too subtle for a sermon to the nobles, gentry, and labor-
ers of the Rhine Valley.[10] We also learn from Tauler and Suso
why Eckhart's adversaries did not find it too difficult after
his death to secure from John XXII a condemnation of
some of his statements. Eckhart, as is well known, had previously retracted, denied any heterodox or purely subjectivist intentions that may be derived from any of his elliptic
assertions. At the same time he pointed out that unless certain assertions concerning the divine doctrine are elliptic in
nature there is little hope of ever being able to teach the
doctrine, since words themselves are already oblique, never
direct. This is a fact, however, that the formal logician is
rarely able to understand.

As for speaking of the most profound insights concerning Divine Knowledge in the presence of those untrained in
theology, he replied by saying that even a person without a
specialized formal education may, with the help of God, be
capable of sustaining a suprarational insight. Moreover, if
the ignorant are not taught, no one will ever attain knowledge. After all, Christ himself said: "It is not the healthy that
need a doctor."[11] And the purpose of teaching is to dispel
ignorance by exposing all things, not in their own delusive
light, but in the light of the Word, or Divine Knowledge itself. Was not St. John's Gospel written for all human
beings, wise and ignorant, believers and nonbeliev-

ers? Yet the prologue to that Gospel contains the most profound and elliptic sentences that have ever been written concerning the unrestricted act of Godhead.[12]

It is now admitted by practically all Eckhartian scholars that had the fourteenth-century authorities intelligently and dispassionately investigated all the Meister's writings, he would probably never have suffered a condemnation.[13] But the flair for condemnation without intelligent cause was just as prevalent in the high Middle Ages as it is in our own twentieth century, as for example the prohibitions placed on the works of St. Thomas Aquinas only a few years after his death.

Though jealousy and certain political issues influenced his attackers, it was clearly their die-hard adherence to a closed systematic theology and their insistence on the primacy of a restricted ontology that primarily accounted for their determination to silence Eckhart. He had no quarrel with formal theology in its rightful province, but his censors failed to understand what he and his students clearly understood: formal theology, like ontology, is at best no more than a participation in the supreme Principle, and if separated from or substituted for that Principle it is of no more perennial worth than the abstractions enjoyed by a mouse. For the Word, like reality itself, is not even initially known by insisting on mentally gazing at it. And participatory knowledge, even at its mystical heights and no matter how extensive, is still short of and never to be confused with pure knowledge, from which all-inclusive standpoint every limited mode of knowledge is relationally naught. It is the relational ignorance of those who confound participatory knowledge with pure knowledge, as well as the total ignorance of those who think they know by adopting a stance of "looking at" reality, that the doctrine of Divine Knowledge is ordained to destroy.

Eckhart makes no claim to setting forth a complete exposition of the doctrine of Divine Knowledge in its strict totality, even regarding a single point. Such an understanding would be impossible, not only in terms of the unending labor it would involve, but primarily because of the very nature of the doctrine. Furthermore, any such enterprise would be self-defeating in that it would inevitably take on the appearance of systematization, which is incompatible with what is essential in the transcendent consideration. Eckhart's exposition is such that it is intentionally designed to discourage those who by their very mental habits are determined, despite all warnings, to extract systems even where none exist. His method is to treat a particular theme or one more or less definite aspect of the doctrine at a time, leaving himself free to introduce other equally important aspects later on in order to make them, in their turn, points for further reflective study.

It is in the light of the foregoing remarks that the intention of this book is to be understood. The purpose is to introduce the reader not only to the insights of Meister Eckhart, but primarily to the doctrine of Divine Knowledge which, as expounded by him, is to be found in the Word. Likewise, and to avoid any appearance of systematization, the six themes or aspects of the doctrine (which are distinctively considered in Part II, under the chapter titles "God and the Human Self," "The Word," "The Primal Distinction," "The Inversion," "The Veils of God," and "The Detachment") are not necessarily set forth in the form of a logical hierarchy; they may be considered in a nonsequential order. Though they by no means exhaust the themes expounded by Eckhart, they are those most essentially and repeatedly marked out by him as equivalent aspects of the doctrine. When reflected upon they may best assist us in attaining a deeper understanding of what is the fundamental teaching and primordial meaning inherent in God's communication to man.

But before these aspects of the doctrine are presented certain preparatory remarks and philosophical considerations should be made. If not strictly requisite, they may at least prove helpful as supports for an understanding of the doctrine. We in our time are so spiritually and intellectually crippled that we are almost rendered incapable of understanding the essential teachings of Eckhart. And no doubt

there will always be those who will make the fundamental
mistake of adapting his insights to techniques for dealing
with workaday emotional problems without first preparing
themselves philosophically and morally.

Obviously some attempt should be made, therefore, to
point out the main difficulties that our contemporary
modes of thought place in the way of comprehending
Eckhart's exposition of the doctrine. After all, we are separated from him in time by almost seven centuries, and our
educational system is anything but theologically or even
philosophically oriented. The spiritual and intellectual influences on the mind of Eckhart, so unlike the influences that
normally shape our mental attitudes, should also be brought
to light, as well as the type of misconceptions we in our day
are especially prone to adopt concerning his exposition.
Moreover, we should properly understand from Eckhart's
own statements how his ardent belief in and full intellectual
acceptance of God's communication of Divine Knowledge is
to be rationally justified. This involves a consideration of his
philosophical demonstration of the reality of God and, consequently, his indisputable reasons for understanding this
world as a time-place continuum of contingent and dependent existence.

Inasmuch as they are preparatory these remarks and considerations will be undertaken in Part I; indeed, without
them the doctrine itself would more likely than not remain
alien to our intellectual quest. Though important in their
own right, they are nevertheless concessions to our present
human situation and to a philosophical and therefore external mode of knowledge—"concessions" inasmuch as they
may be said ultimately to derive their intelligibility from the
transcendent mode of pure knowledge. The fundamental
thread that binds this entire study together should be clearly
evident once the relation of the human self to God is theoretically understood. Eckhart's exposition of the doctrine of
Divine Knowledge unfolds step by step the requisite considerations involved in that relationship and culminates in that
detachment which alone makes possible the reintegration
of *theoria* and *praxis*.

For good reason references to Eckhart's world or to our own contemporary situation are intended only to assist the reader in attaining an understanding of his essential teaching. At the same time it should be clearly stated that the doctrine he expounds transcends comparatives and the relative generalities that historians use to designate an "age of faith and qualitative intellectuality" in contrast to one, such as our own, of "marked quantitative and sensate tendencies." Any generalized attempt to relate the doctrine to Eckhart's situation, to our own, or to any other human situation in the sense of showing a special individual concern for the march of the times would obviously tend to particularize and therefore distort its timelessness and transcendence.

It is rather for each student of Eckhart, regardless of time and place, to relate himself to the doctrine and its divine source. Thus he must start with himself, the personal world he alone knows, and rise above his own situation and finally above the realm of historical particularity to that of detached intellection "in the fullness of time." In the process only he can modify and adapt the exposition of the doctrine to a limited degree externally and for the sake of his own personal needs.

Let it again be said that understanding and not erudition is our concern. This study is not to be regarded as equivalent to what the specialists call a "research paper," because the basic metaphysical principles as affirmed by Eckhart will be necessarily repeated and kept central throughout. The derivative points themselves are only to be considered as direct or indirect applications of those eternal principles which are all contained within the supreme Principle from which all else derives. When it is a matter of considering the transcendent and unconditioned Principle, which is the synthesizing objective of this study, "specialization" is out of the question. Though there will be need to deal with other subjects, which initially may appear as extraneous, they will be introduced in reference to the main objective. So long as the reader keeps in mind that the principles themselves have a range far exceeding the entire realm of their possible applications, no objection should be found to expound-

ing them, whenever possible, in relation to this or that application. Nor should the reader fall into the danger of finding
anything in this presentation, or even in the writings of
Eckhart, that may be taken as the last word on the doctrine.

Part I

Preparatory Considerations

1

Difficulties and Misconceptions

The general remarks set forth in this chapter and certain considerations undertaken in the next should help prepare the way for an understanding of the doctrine of Divine Knowledge which Eckhart expounds. These remarks and considerations, which are concessions to our present human condition, pertain to the essential qualifications and well-grounded judgments requisite for any genuine understanding of his teaching. Yet such an understanding can only come about through an intellectual discipline which culminates in a realization of "uncreated wisdom." Inasmuch as that wisdom is always present and accessible to the person capable of receiving it, any conception that it is specifically ancient, medieval, or modern is false.

Because Eckhart expounded the doctrine of Divine Knowledge at the height of the so-called Middle Ages and before the general breakdown of the tradition which maintained the pre-eminence of "unitive knowledge," these initial remarks are meant to help us place ourselves in the tradition to which he belonged. They might also assist us in surmounting difficulties that modern modes of education and thought place in the way of a true understanding of the doctrine. It can even be said that by a genuine assimilation of the essential content of the doctrine of Divine Knowledge, we might recapture the spirit that dwells at the core of Christianity itself. This instead of restricting ourselves, as generally happens, to a humanistic transcription of the doctrine that relies for its authority almost exclusively on "historical facts," thus relegating to the background the all-inclusive and eternal character of its fundamental truth.

In this sense our present situation may be compared to that of the foolish virgins who, through the direction of their attention to individual and timely interests, allowed their lamps to go out. In order to rekindle the divine fire, which in its essence is always the same whenever and wherever it may be burning, we must have recourse to the lamps kept alight by our wiser companions among the contemplative faithful. But once lighted, it will still be our own lamps that we shall be lighted by, and all that we shall then have to do is to keep them properly fueled by ever present divine grace as is needed for that knowledge of reality which transcends our mere human limitations.

THE CHIEF DIFFICUTLY

In our contemporary age many difficulties stand in the way of any endeavor at a serious and intimate study of Meister Eckhart's teaching. Even though the student may now gain access to the genuine Latin and German texts of the Meister, these difficulties remain. Surely the greatest obstacles originate not from Eckhart but from ourselves; or rather from our own mental attitudes, which are grounded in prejudices and limitations wholly foreign to him.

Obviously the first condition for such a study, and the most necessary, is to possess the intellectual qualifications for understanding the doctrine in question, and by this we mean for understanding it essentially and in truth. In the prologue of his major work, the *Opus Tripartitum*, Eckhart cautions his readers not to rest on the apparent sense of his words, but to exert great effort to apprehend the true meaning: "It should be noted that some of the following propositions, inquiries, and expositions will appear at first monstrous, doubtful, or false, but not if they are studied with detached understanding and consideration."[1]

It is this aptitude of detached intellection which, with very few exceptions, is lacking among would-be students of a doctrine which by its very nature is transcendent to our human and therefore restricted modes of understanding. On the other hand, the fulfillment of this one necessary condition can be considered a sufficient qualification, for once it is actualized there is no major difficulty in grasping the integrality of Eckhart's teaching.

But if there is really no other serious obstacle to the study of his exposition except this failure to understand in terms of detached intellection, how is it that so far most scholars who devote themselves to this subject have not managed to overcome the difficulty? One could hardly be accused of exaggeration in maintaining that they have not actually overcome it, since so far they have only succeeded in producing specialized works of erudition.[2] Though these works are no doubt valuable from a certain standpoint, they are of little interest when it comes to the question of understanding the most direct of all true intellections.

For instance, take one of many examples to be found in Eckhart's writings: "When I flowed out of God, then all things proclaimed 'There is a God.' Now this cannot make me blessed, for hereby I realize myself as creature. But in the breaking through into Divine Knowledge I transcend all creatures and there I am neither 'God' nor creature; I am that which I was and shall remain, now and forever more. . . By this breakthrough I become so rich that God is not sufficient for me, insofar as he is only 'God' or even God in his divine works. For in thus breaking through, I realize that God and I are one. There I am what I was, there I neither increase nor decrease, for there my innermost I is the immutable Principle of all things."[3]

Much more than a knowledge of words and grammar, more than the use of textual criticism, more than the so-called historical method, even more than philosophical scholarship is needed to understand such statements. The habits that grow with the use of such methods, the relative value of which should not be disputed, tend to narrow the intellectual horizon. They introduce preconceived notions that go to make up a mental attitude with the manifest intention of forcing the doctrine under study into the framework of modern thought. In short, questions of specialized method apart, the chief error on the part of many who attempt to understand Eckhart's teaching is to consider everything from an individual standpoint, whereas the first condition for the true understanding of the doctrine is to make an effort to assimilate it by placing oneself as far as possible at the intellectual standpoint of the one who expounds it.

Eckhart speaks essentially and intentionally, as he himself indicates, "in terms of pure Intellect," that is, "as it were from the summit of eternity" or "as from within the infinite Principle." In other words, he speaks primarily from the standpoint of *principial*[4] knowledge. If he is able to do this, it is because the intellectual tradition in which he grew and matured was one that placed no serious obstacles in the way of cultivating the habit of considering everything, not from the points of view of restricted comprehension, but as it were from there within the Godhead. With others in the tradition to which he adhered he was able to affirm: "There is a principle in the intellective soul, untouched by time and corporeality, flowing from pure Intellect, remaining in pure Intellect, itself wholly intellectual. In this principle is God, ever verdant, ever flowering in all the fullness and glory of his actual Self. . . . It is free of all names and void of all structures. It is one and unconditioned, as God is one and unconditioned, and no man can in any way behold it mentally."[5]

No, the Principle cannot be mentally beheld, looked at, or conceived, and any attempt to do so, as though it were "out there somewhere or in here somewhere," is illusory. The Principle, which is unrestricted Intellect itself, or God *in se*, is that in which we either choose to participate or not. But by participating in it we may come to realize that our truest identity is with it, rather than with our outward or inner self. We choose to participate in the Principle insofar as our unlimited will to know, or our intellectual desire, is maintained. We may understand our true identity with the Principle once we gain direct knowledge of the truth that "in the innermost Intellect God's ground is my ground and my ground is God's ground." After all, "the knower and the known are one in knowledge. . . . Some people think that they shall know God as standing there and they here. Not so. God and I, we are one in pure knowledge,"[6] But such an understanding is actualized, insists Eckhart, only by the complete communication of God himself in his Word.

INTELLECTUAL INFLUENCES ON ECKHART

If we are to place ourselves as far as possible at the stand-point from which Eckhart expounds the doctrine of Divine Knowledge, it may be of initial help to understand something of the intellectual tradition in which he was grounded and the major spiritual influences that made it not unnatural for him to consider "all things eternal wise."

Eckhart's adult life spans the last quarter of the thirteenth century and more than the first quarter of the fourteenth. He was a fully committed Christian, a prominent member of the Dominican Order of the Church, and one of the foremost metaphysicians of his time. To a Christian, Holy Scripture totally preceded in import and influence all other writings or speculations. As a Dominican and in the direct line of St. Albert the Great and St. Thomas Aquinas, Eckhart was a chief upholder of the teaching on "the primacy of intellect," which was the distinguishing mark of that order. And for Eckhart, with a genuine tradition to support him, the primacy of intellect meant not only the primacy of knowledge over action, but the primacy of Godhead or pure Intellect itself, of which everything else is in function. Otherwise the Scriptures would have only an extrinsic rather than an intrinsic meaning. But the very fact that they actually reveal the Word of God signifies the assured disclosure of the primacy of pure Intellect.[7]

That Eckhart knew the Scriptures backwards and forwards and acknowledged their supreme authority is well attested to by a study of his Latin works in particular. In his commentary *In Sapientiae*, thirty-six books of the Bible are quoted to substantiate his exposition. In one short Latin treatise alone at least twenty scriptural texts are authoritatively cited from ten different books of the Old and New Testaments.[8] If "originality" is recognized in many of his interpretations it is because his exposition is intended *sub specie aeternitatis*, which necessitates a transposition from the ordinarily accepted meaning, but a transposition that in no way contradicts it. For instance, in the first chapter of St. John's Gospel we are told that "the light shines in dark-

ness." Understood by Eckhart to indicate the light of God
the Father shining in "the darkness or unknowing of the
unmanifest Godhead"[9] signifies a clear transposition to a
purely metaphysical order of knowledge.

Apart from Holy Scripture the main intellectual influences on Eckhart were St. Thomas (d. 1274), St. Augustine
(d. 430), and Pseudo-Dionysius the Areopagite (writing
c. 500). Schooled on St. Thomas's writings and later professor at both St. Jacques in Paris and the famous *Studium
Generale* in Cologne, at which schools both St. Albert and the
Angelic Doctor had lived and taught, it is understandable
that he should be greatly imbued with their teachings. But
St. Augustine was still acknowledged as the Father of
Western Christendom and the voice of theological authority. One could not become a professor of theology at that
time unless he was well grounded in Augustine's teaching.
As for the Pseudo-Dionysius, he not only pointed out the
responsibility of theologians for all time to discover the hierarchical structure of manifest reality, but suggested precise
terminology to be employed when designating the order of
transcendence.

Eckhart was well acquainted with the doctrines of Plato
and the neo-Platonists such as Plotinus, Proclus, and the author of the *Book of Causes*, and he does not hesitate to quote
from them frequently. But as might be expected, he is far
more indebted to Aristotle. His familiarity with the peripatetic philosopher's major works was extensive, especially
his *Metaphysics, Posterior Analytics*, and the *De Anima, De Caelo*,
and *De Mundi*. With Eckhart, as with St. Thomas, it was
never a question of "Christianizing" either Plato or Aristotle;
rather it was a matter of completely transforming the concepts and terminology of the Greek thinkers by new and
profounder insights and higher principles made known by
the revelation of the Word of God.

In the same way Eckhart did not refrain from citing the
Stoics and the Latin Classics as represented by Seneca,
Cicero, Ovid, and even Virgil. He was also familiar with
the works of Boethius, Macrobius, John Scotus Erigena, and
Alanus de Insules. He often refers with acute under-

standing to the great Arabic thinkers, Avicenna and Averroes; and also admits his indebtedness to the Jewish theologians, Avencebron and especially Moses Maimonides. But although he absorbed many of the genuine insights of these men, he at once applied them in terms of higher principles.

Nor was Eckhart's knowledge slight of both the Greek and Latin Fathers of the Church. Origen, St. Chrysostom, St. Gregory of Nyssa, St. Gregory of Naziensus, and St. John Damascus are particularly referred to in his writings. Likewise we often find him quoting from St. Ambrose, St. Gregory the Great, Hilary of Poitiers, even Isodore of Saville. And there are several citations from later writers, such as St. Bernard, St. Anselm, Peter Lombard, Richard and Hugh of St. Victor, and of course St. Albert of Cologne, whom Eckhart knew personally when a young student.

Eckhart's profound knowledge of philosophy and theology was practically unmatched by any other person throughout his mature years. Professor Clark is right in stating: "As regards his reading in this and other fields, he may have been inferior to St. Thomas in the range and extent of his erudition, but after the death of Duns Scotus in 1308 he had no rival in Germany and very few in Europe." [10] Though Eckhart wrote no treatises on cosmology, natural science, or mathematics, there is abundant evidence that he was extremely well informed in these subjects and in every branch of knowledge then available. He was very familiar with the then current theories of astronomy, anatomy, physiology, and biology. He also knew the principles of social government and the details of both civil and canon law. [11] It is even possible to extract an almost complete philosophy of art from his writings. Moreover, his high administrative duties in the Dominican Order caused him to be well traveled throughout the Empire and other parts of Europe.

It must be repeated, however, that we should turn to St. Thomas, St. Augustine, and the Pseudo-Dionysius in order to appreciate the major preparatory influences on the mind of Eckhart. He was extraordinarily imbued with their teachings and he acknowledged them as complementary in every respect. Yet the designations of "Thomist," "Augustianian," or "Neo-Platonist" are wholly out of place applied to Eckhart's teaching. This becomes very clear once it is understood that the standpoint from which Eckhart essentially expounds the doctrine of Divine Knowledge is as it were wholly within God and not as one in direction toward God, as was the intended concern of his predecessors. His use of their terminology, his reliance on them for supportive pointers should not mislead the student of Eckhart.

The Pseudo-Dionysius affirms God as Wisdom, Goodness, and Being in a theological manner, and shows how these terms are applicable to creatures only in virtue of their derivation from God and their degree of participation in him.[12] When, in the *Divine Names*, he speaks of "One" as "the most important title of all,"[13] he makes it clear that God is the ultimate Principle of all that is. In his *Mystical Theology*, however, he explains the negative way of approaching God, that is, the way of excluding from God all the imperfections of creatures and universal manifestation. Starting by denying of God those things which are farthest removed from him, such as "drunkenness or fury," the intellect proceeds upwards by progressively denying of God all the attributes and qualities known in creation until it reaches "the superessential Darkness."[14] When all the human ideas and modes of thought have been stripped away from the intellect's quest for God, it enters upon the "darkness of unknowing," wherein "it renounces all the apprehensions of the understanding and is wrapped in that which is wholly intangible and incomprehensible . . . and is united to him."[15] Then God is known as the "superessential Intellect."

Thus when we speak of the transcendent, all-inclusive Godhead as Unity and Trinity, it is not Unity and Trinity such as can be understood by us. The Pseudo-Dionysius goes on to say: "We apply the titles of 'Trinity' and 'Unity' to that which is beyond all titles, designating under the form of Being that which is beyond Being. . . . Godhead has no name, nor can it be grasped by reason," since it is "unconditioned Knowledge in itself."[16] The transcendent

Godhead "is not *a* unity or goodness, nor *a* Spirit, is not Sonship nor Fatherhood . . . nor does it belong to the determinations of non-Being or to that of Being."[17]

With regard to the relation of the world to God the Pseudo-Dionysius speaks of the manifold manifestation of God in the universe of things. At the same time God remains indivisibly One even in the act of "Self-manifestation" and without differentiation even in the process of structureless or structured manifestation. God is eternally "the Principle and end of all things."[18]

With the Pseudo-Dionysius Eckhart acknowledged the indispensability of the negative approach to God as well as the hierarchical structure of all being. But the Areopagite's terms "darkness", "desert," "nothing" as applied to God are transformed by Eckhart to indicate God as unmanifest All-possibility and really distinct from manifest individual reality. The negative approach to God is reinforced by Augustine's assertion that "though we can know that God is, we cannot know what God is," and also by Aquinas's "way of remotion." As Eckhart says: "Nobody is God, no created rational being as such is God. The demonstration of a knowable thing is made either to the senses or to the intellect, but as to the knowledge of *what* God is there can be neither a demonstration from sense experience, since he is incorporeal, nor from intellect, since he is without quality or structure, but is known only through remotion from structures known to us. Hence God is, so to speak, affirmed from other beings by discrimination and discriminated by affirmation."[19] But, as we shall discover, the negative way, though superior to the way of rational analogy, is still in direction toward God; it does not constitute what Eckhart discriminates as the "mode" of knowledge *in principio,* or *Intellectus in divinis.*

Mention has already been made of Eckhart's great indebtedness to Aquinas for his understanding of the primacy of intellect over reason and will. We shall further consider this particular influence in the next section and, indeed, have occasion to refer to it throughout. This teaching is of prime importance, especially as it prepares the way for an under-

standing of the full implications to be derived from
Aquinas's clues regarding inverse analogy and knowledge
through identity.

First, however, we should acknowledge the fact that the
teachings of both Augustine and Aquinas on time and eternity, on the finite and infinite orders, are most evident in
Eckhart writings. These teachings have little in common
with those of the Greek philosophers, for whom eternity
and infinite designate merely unending duration and the
indefinite, rather than strict timelessness and the purely unconditioned. In other words, the Christian notion of transcendence is of that which is strictly beyond and really distinct from every possible extension of individuality and universal manifestation.

After St. Thomas, Eckhart cites St. Augustine more than
any other author for support on this theme. Augustine insists that the world of time and finitude reflects and manifests eternal and infinite God. "If anything worthy of consideration is noticed in the nature of things, whether it be
judged worthy of slight consideration or of great, it must be
applied to the most excellent and ineffable consideration of
the Creator." "The order and stability of the universe manifest the Intelligence of God." God transcends the finite and
the indefinite, which is merely an extension of the finite; his
essence is purely unconditioned and without accidents.[20]

Augustine also says that "God is himself in no interval
nor extension of place, but in his immutable, pre-eminent
all-possibility is both within everything because all things are
in him and without everything because he transcends all
things. So too he is in no interval nor extension of time, but
in his immutable eternity is the principle of all things
because he is [metaphysically] prior to all things and the
end of all things because the same he is after all things."
God is pure Knowledge; he knows all that he would make
manifest, but his knowledge is not distinct acts of knowledge, rather "one eternal, immutable, and ineffable comprehension."[21]

Contemplating his own eternal essence, God, says Augustine, "knows himself and all-possibility," including finite es-

sences, the structural reflection of his infinite Selfhood, so
that the *rationes* (reasons or principles) of things, including
manifest intellects, are present in the divine Intellect from
all eternity as the "divine ideas." These "divine ideas are
archetypal forms or permanent and unchanging *rationes* of
things which are not themselves formed but are contained
in the divine Intellect eternally and are always the same.
They neither arise nor pass away, but whatever arises and
passes away is formed according to them."[22] This is the
famous doctrine of exemplarism, but in order not to impair
the identity of God and of all things in God, Eckhart, following Aquinas, insists that the "divine ideas" are really
indistinct in God, in contrast to the position held by many
of their contemporary Augustinians.

From Aquinas, who was greatly influenced by the Pseudo-
Dionysius on this point, Eckhart came to understand that
God is completely without form and duality. From Aquinas
he also learned that "we must go through time to come to
the knowledge of eternity. . . . There is no *before* or *after* to be
reckoned with in constant changeless Reality. Eternity lies
in the apprehension of that identity. . . . Eternity is signified
by these two clauses: first, that a thing in eternity cannot be
closed either prospectively or retrospectively; second, that
it is all-inclusive and all at once without any succes-
siveness." Aquinas goes on to say that "eternity is the measure of permanence; time the measure of change." More
over, "the *now* of time is not time; the *now* of eternity is really
the same as eternity."[23]

The influence of these teachings explains why Eckhart
could say "the world has always *existed*," for the term "existence" pertains not to eternity and the unconditioned order,
but only to the manifest order of time and finitude. "For
there never was a *time* when the world did not *exist* or when
the world did not yet *exist*."[24] Because eternity, or the unconditioned, simply *is*, it does not exist, does not stand-
from something else, nor is it manifested in any way. Rather
it is for us to consider all manifest reality in terms of pure
isness[25] if we would truly understand the relation of time to
eternity, of the finite to the infinite.

But can any of this be truly understood without first understanding the distinction between intellectual knowledge and rational knowledge?

The Special Influence of St. Thomas Aquinas

It has been stated that a sustained insight into "pure Intellect" is the chief qualification necessary in order to understand the essential teaching of Meister Eckhart. It has also been noted that the great influence of St. Thomas Aquinas on Eckhart largely accounts for the sense of confidence the Meister had in expounding the doctrine in terms of pure Intellect.

St. Thomas died in 1274, only a year or two prior to Eckhart's entrance into the Dominican house of studies in Erfurt where he began his long years of higher formal study. The young Dominican came from a well-educated family of nobility who were large landowners in the countryside of nearby Gotha and benefactors of the Church in this part of central Germany. He was a gifted student and also endowed with administrative ability, for after serving as Sentenzenlektor (1293–94) at the University of Paris his extensive formal studies were interrupted when he was chosen to be Prior of Erfurt and Vicar of Thuringia. But in 1298, or shortly thereafter, he was again sent to the Dominican house of St. Jacques in Paris where the teachings of Aquinas still held undisputed sway. Here he studied and fulfilled his lecturing assignments for the degree of doctor of theology, which he received from the University of Paris in 1302. He was to return to St. Jacques as a professor almost a decade later, at which time he began to compose his major work, the *Opus Tripartitum.* After a couple years he was called back to Germany, first to Strasbourg and then to Cologne, where he taught and fulfilled other administrative duties.

Though Eckhart was one of the most erudite scholars of his time, he insisted that erudition, no matter how scientific or comprehensive, is at best only ancillary to the direct knowledge gained by detached intellection.[26] He never gave any prior claim to learning or to the discursive operations of reason and its objective. Priority is always placed on the objective of the unlimited will to know which is the unrestricted act of knowledge itself. "One should be stripped of and detached from reasoning and withdrawn into detached intellection." The will to know must be kept unlimited and not primarily directed toward the objects of limited reason. Moreover, the unlimited will to know can only be sustained by divine grace, for "there God works in the highest and purest act." After all, "reason apprehends God only insofar as he is known to it. There it can never comprehend him in the ocean of his unfathomableness." "From this one can deduce that an unlearned man can, by means of love or the unlimited will to know, obtain knowledge and teach others."[27] Recall that Nathanael, who had not detached himself from his own erudition, was not chosen to be an Apostle, "for to this rank neither the mere learned nor the humanly wise were selected."[28]

This calls for a few additional remarks pertaining to the special influence on the mind of Eckhart of Aquinas's understanding of both manifest and unmanifest intellect. In fact Eckhart regarded this understanding as fundamental to the entire structure of Aquinas's teaching.

First of all, Aquinas makes it very clear that "reason differs from intellect as multitude from unity, as time from eternity."[29] But "intellect and reason are not separate faculties. To know intellectually is to apprehend intelligible truth directly; to reason is to proceed from one understanding to another. Reason is compared to intellect as activity to rest, as acquiring to already having. One is a process, the other is an achievement." By intellect "a man is intent on things eternal, contemplating them in themselves and consulting them for rules of action, while by reason he is intent on things temporal.. . . In the order of intellection we judge of temporal matters according to eternal principles. Intellect and reason are distinguished by different habits and active functions. Unitive knowledge is attributed to intellect, scientific or discursive knowledge to reason."[30]

"Rational knowledge," says Aquinas, "is the middle stage between sensation and detached intellection. . . . It is properly concerned with structures that in fact exist in all indi-

vidual beings." Intellectual knowledge, however, "is concerned with eternal principles which are apprehended by
intellectual intuition." That which is "directly known in the
intellect is isness. A thing is knowable because isness is
pointed to. Isness is the proper object of intellect; it is the
primary intelligible." And this is why "the actually known is
the knower as actual."[31]

Aquinas goes on to say that intellectual knowledge
"means the presence of the known in the knower in the
knower's own way." The unaided intellect, however, can only
know manifest, dependent isness, and it does so naturally.
However, "to know self-subsisting [unmanifest] isness is
natural to the divine Intellect alone . . . a created intellect cannot know the divine essence [which *is* God's is-
ness] except God by his grace shows and gives himself."[32]
Nevertheless, "the intellect which is potential to all knowability [and 'God is the supreme, total knowability'] we term
the *intellectus possibilis*," that is, the intellect able to know all
things and even God in himself. "There is nothing that the
divine Intellect does not know actually, nor the human intellect potentially." But "no potentiality is actualized save by
that which is in act," which means that only pure Act, or
God, can actualize the potentiality of the intellect to know
all things and God himself. It is by this actualization that
"the intellect is transposed into God" and "that which is in
God is God."[33]

It is precisely this actualization by God that makes for
unrestricted knowledge through identity. Aquinas affirms
that "God's understanding, the object understood, and the
act of understanding are identical." Moreover, "God knows
everything simultaneously." "It is the infusion of supernatural light which enables the intellective soul to know everything and even to realize God himself."[34] Were one to consider "the *intellectus possibilis* as fully actualized," then "all
would be known directly as indistinct from God's knowledge and in eternal unity." In this sense he reminds us how
"Dionysius notes that Hierotheus was taught by actually un-
dergoing divinity, not only by learning about it." "To the

lover of divinity is divinely given the ability to know and determine it directly. He is identified with it."[35]

"The human soul," says Aquinas, "is termed intellectual because it reflects and shares in the power of pure Intellect." "There is in the soul a power directly derived from transcendent Intellect itself." "Divine Knowledge is the first Principle of all intellectual knowledge."[36] Our natural "intellectual desire," or unlimited will to know, "is never quieted until we know the first Principle, not from its reflection [in universal manifestation] but directly by its very essence. The first Principle is God. Therefore the ultimate end of rational creatures is immediate knowledge of the essence of God." Indeed, "this desire to know is not quieted but rather excited by the knowledge of faith [in the Word of God], for everyone desires to know immediately what he believes. Therefore man's end does not consist in believing things about God but in knowing within God." "When the end is attained the natural desire [to know] is stilled, for God's knowledge united to the intellect is the principle of knowing God and all things."[37]

The exposition of divine doctrine "is the reverse of philosophical exposition," says Aquinas. Whereas with the latter "creatures come in at the start, God at the end," with the former "God comes first . . . is liker to God, who in knowing himself knows creatures."[38] Yet the highest possible exposition is that which is presented from the standpoint of "knowing as it were within God." And here is one of several pointers he gives for such an exposition:

"First, with regard to knowledge, note that temporal events stand in a different relation to a mind that is inside the time-series and to a mind that is entirely above it. . . . Imagine many people marching in a column along a road. Each of them knows the men in front and behind him by reference to his own position. But an observer high above, while he sees how one precedes another, takes in the column as a whole without working from a position inside it. . . . Now God completely transcends any system measured by time. He is the summit of eternity where all is at once entire and complete. The whole stream of things falls under his single and unrestricted intellection. With one glance he sees [analogically speaking] all things that take place in time, and he sees them just as they are in themselves. The causal order is appreciated, but things are not seen as past and future to him. They are entirely in his presence." "Now the intellect which, by God's grace, is united to the divine essence understands all things as from God's understanding."[39]

Thus imbued with this unassailable teaching Eckhart had no qualms in attempting to expound the doctrine from this highest possible standpoint. And this means no less than a consideration of all that is in terms of "the possible intellect as it were fully actualized" and hence as "indistinct from pure Intellect, or God in his Godhead." Aquinas admits in his prologue to the *Summa Theologica* that he is expounding the doctrine according to St. Paul's intention: "Even as babes unto Christ I have fed you with milk and not with meat."[40] Eckhart undoubtedly thought that some of the children of Christ whom he addressed were capable of being fed meat. If many still could digest only milk, there was always Aquinas and Augustine to turn to, as he himself counseled.

Aquinas stands out for Eckhart over all predecessors in the tradition because he most clearly affirmed the isness of Divine Knowledge as the supreme Principle. He also insisted that Divine Knowledge is the inverse of all manifest modes of knowledge. Thus a consideration of all things principially means, for Eckhart, nothing less than the transposition of our natural consideration from the standpoint of time and limitation to one of God in his Godhead. This transposition is made possible through knowledge of the Word incarnate who, in his return to the Father, signified the inversion of manifest intellect into its Principle, the unmanifest pure Intellect. Thus it is that when Augustine, in his *De Trinitate*, for example, refers to knowledge *sub ratione aeternitatis*, or when Aquinas in his *De Veritate* considers truth in terms of *Intellectus in divinis*, Eckhart gets his primany inducements to expound the doctrine of Divine Knowledge principiallv.

That Eckhart should be so intent on doing this in a manner never done before and in such a way that it is the essential ground of all his teaching should not surprise us. The long tradition in which he so thoroughly disciplined his intellect made it almost inevitable. For a genuine understanding of the teachings of Aquinas, Augustine, and the Pseudo-Areopagite indicates that they well serve as supportive pointers to and springboards for a vault into that mode of knowledge *tamquam in principio infinito.* And Eckhart acknowledged them as just that, supportive pointers and springboards which, when united with the primary meaning of Holy Scripture, make the supports secure and the vault certain.

Another factor should be noted regarding Eckhart's intent in expounding the doctrine from the supreme standpoint. With the advent of the fourteenth century, scholarship in Europe had begun its long decline and the teachings of Aquinas were entering upon an extended period of almost total neglect. Masters who placed primary emphasis on analytical reason and theologians who preached a radical form of fideism were on the rise. As a Dominican called to uphold the banner of genuine learning and the torch of intellectual knowledge, Eckhart could ascertain no truer way of doing so than to throw himself wholeheartedly into the task of dispelling ignorance by stressing the inversion of intellect "into the Light of eternal Truth."

Once we understand that no other mode of knowledge is more eminent or even more "practical" in the long run, we should not be surprised that some of the new masters and theologians, who minimized intellectual discipline, were determined to silence Eckhart. Eckhart had made it clear that they were in misdirection insofar as they were intent on "mentally looking" at being and at God, in either extroverted or introverted ways, rather than participate in being and in God. Furthermore, the risk involved in the chance that some will misunderstand the doctrine and turn it into form of erroneous subjectivism is not nearly as great as the risk involved in the discouragement of intellectual knowledge.

"No one is so foolish as not to desire wisdom, yet why do so many remain ignorant?" asked Eckhart. Because, first, they forsake their unlimited and detached will to know and think instead that reality is something to behold. Second, wisdom cannot be acquired without disciplined intellection sustained by divine grace. "If a man is rich [even in reasoning or in faith], that does not make him wise. But if a man is transformed and conformed [by God] to the essence and nature of wisdom and becomes wisdom itself, then he is wise."[41]

What particularly amazes, from the human standpoint, is that Eckhart persisted in expounding the doctrine of Divine Knowledge in principial mode when practically all the great minds of his time were preoccupied with political and ecclesiastical struggles. Throughout his adult life the problem of church and state was regarded by most professors in the universities and, in fact, by most people in the whole of Christendom as uppermost, and they had to agonize through several decades before a *via media* was found. Consumed by a sense of absolute royal power, Phillip the Fair marked his reign from beginning to end (1285–1314) with insidious attacks against papal authority even in spiritual matters. No less a would-be absolutist, the vacillating Emperor sustained an enmity for both France and the Holy See. Though the ministers of England were biding their time until they could open the Hundred Years War with France, they were patiently seeking allies on the continent. Then there was restless Constantinople, seat of the Eastern empire, and just beyond the ever-menacing Turks. Meanwhile, heretical sects, such as the Franciscan Spirituals, the Beghards, and the Free Spirits, were constantly seeking political favors and military support from rebellious princes to enhance their ideological causes.

The papacy was in a state of near total confusion. With the death of Clement V, Christendom had to wait over two years before the various factions could elect a new pope—a pope, what is more, who was exiled in Avignon from Rome. John XXII, a hot-tempered Frenchman, was seventy-two years old when elected in 1316. He then proceeded to take direct charge of the Inquisition and proclaim many acts of excommunication, notably that of Ludwig the Emperor. Though the pope himself was later accused of heresy on purely doctrinal grounds, he retracted his dissenting opinions on his deathbed in 1334. It was this same pope who, in a frustrated and senile condition, was persuaded to condemn some of Eckhart's statements in 1329. The Meister had gone to Avignon to defend his exposition and died— where or how remains unknown—before the condemnation was pronounced. We are made mindful of the canon of the Lateran Council of 1215, which stated that Scripture bids us to beware of being more just than justice.

None of these particular human situations seem to have deterred Eckhart; we search in vain throughout his work to find reference to any political or ecclesiastical problem. But the breakthrough into Divine Knowledge was never regarded by Eckhart as an escape from the human situation, from which there are no escapes. To get to eternity we must go through time, as Aquinas counseled, but we cannot stop on the way. And if we would truly understand and reply to our human situation, no matter where or when, we must understand it "eternal wise" and reply to it principially in terms of "unrestricted Truth, the Son of the Father of all."[42]

The Distinction between Primary and Secondary

As corollary to the self-affirmation of intellect and its primacy over reason and action, the serious student of Eckhart must also qualify himself by an ability to discriminate intelligently. "Truly to discriminate," the Meister says, "means not the mere distinction of one thing from another but the determination of that which is primary and that which is secondary."[43] A few remarks on this point might prove helpful.

In expounding the doctrine of Divine Knowledge Eckhart endeavors to dispel ignorance by ascertaining princi-

ples, priorities, and values, and his language is meant to
serve his purpose of evaluating realities. Throughout his
entire exposition, no matter what aspect of the doctrine he
takes into consideration, we always find the key distinction
between "that which is primary and that which is secondary." This distinction becomes self-evident once the relation
of intellect to pure Intellect is truly understood.

The primary is usually designated by Eckhart in affirmative terms. For instance, Divine Knowledge means "the
act[44] or isness of pure knowledge itself, or Godhead,"
whereas "imperfect knowledge," when designated of the
manifest knower, means "active, evolving, and therefore restricted knowledge." Again, pure isness, which is identically
pure knowledge, means the all-inclusive Reality itself,
whereas "nothing," when said of the manifest world as such,
means the changing, temporal, and contingently real, or
"un-Reality."[45]

Now simply to consider "the manifest knower *as such*" or
"the created world *as such*" is, according to Eckhart, to consider them as separated from all else, that is, exclusively and
independently. It is actually to regard them without their
principle, for "nothing manifested contains its original unmanifested source." To value them exclusively in this way is
to regard that which is secondary as primary—a regard
which is "the root of all fallacy." Considerations solely of this
kind make for their un-Reality, for "apart from pure isness
itself [the primary Reality] there is nothing."[46] Secondary
realities, when considered not in themselves as such but correctly as dependent upon and participating in that which is
primary, are still only relationally real, but certainly so in
participatory knowledge. And when they are considered
wholly within the primary, that is to say in principle, then
they are indistinct from it, for "that which is within isness is
not other than isness."

A fundamental qualification laid down by Eckhart for the
study of the doctrine is the capacity to discriminate between
eternal and temporal realities. The student must acquire the
habit of distinguishing perfect from imperfect knowledge, pure isness from participative being, all-possibility

from certain possibilities, all-inclusive from exclusive, personality from individuality, pure spirit from composite structure, cause from effect, necessity from contingency; important from insignificant, excellent from pleasant. In other words, primary from secondary or the principle from its manifestation.

When one considers all the goals a human being may have—wealth, honor, power, private enjoyment, community peace, multifarious experience, aesthetic awareness, scientific cognition—all of which are delusive in their contingency, surely the pre-eminent goal is liberation from delusiveness. It alone eliminates all tension, pain, and dissatisfaction. It alone, says Eckhart, culminates the striving of the detached and unlimited will to know—that intellectual appetite which is innate in all knowing beings and the essential mark of their distinction from other beings.[47] The term of the unlimited will to know is nothing less than the actualization of unrestricted knowledge itself. Since true knowledge alone carries its own fruit within itself, it is the ultimate end as well as the direct "way"; only true knowledge can dispel ignorance, which is the root of all delusion.[48] Sacramental rites serve only as a preparation; even selfless activity can at best induce a favorable disposition. Spiritual exercises and techniques are useless except insofar as they discipline the inner self for the advent of true knowledge. As to the love of God, it must be directed by the light of true knowledge if it is to preserve itself from devotion to an anthropomorphic deity or to an idea of God that is, by definition, less than true God.

Eckhart insists that at our human disposal there are different sources of valid knowledge: sense perception, reasoning, intellection, and testimony. Sense perception comes first in time, but certainly not in truth value. Though superior to dreaming, it can nevertheless err; moreover, it is only concerned with fleeting, accidental realities.[49] Reasoning suffers similar defects in virtue of its dependence on sense perception; it is restricted to comprehensible structures of finite being and cognition in terms of twoness.

As previously noted, intellection, or direct insight into reality, is superior to sense perception and reasoning, though without sense experience and reasoning it could not affirm or negate the isness of anything comprehended. Intellection furnishes the human mind with unchanging principles that ground reasoning in being and enable it to establish with certainty the necessity of transcendent Reality, as well as the relation between secondary and primary realities. Nonetheless, it is restricted in its natural ability to enjoy an unrestricted act of comprehension or comprehend the nature of that which is ultimately primary and the mode of pure knowledge.[50]

As for testimony, it originates either from a genuine witness directly inspired by the Word of Divine Knowledge and effected by its Spirit, or it does not.[51] There is the human tradition of the testimony of profound intellects and saints, but that tradition is defective, for all men and women are fallible. But the Divine Word, or God-Man, who is infinitely more than a seer or a prophet, is infallible, and the Holy Scriptures that reveal that Word are substantially free from dependence upon the restricted capacities of individual authors. Hence that testimony is the supreme and primary source of knowledge.

Any attempt to rank any other source of knowledge as primary to the testimony of Holy Scripture must, according to Eckhart, be vigorously combatted.[52] As to those who pay heartfelt allegiance to it, our responsibility is to evaluate their teachings by studying them in the light of Holy Scripture. But to do this we require the guidance of the indestructible Church, whose function is to preserve and teach the divine doctrine. Thus we shall be able to sift away the defects that mar all human teachings and writings, including Eckhart's. What in them conforms to the primary meaning of the Divine Word should be retained as ancillary to our quest.[53]

Indeed, the primacy of the teaching of Holy Scripture—especially the New Testament, which fulfills and supersedes the Old—must be accepted on faith. But that faith, says Eckhart, requires reasonable justification.[54] Not only should we study the Scriptures in such a way as to discover their primary meaning and mutual harmony, but we should avail ourselves of all the rational means of dialectics by drawing upon all the secondary sources of knowledge. Only then can we refute all possible objections against that ascertained all-inclusive meaning and establish final conclusions. By thus uniting the light of intellect with the light of faith we may undertake a personal process of assimilation unimpeded by any remaining doubt, a process that culminates in a mode of knowledge situated as it were in the infinite Principle and that is in perfect conformity to the pure reality of Divine Knowledge indicated by the texts. Thus the act of faith, effected and sustained by recreated act and fully supported by reason, becomes initially validated at the very moment it is transformed into that transcendent principial knowledge and finally in the actual realization of Godhead.

Inasmuch as the reality of Divine Knowledge is ever present to us, it is not an accomplishment. Strictly speaking there are no "means" as such, for "means" designates effects to be accomplished and the reality of Divine Knowledge is not an effect but the primary Principle of all cause and effect. Divine Knowledge is an awakening. "When all individuality is asleep in you, then you are awake in God." In fact, "directly God awakens the ground [of the intellective soul] with truth, light darts into the powers, and that man knows more than anyone could teach him."[55] But just as there are degrees between sound sleep and waking awareness, so we may find ourselves in distant or close proximity to that divine awakening according to our state of awareness, way of life, character, and inner disposition. Since, however, these conditions are not "means," the awakening may, strictly speaking, occur to any person independent of his temporal condition.

To determine what is primary in Holy Scripture, we should first of all distinguish between indicative assertions and declaratory assertions.[56] Indicative or symbolic assertions point to the proper object of Holy Scripture: "Christ the God-Man," the "eternal Word of God." Declaratory or public assertions are preparatory injunctions, discussions, analects, or recordings of events, and therefore secondary and preparatory. But even in the multitude of indicative assertions we find some that designate only temporal or finite entities, others that designate the principles of sensate or rational awareness. All such statements are secondary and should never be granted ultimate value, for their concern is only with temporal realities that can be known by human cognition.

It is not in Holy Scripture that we should seek knowledge and the dispelling of ignorance in matters that are within the range of experience, for this double aim can be attained through sense perception and reasoning.[57] Nor is it the primary function of Holy Scripture to inform us about our manifest universe and its natural ontological and cosmological structure, for we are not told by God that the ultimate well-being of man essentially depends on such information. Nor have we any right to assume such a claim, inasmuch as all the passages setting forth the creation, the fall of man, the quest for knowledge of Nature are wholly subservient to the purpose of communicating the all-inclusiveness of God and Divine Knowledge upon which our very being is primarily dependent. It is rather That about which human experience and intellection tell us nothing, That which transcends all restriction, which is to be considered as the primary theme of all scriptural texts. Only those which communicate the intrinsic reality of God in his Godhead, which is Divine Knowledge, possess primacy and independent authority.

Yet even in these assertions which designate the knowledge, isness, and beatified love which God intrinsically is, we must seek, says Eckhart, the highest meaning, free from all imagination, conceptualization, and individuality. Otherwise they can only serve as useful pointers to that true meaning which alone satisfies the unlimited will to know. We must, then, distinguish three modes of divine designations: analogical, negative, and principial.[58] For while designations such as knowledge, isness, and love can be expressive of realities in finite manifestation, they can only be indicative when considering unmanifested God.

Analogical designations of God point to their object as to

that which they merely determine by reference to a relationship intrinsic in something that is known in manifestation. But in the case of God no relationship to anything in the manifest universe can be said to be intrinsic.[59] Therefore all such determinations, to the extent that they are merely analogous relationships, must be negated. And this negation is the function of our negative, or "not this, not that," indications, for they point to God by excluding from him all unsuitable predicates. Thus our quest is narrowed down to those assertions which indicate God's affirmation of himself as all-inclusive knowledge, isness, and love in principle. It is to these principial designations that all the previous steps have led us.

When we understand "isness" according to its meaning in manifestation it applies to things existing, but the context makes it clear that it is not in that sense that it applies to their ultimate Principle. Indeed, the designation of "knowledge" is there to warn us that God is not impersonal, unconscious reality, but the actuality of pure knowledge itself, the content of which is all-possibility; it also indicates that isness is in function of knowledge. Or we might understand "knowledge" in its active, manifest sense and think that God *has* knowledge as one of several qualities; but the terms "all-inclusive," "omnipotent," "on high" oblige us to deny this and affirm that God is Knowledge-in-itself and in Principle.[60] Similarly with those texts which communicate his love and beatitude, or his holding in oneness that which is eternally united. And since the designation of God as Father, Son, and Holy Spirit in the unity and identity of his Godhead discloses the transcendent, principial mode of Divine Knowledge, then the highest of all meanings indicates that which otherwise could never be ascertained—that is, knowledge by identity in the supreme Principle that God in his undifferentiated Godhead is.[61]

BASIC MISCONCEPTIONS

On the basis of direct testimony of the Word of God Eckhart presents us with a truly principial doctrine of Divine Knowledge. It is a doctrine worked out and expounded in terms of pure metaphysical intellection of which well-grounded faith is the animating principle and reasoning the supporting instrument. As for a corresponding philosophy of man and the manifested world of nature, we should not expect a detailed exposition. Why? Because he explicitly considered that as secondary and did not intend to produce one.[62] All that he has to say on the subject of man and the reflected order of existence is merely consequential upon what he intends to say about God and Divine Knowledge. In fact it is for the most part expressed in a relative or negative manner. Moreover, there is little need to repeat in terms of philosophical method what Augustine and Aquinas have already said.

What he does say is this: The entire manifest order of reflection, including man, cannot be truly understood apart from and independently of God. This is so because it depends entirely upon him as upon its transcendent-immanent Principle.[63] Furthermore, inasmuch as it is universally his manifest reflection, it is, as such, nothing in itself, yet by him it is in its imperfect way what he is in his infinitely perfect way. Thus it is neither sheer non-reality nor unconditioned Reality.

If Eckhart speaks of man and the existential world in a language which, for the most part, confines itself to the use of terms in their principial sense, it is because he was convinced that it was necessary, even at the risk of being misunderstood. It was a language which Augustine and Aquinas also used, but which they employed sparingly, for it can mislead the unqualified intelligence. But someone had to do it, for the simple reason that in affirming Knowledge-Reality as in our primal Principle and final end, it grounds all other true expositions. It states directly what is actually implied in all true indirect statements, and unless that which is implied is somehow rendered explicit, the implied, which in this case is primary, is too easily relegated to a secondary consideration and then neglected.

Of course the unqualified intelligence is more likely than not to read some form of pantheism or philosophical monism into Eckhart's principial knowledge; in spite of the fact that such forms of thought were completely foreign to his doctrine and actually refuted by him. But his language kept to such heights that the lower genius of many who came to regard themselves disciples or influenced by his teaching could not keep pace with him, and so turned his doctrine of transcendence into some heretical or heterodox form of thought.

When Eckhart says that the manifest universe, including man, is to God as "the reflected light is to its uncreated source," or as "the production of our dreams is to the world of our awakened intellect,"[64] many mistakenly understand him to say that the manifest world is sheer illusion. They forget that comparisons are meant to reach their object through a process of purification and transposition. When he says "my innermost Self is God," or "I am the Son and not other," they neglect his subtle but correct interpretation by precise discrimination and simply endow our finite self with divinity. These are errors that he is most emphatic in refuting, since for him the essence of ignorance is to superimpose finiteness upon God and divinity upon the finite.[65]

These remarks should indicate why it is hazardous to speak of Eckhart's influence on later writers and thinkers. That he was a major influence on those immediate fourteenth-century disciples such as Tauler, Suso, Ruysbroeck, and others who, for practical purposes, lowered his teaching to the level of a determinate mystical theology is beyond dispute. That this school of religious mysticism has been the major intellectual influence on subsequent mystical movements in Europe, such as in the seventeenth century, is also indisputable.[66] We also recognize his influence in the metaphysical aspects of the writings of Cajetan, Gerson, and Nicholas of Cusa. But to claim that Eckhart anticipated the theology of the Protestant Reformers, as some have asserted, is wholly mistaken and based on prejudice. Others have tried to affirm his influence on the philosophies of Kant and Hegel and even of modern Existentialism, but such affirmations are based almost entirely on mistaken attempts to read these philosophies into Eckhart's teachings.[67]

In the same way twentieth-century students of "mysticism" have tried to force Eckhart into conformity with their own brand of that subject, but these attempts have relied almost exclusively upon the Meister's German works; even, as often as not, on writings falsely attributed to Eckhart.[68] Deliberately ignoring his teachings on the indispensability of uncreated grace and the Incarnate Word, certain adherents of Far Eastern traditions have tried to acknowledge him as a fellow Zen Buddhist or as a Brahmanic seer.[69] Even some Nazi apologists tried to claim him as one of their own! Philologists, however, are on a far surer ground when they assert Eckhart's considerable contribution to the German vocabulary, which he enriched by the addition of many new and precise terms.

Sincere study in terms of the requisite qualifications previously noted can eliminate gross misrepresentations of Eckhart's teaching. It can do this to such a degree that the doctrine must be acknowledged as central in Christianity, inasmuch as it is a doctrine essentially situated as it were within Christ the Word of God. To do this, however, the student must first redress certain fundamental wrong considerations which the unqualified intellect is prone to adopt. Generally speaking they are as follows:

First, there is the point of view of radical fideism, which reads into Eckhart a rejection as impossible of a rational demonstration of the reality of God and his infinite, unconditioned nature. Second is the viewpoint that overlooks his full recognition of Holy Scripture as the highest source of knowledge and the fulfillment of our rational quest for transcendent Truth. Third, there is the attempt, entirely subjective, to consider Eckhart as not wholly committed to the Catholic Church as the divine dispenser and protector of the doctrine. Fourth is the consideration that ignores his insistence on the supranatural order of divine initiative and transposition by recreated grace, that is, by the Holy Spirit. Fifth, and consequently, is the affirmation that pure intellection or principial knowledge, as understood by Eckhart, is an achievement well within the natural power of man, rather than a pure Self-gift of God undue and inaccessible to our unaided effort. Sixth, there is a consideration that confuses his doctrine of identity through knowledge with identity through nature or substantial being. Seventh is a viewpoint ignorant of his precise theory of divine causality, which is to be praised in that it maintains the unrestricted freedom and transcendence of God and his immanence in the manifested effects that he originates, sustains, and directs. And finally, there is an external consideration that is wholly constituted in a mystical approach toward God, rather than a purely intellectual consideration situated as it were *in divinis*.

Once set right on these points, the student of Eckhart's teaching may then understand that the doctrine does not fall short in its application of "personality" either to all manifest knowing subjects or to God. For "where there is knowledge there is personality."[70] God is not infinite Personality primarily because man is a person. When we attribute this designation of God by analogy we do so in the context of secondary truth. The primary truth, according to Eckhart, is the inverse of this analogy: Man is a person because he is a direct image of pure Personality itself, or *Intellectus in se*, as indicated by the primary meaning of scriptural texts.

What therefore vitiates these several incorrect considerations of the doctrine is essentially their conscious opposition to infinite transcendence. The root of all false or inadequate considerations is basically either the notion of the detached intellectual act as inevitably relational or the view of reality as exactly corresponding to the relational and contingent character of mere human judgment. It is at the very moment when we refuse to apply Eckhart's theory of discrimination and principial knowledge to the enunciations of God and Divine Knowledge that we turn away from the most fundamental truth of the doctrine. That truth is simply that God in himself can have no ways of action or approach, for he is identically all-inclusive Knowledge-Reality, the pure identity of knowledge, isness, and beatified love.

We inevitably miss that truth as long as we think of God as a Being and therefore as approachable through other beings or conditions of being.[71] For Eckhart such thinking "never breaks through the bounds of creaturehood." And what, after all, does "creaturehood" mean? It means individuality; it means, in Aquinas's terminology, "a being divided from each and every other being while remaining undivided in itself."[72]   We must understand, therefore, that the designation "highest among beings" is no more than a designation of the highest individual or creature, say the highest angel.[73] Only when, as Eckhart says, the entire order of individuality, or of "self and other," is shattered by "the birth of the Word" is it possible to understand that in truth we have never been outside God, " in whom there is no otherness." For the birth of the Word initiates a transposition of our understanding from one limited by and attached to individuality to that of transcendent all-inclusiveness and all-possibility. What externally appears as approaches to God or actions in God are recognized as delusions once the transposition is effected.

It must be repeated that perhaps the most significant factor which distinguishes Eckhart's teaching from all others in the tradition to which he belonged is his persistent consideration of pure metaphysics which completely transcends individuality and universal manifestation in every respect. For him a metaphysics oriented externally to the revealed Word of God is incomplete. It is complete and pure only when its considerations are grounded as it were wholly within the eternal Word. When metaphysics, or detached intellection, is so considered, then and only then are the last vestiges of limitation, present in its subordinate and externalized role, removed. For divine intellection, which the term "pure metaphysics" designates, pertains to God alone and only to the unrestricted knowledge which he is in his Godhead.

When the light of intellect is perfectly united to the light of well-grounded faith in the Word of God, the possibility of understanding all things as it were within God is granted. This is axial in Eckhart's teaching.[74] For that perfect unification means the intellectual detachment from all considerations of time and place, from all external modes of knowing and indeed from the entire universe of existence and individuality. It is brought about by the birth of the Son, the Word of God, in the very ground of the intellective soul— and our willingness to accept it and to know.

Eckhart's teaching on "the birth of the Word" is one of the most repeated themes in his exposition of the doctrine. The realization of this "birth," which is actually a realization that one eternally dwells in God, effects the knowledge of God through identity, that is principially. Since Aquinas had taught Eckhart that from the immutable and all-inclusive standpoint of God "there is nothing apart from God" and "that which is in God is God," then an exposition of Divine Knowledge from that standpoint is not only possible but indeed the primary mode of exposition.

Anything short of this, that is to say any intended external mode of exposition, must of necessity introduce an obviously sentimental or consoling element into the doctrine. To the degree that it does it represents a falling away from pure metaphysical insight. This, of course, is inevitable once it is understood what pure Intellect is not. If the doctrine was to be adapted to the mentality of the men and women for whom it was especially being framed, that is, people in whom feeling and the desire for consolation were stronger than intelligence, then Augustine and Aquinas were not wrong in taking these factors into consideration. Nor was Eckhart in some of his Sermons or when he composed his *Book of Divine Consolation* for the Queen of Hungary, who had recently undergone a great personal tragedy.

Nevertheless, it remains true that feeling and the desire for consolation are relative and contingent, so that, to the degree to which an exposition of the doctrine makes an appeal to it, it is bound to be relative and contingent. Far more than any of his predecessors Eckhart intended his exposition of the doctrine to be free of such consoling elements, with the hope that perhaps a few might be qualified to accept it in its purity. And it only takes a meager few in each generation to keep the light of reconditioned truth aflame. After all, truth in itself has no need to be consoling. If anyone finds it so, then obviously so much the better for him.[75] But the consolation he feels emanates from himself and from the particular dispositions of his own feelings, not from the doctrine. On more than one occasion Eckhart states that the doctrine should be expounded in its purity even if it is not fully understood by those who hear it.

The preparatory considerations to be undertaken in the next chapter and the consideration of the doctrine of Divine Knowledge according to Eckhart's exposition in all that follows in Part II should go a long way toward removing the many misconceptions outlined above to which the unqualified student of Eckhart is subject. It should also become clear that misdirected considerations are of value only insofar as they indicate their own need of correction.

As understood by Eckhart, what distinguishes true Christian doctrine from all other actual and possible teachings is the essential starting point. In all other teachings the human being is regarded as the starting point. The human being starts thinking about God, and is inevitably misled into misrepresenting him either as an impersonal absolute or as hiding behind innumerable myths. In true Christianity God is the starting point; he initiates the knowledge of himself, by his Self-revelation in Jesus Christ, as the God of unrestricted knowledge, isness, and love.

But we human beings in our unregenerate condition do not know that God is the starting point and the initiator of true knowledge. We do not even know that God is real, that his unrestricted isness and love are identically the unrestricted knowledge which he is. Before we consider the essential doctrine as expounded by Eckhart, we must first seek reasonable justification for that doctrine. Or, as he says, "we must prepare ourselves rationally and spiritually for the eternal birth of his Word,"[76] We must first know that God is real before we can affirm him as the starter and supreme Principle of all that is. Though this "preparation" involves a concession to philosophical considerations, it derives its immediate justification from truths known directly by reasonable judgment and disciplined intellection. It derives its ultimate justification from the consideration of pure Intellect, for after all is said that can be said, God is also responsible for the preparation.

2

The Reality of the Divine Self

In undertaking certain philosophical considerations, as is our concern in this chapter, it should be said that it is done in order to show, as Eckhart says, "that the affirmation of God as the primal source of all being and knowledge is intellectually justified."[1] In other words, blind faith, or commitment unsupported by reasonableness, is an act that the seeking intellect cannot tolerate. But any intellectual justification for a doctrine of Divine Knowledge, which is transcendently distinct from all other doctrines, must begin by considering the human being in his unregenerate condition.

Thus considered the human intellect does not have a direct and immediate knowledge of any distinctions except those existing between his own reality and the reality of individual beings other than himself, and also those distinctions which are the result of the extensions of the human self, such as general and particular concepts. As each human being starts with himself he cannot yet know that his cognitional activity is an externalization of God's knowledge. In other words, the unregenerate human being does not have a direct and immediate knowledge that there actually is the all-inclusive God who must be really distinguished from the entire order of manifest existence, including the human intellect.

The acquisition of knowledge that God is real and hence of the essential distinction between universal manifestation and its nonmanifest Principle, is the conclusion of a highly disciplined and reasonable reflection grounded in a detached and unlimited will to know. The unlimited will to know, which is immediate in the human being, urges the intellect on in its search for the ultimate principle of all that is actually known and remains to be known.[2] Unless the will to know is aborted by other desires, this search continues until the intellect is able to answer the question of the actuality of that supreme Principle. It must answer this question by a well-grounded affirmation that the Principle itself necessarily, objectively, and really is, that it is transcendently distinct from the entire order of manifestation and every modality thereof, that it is the ultimate Principle of all manifestation and that God is the Principle.

"I AM A KNOWER"

If one's own individual self is now considered as the starting point—and each human self must start with himself and on his own—then, as Eckhart reminds us, the one primordial and intelligent assertion is: "I am a knower." Indeed, "Before all else I am a knower." "I naturally and preeminently desire knowledge. . . . What I will, that I seek, and knowledge comes first." "The very nature and life of man, as man, is to know and be a knower."[3] The immanent will to know is totally unsatisfied with any other initial determination. For if the human self is not a knower, then he is obliged to remain in brute ignorance and silence so far as knowing anything whatsoever goes; even contradictions, such as "I know that I am not a knower."

Furthermore, knowing that he is "before all else a knower" distinguishes each human being from all other knowers and also from all nonknowing beings. As an individual knower he not only knows himself as an individual, but also knows that he is not the whole of reality, that there are beings that are really, and not just mentally, other than himself. These other beings are known objectively. Not merely because the knower experiences and has concepts of what he experiences, but primarily because their actual existence is directly determined by a well-grounded and necessary judgment: a "yes," an "it is so," designating that "this (house, person, or whatever) is." Only thus is the knowable directly and actually known and known as real being. This is what Eckhart means when he says that "the object of the intellect is being."[4] In other words, that which makes for truth or conformity of the intellect with reality[5] is the affirmation primarily of the isness of "this" or "that" knowable, and only secondarily its "whatness."

"I *am* a knower and things other than myself are." This is a determination that is insusceptible to any "proof," not because it is not true but because it is known to the reflective human knower as immediately given in a direct and necessarily affirmed insight into the principle of being (*being is being*). As understood by Eckhart, as indeed by Aristotle, being is prior to any demonstration and that upon which all demonstrations of anything else are to be grounded. Being, in which both the human self and other individualities are grounded by their actuality, or isness, is neither experienceable nor conceivable. It is directly known as the objective of the unlimited will to know which is open to all-possibility. In this sense, being designates itself as all that is known and all that is to be known,[6] as that apart from which there is nothing, as that which is known by any and all true determinations.

Being, then, is all-possible substantiality, which means that being is at once thoroughly concrete and everywhere present. It also means that being is not divided from without; rather it divides itself from within, such as into subject and object.[7] Moreover, being and reality are identical in that the real, as also being, is not merely the object of thought but that which is known actually *to be* by true determinations.[8] In the affirmation of being it is the actuality of being, or *isness*, that is fundamentally affirmed. In fact the identity of being and the real involves a consent to the course of the unlimited will to know and an exclusion of all other intruding desires, for only "as long as this will (to know) remains unmoved by creatures and creaturehood, is it free and unlimited."[9] And the unlimited will to know is satisfied with neither sensory nor conceptual knowledge, with which most modern philosophy stops short, but only with well-grounded determinations of concrete facts and ultimately when all questions for intelligence are exhausted.

"The intellect directly receives being first, even before it receives truth, though truth is present along with being."[10] The knower does not "go outside himself to a known," for

being, in which both the knower and the known are constituted as real, "has no outside." There is no beholding of
oneself and a beholding of something else. There is simply a
direction toward the knowable by participation in being,
within which there are no separations but only real distinctions, and self and other is one of those distinctions. Of
course, if one forgets that real distinctions are not separations, or that subject and object are not strict differentia-
tions from but divisions within being, then understanding
in the direction of the unlimited will to know is halted and
knowledge is aborted.

We know things through our senses, says Eckhart.[11] But
experiencing, thinking, comprehending, questioning as
such never establish real existence. Only the reasonable
determination "it is" or "this is" does that, inasmuch as well-
grounded determination is the culminating act of the knowing course as a cumulative increase of sense experience,
comprehension, and reflection. Yet every reasonable affirmation raises a further question, for the ultimate term of
the unlimited will to know is the unlimited *act* of comprehension which knows all about all. Considered in its fundamental isness, being is not an experience, nor is it a concept or idea pertaining to any general or particular order of
individuality. Rather it is the human intellect's primary intention or notion of the entire content of the unlimited will
to know, and that content is nothing less than all-possible
knowability.

"Being and knowledge are all one, for whatever is not
cannot be known."[12] Being and the knowable are identical
and are reality. Furthermore, "knower and known are one
in knowledge." Knowing is "a participation in being," and
not a mental gazing at it, not the result of any attempt to
reach *out there* or *in here* to grasp being as though it were a
conceivable and analyzable essence, or whatness, and thus
differentiated from something else. Apart from being there
is nothing. The isness of being is not a whatness, but every
essence or whatness is in potentiality to it and therefore
nothing if separated from it.[13]

THE REALITY OF GOD

Were the human knower in himself capable of the unlimited act of comprehension there would, of course, be no questions whatsoever, for then he would be that act and know all about all. He would then *be* the Principle substantially and not subject to individuality in any way. However, despite the fact that he is incapable of that unlimited act of comprehension, he does have an unlimited will to know which, if sustained, grants a profound insight. This insight reveals that God, if he really is, must not only be knowable but also total knowability, that God must be unrestricted and unconditioned reality and therefore the infinite Knower, the divine Self and Principle of all actuality and possibility. The human knower is presented, then, as Eckhart says, with a twofold question: What is God, and whether God is?[14] Or to put it another way: What is the ultimate Principle, and is it real?

Sooner or later the human knower who wills to know without attachment or the intrusion of other aims must meditate on the question: Is God only a mental object, or is God real? To say, as some have, that Eckhart needed no demonstration that God really is shows a complete misunderstanding of his teaching. It is certainly true that he believed in the revelation of the Word and that the Word told him that God is and is to be known as "I am who I am" and as "the Principle identical with the Word."[15] But believing is not knowing, and in order to believe the communication from God it is, he says, essential to *know*, and not merely believe, that God really is. For "how can one believe anything about God if one does not know that he *is*?"[16] The reality of God is not an article of faith, nor is it known by any human experience, mystical or otherwise. God is actually known to be real only by intellection, reflection, and well-grounded determination.

Nor is the reality of God to be known by any essentialist answer to the question: What is God? Since the human knower cannot conceive or have an idea of pure isness, he certainly cannot conceive or have an idea of what the unlimited act of comprehension actually is, the full content of which is knowing all about all. Knowledge of *what* God is is not possible for the human knower, inasmuch as the what-ness of God infinitely transcends the grasp of that which is confined to individuality.[17] But if the unconditioned Knower actually is, then his isness must be that unlimited act of comprehension, and it must be a single act for him to know what he is and that he is. As the comprehension answers the "what?", so the unlimited answers the "is?" For the human knower there is no single answer to these two questions.[18]

The human knower may come to know that pure isness is all-inclusive as the ground of being, but what it is he can-not know, inasmuch as *isness* is not a *what*. Isness is simply is-ness, is wholly inconceivable, but is that without which all actual knowledge is impossible, without which all concepts and ideas and essences are dead, without which there is nothing.[19] The knowledge that God really is, then, must depend on disciplined reflection and be the conclusion of a demonstration, which is simply the meditative framework for a well-grounded affirmation. In other words, the reflec-tion, demonstration, and affirmation are dependent upon the knower's participation in being.

Eckhart fully accepts the traditional ways of demon-strating the reality of God, and he sums them up by the necessary recognition of the identity of real unrestricted isness with total knowability.[20] In other words, to affirm the total knowability of real isness is to affirm the total knowa-bility of all that is to be reasonably affirmed. Since one can-not affirm the isness of all that is to be reasonably affirmed without in the same stroke affirming unrestricted and all-possible isness, then reasonably to affirm it is to know that it *is*.

Now, that total knowability cannot be a knowability that is in any way conditioned, restricted, or affected by any being whatsoever, for apart from total knowability there is strictly nothing.[21] It cannot be a knowability for which further ques-tions are possible, as in the case with any limited isness or the sum of all individual acts of being. Hence it must be that knowability that is purely spiritual, nondependent, non-abstract, and therefore wholly real. It must be the identity of all-inclusive knowability in act with all-inclusive knowledge in act. In fact it must be pure reconditioned reality itself, fully self-explanatory and self-sufficient, the unlimited act of comprehension itself. Indeed, it must be the unrestricted Knower who cannot question because he knows all about all. Such is what is meant by God. Thus "unrestricted isness is God, and if God is not then there is strictly nothing, which is absurd. It follows that everything that is, is through unrestricted isness. But unrestricted isness is God."[22]

Now this or any other philosophical demonstration of the reality of God is, according to Eckhart, little more than a rather formalized expression of a far more intimate demonstration which indicates the very heart of the doctrine Eckhart expounds. Indeed the truly intimate demonstration more directly unfolds the orientation of pure metaphysics or principial knowledge. This calls for further consideration.

"MY TRUEST *I* IS GOD"

Eckhart is constantly directing the human knower to reflect on the immaterial nature and detached spirituality of intelligence. This is central throughout his teaching, as already noted. He points out that in this reflection a profound insight can be gained that will lead to a knowledge that the reconditioned Principle is God, and also a knowledge of the knower's direct relation with God. In this most personal reflection the human knower is not basically intent either on any known fact of experience or on any succession of causes. Rather he is now intent on that prelogical awareness wherein certainty unfolds in an intimate knowledge "within the proper existence of the intellect itself."[23]

Ordinarily the human knower is aware of the intellect's development insofar as it is related to human life as it occurs in the course of private, social, and vocational endeavors. In this respect the activity of the intellect consists of a process of operations implanted in time and hence

operations of sense experience and sense presentations
maintained and directed by the intellect to comprehensions
and actual determinations and decisions. Yet the activity of
the intellect itself, as Eckhart points out, exists primarily and
pre-eminently in a process related not to human life but to
detached intellectuality itself. "There is a power in the soul
[the act of intellect itself] which touches neither time nor
flesh. It flows out of the spirit and abides in the spirit and is
altogether spiritual."

In this respect intellectuality is not a series of operations
in time and of sense and images. Rather this spiritual act is
thoroughly withdrawn in intellection itself and constituted
above sense and images. Grounded only in knowable objec-
tivity, it is removed from time. "There is this power: intellect, which is of prime importance for making the self
aware of, for detecting, God. It has five properties: First, it
is detached from time. Next, it is like nothing sensed or
conceived. Third, it is pure and uncompounded [by materiality or corporeality]. Fourth, it is in itself in act and self-
searching [or reflective, meditative]. Fifth, it is a reflection
or spiritual image."

Now when the human self is wholly absorbed in such an
act of intellection, or detached meditation, he is engaged in
concentrating on a certain truth, for instance: "Apart from
isness there is nothing." Nothing else enters his intellect. He
is now completely at one with the act of intellection, identified with the intellectual apprehension and the knowing of
that which is. It is now that the profound insight unfolds.
For suddenly he is brought up sharply with a question: "Is it
possible that that which is now in the act of detached knowing once was nothing, nonexistent:" It is then that the
knower immediately realizes that he, who is now at one with
the act of intellection itself and fully aware of his knowing,
was never a strict nothing, never nonexistent. "It is not
possible that that which is now knowing and reflecting was
once upon a time nothing, for this act of intellection, with
which the knower is identified, could not have come into
existence."

The knower is now not knowing essentially in terms of sense experience or sense presentations, that is, of operations implanted in time. On the contrary, "he is at one with this wholly spiritual and supratemporal act of intellection itself and thus has always been. . . . Nothing could be more certain or immediate in this timeless 'now.'" It is only when the knower turns away from this detached reflective act of intellection and begins to philosophize about it from a psychological standpoint that he regards the insight as strange and question-raising. In this act, however, "there is the intimate and direct awareness of actual knowing and knowability," of an intellectual reality that "transcends the series of operations in time."

Of course the knower is certain of his human individuality and existence. He is "aware of his temporal parents," his childhood, his time-space environment and "the fact that he was born in time." But now in the detached intellective act he is also fully and immediately certain, inasmuch as the essential immateriality of intelligence is in act, that his existence now as a knowing intellective act "is neither the consequence of strict nothing nor of something beginning in time." Thus he is aware of two certitudes: "he was born in time," yet "he who is now the supratemporal intellective act [or reality] is not born." He is also aware of the fact that unless his unlimited will to know is maintained and prompts him to reflect in this intellectual awareness, he would not know the second certitude, for the first certitude "greatly tends to cloud it over." But he has sustained and followed the unlimited will to know, is now reflecting, and now gains this knowledge.

In other words, the knower who is now fully concentrated in detached intellection and identified with this actuality has always been. Not of course in his temporal self or within the conditions of his own distinct personality. Nor has he always been in and by an impersonal Being, for "there is no intellection or knowledge without personality." Where, then, has this self now identified with the act of intellection always been? "He has always been in and by infinite and eternal Intellect," that is, necessarily in transcendent Personality or pure Spirit itself, in whom all there is of perfection in all knowing is in an unrestricted mode.

Metaphysically "prior to the existence of the individual self, that unrestricted Knower is and is his own infinite Selfhood, knowing himself by himself." And though the individual self now is, that all-inclusive Self is infinitely transcendent, is eternal and unconditioned isness itself. "It is in pure Spirit itself, which is infinite Intellect-as-such, that this self who is now at one with the act of intellection now *is*." And it is from pure Spirit that this self "issued forth one day into temporal existence in its own structure and personality." Pure Spirit, unconditioned Isness, infinite Selfhood, the unlimited Knower, we call God, or the divine Self, which is identically the unrestricted Principle. "Unconditioned Intellect . . . as the first Principle of all things, is entirely Intellect, transcendently pure Intelligence. In him indeed Reality and Intellect are identical."

Once this certitude is attained, the human knower then realizes that he alone is not fully responsible for the attainment. He now knows that to actualize a firm and stable affirmation of God as real is not possible without the divine help that sustains the unlimited and detached will to know and the participation in being that makes the insight true. From a nonparticipative viewpoint no demonstration of God's reality is free of "loopholes," but as Eckhart has explained, such a "view" is illusory to begin with inasmuch as it is "separated from the intelligibility of being." It is not that this fundamental and demonstrative knowledge of the reality of God is indecisive. It is simply that the human knower, enmeshed in dualities and the indefinite extensions of the temporal self, plagued by corporate selfishness and weakened by his own inward adherence to unsuccesses in willing to know, needs help to sustain himself on the level of participatory intelligence "wherein it is realized that every actual human knower lives in a grace-enveloped order of being."

To realize the significance of the certitude of God's reality we must, as Eckhart says, correctly understand that "intellect is above time." "Intellect is the summit of the soul

. . . time cannot touch the intellect." What is time? "Time is
the proper duration of materiality." But the intellect is immaterial, spiritual. The intellect "enjoys a wondrous pre-
eminence, so much so that the light of intellect raises a
stone above the realm of sense and temporality." In fact,
"the intellect [being wholly spiritual] has the power to know
all things and never rests until it returns to the first *ratio*, in
which all things are one, that is, in God."

Indeed, the outward, progressive operations of the
human intellect are in time, and inasmuch as the movements of sense and images are restricted to materiality these
operations are subject to time. But in themselves these operations are grounded above time and are not subject to the
flow of matter's own duration. How do they then exist in
themselves? They exist in a way that is "a direct reflection of
eternity," for their way of existing is "the constancy in isness
of the spiritual acts of intellection." This way of existence is
without flow, movement, or series: "It consists of a direct
reflection of eternity, of an absence or negation of time."
Such is the nature of detached intellection in itself, which is
not in time and not subject to time.

In itself the spiritual or intellectual act is supratemporal.
"In that act knower and known are one without interval,
without medium, and the act itself is without beginning and
end." Insofar as it is "an actual [concrete] happening" it
occurs in time, in process, in history. But its content pertains wholly to an order transcending the materiality of
sense experience, sense presentations, of flow, movement,
and series. The "word-happening as such" is allusive, a *lapses
linguae*, wherein more is meant than meets the ear. That
which "happens" acts on stage, so to speak, for a moment in
temporal existence, but acts without beginning and end "in
the ground of the intellective soul and in detached intellection itself."

All operations proceed from a subject, and intellectual
operations proceed from a knowing subject. And what operation is more truly personal than intellection itself?
The human knower engages in intellection. This intellection is performed by human selves, and each human self is

"a composite of spirituality and materiality." Where is this self? This self is in time and was born in time. But in that it fully engages in the spiritual and detached act of intellection, in that it identifies itself with the spiritual act and so is capable of being in and by the immaterial ground of the act of intellection, then this self is also supratemporal, as is intellection itself. In this ground of the intellective soul, this self transcends the limits of time. True, this self began in time. But does anything begin unconditionally? Doesn't everything that begins "exist before itself in its causes?" Insofar as it is material or corporeal, this self "existed before itself in time," that is, in the ancestral cells, the physico-chemical and psychic materials and energies utilized by life all along the evolving process from which this self emerged. That of it which existed before pre-existed in time.

Nevertheless, this self as spiritual, as performing and identified with the supratemporal act of intelligence; it is not possible that it could have pre-existed in time. Why? Simply because "intellect can only proceed from Intellect; intellection can only proceed from Intellection itself and hence from that unrestricted isness which is supratemporal, without beginning or end." Furthermore, intellection is fundamentally and truly personal, as previously explained. It follows, then, that when intellection is enacted as the operation of this or that knower born into temporal existence, it cannot proceed from that which transcends time, sense, and images *unless* this self that is now performing the fully concentrated act of intellection somehow is prior to and above time, sense, and images.

We are not, Eckhart warns, here confronted with two separate selves. This self, which the human knower is, is born in time. But insofar as the self is now wholly absorbed in intellection, it is not born in time. "It proceeds from eternity." It necessarily is prior *in* that transcendent, ultimate, and "divine Selfhood" in whom there is no temporality or individuality. Hence "it is not there in its own human nature," for in its proper nature it came to exist only by being born in time. But "all that there is in this spiritual self of detached intellection, knowing, personality, and isness" is first there "in the unrestricted Knower" in a way "infinitely other to any way in itself." This self "is thus a reflection or image of its object, the divine Selfhood." But "object and image are bound up with one another so that we cannot separate them. We can think of fire apart from heat and heat without fire. We can think of sun apart from light and light as independent of the sun. But we cannot separate the image from its object."

This is so because everything that is in individual existence is "a direct participation" in the unrestricted act of knowledge itself, apart from which there is nothing. That unrestricted act or isness "must contain all things in itself in a perfect way" and be itself personality, intellect, and isness in a strictly transcendent order. This means that unrestricted isness, or total knowability, is the divine Knower, the infinite and eternal Selfhood, and as such "transcendently distinct from all the diversity of individual existence." This also means that unrestricted isness is not the act of being (or isness) of an individual manifestation, "which *has* its isness" from nonindividualized and nonmanifested isness, but that unrestricted isness itself (*esse in se*) "is subsisting completely through itself." And this is what is meant by God.

The divine Selfhood, from which the self now absorbed in detached intellection directly proceeds, is identically God. Hence we are directed to a well-grounded affirmation of that necessary metaphysical principle which transcends conceptualization: "Unrestricted Isness, from which proceeds every being; eternal Intellect, from which proceeds every intellection"; or "divine Selfhood, from which proceeds every self."

But this self that is eternally in God, in what way is it there in God? Not, of course, as it is here in its natural or integral structure. Rather "it is there in God inasmuch as it is known to and not other than unconditioned Intellect." In other words, "it is there in God not other than the divine essence itself"; it is fully "at one with the participality of the divine essence" and thus identical with it. And the divine essence is the immediate and undifferentiated "object" of the unlimited act of comprehension.

Indeed all selves, as they are in this way *in* God, are the divine Selfhood as unfolding its participality. Without existing in themselves they are in and not other than the Selfhood. They are there in the Selfhood "infinitely more perfect and real than in the existence they have in their proper natures." They are in the infinite Intellect "by the very isness that God *is* in his unrestricted act of knowledge." And "that which is in God is God"; the self that is *in* the Self-hood, *is* in Selfhood.

This is eminently true of all selves endowed with intelligence, but it is also true of all other contingent knowables. "Prior to their existing in themselves they, in their isness and knowability, are, as participations of the divine Intellect, known to that Intellect eternally. They are in God by his very isness." They are in God by the participality of his essence "not as particular ideas or universal ideas abstracted by the human intellect from things," but "as the eternal and unrestricted *ratio* which is prior to the manifestation of things . . . and which is identically the *Logos*." And "*in* the primal Intellect [Godhead] properly speaking . . . God always knows in act [isness] and in knowing eternally begets the idea and the idea which this knowing begets is God himself." "God speaks one word; this is his own comprehension of himself [apart from which there is nothing]. . . . In this one comprehension he comprehends all things, he comprehends them as issuing forth from prior nothing [that is, from his unmanifest all-possibility]. . . . As subsisting eternally in him, they are without themselves [in their own proper natures or as individuals]. What they are without themselves, *is* God himself."

Therefore this knowing self can rightly affirm with Eckhart that "I, without my temporal self, always am. I am eternally in God. And inasmuch as that which is in God is not other than God, then in principle my truest *I* [or innermost Self] is God."

Now it is only by proper discrimination that we can avoid falsity and correctly understand this affirmation. It does not assert that in God this spiritual self is eternally performing the act of intellection. It does not assert that this self is even collaborating in the infinite act of Divine Knowledge. This would be nonsense, for "in God the only knower who knows is God himself." No, what is asserted is that the self that is now fully absorbed in detached intellection is eternally in God, not as distinctly performing any act of intellection, but as comprehended by and known to God in his knowledge of himself, that is to say in Divine Knowledge. This self abides there by uncreated and unmanifested personal isness, by that isness which is the eternal and infinite intellective Principle through which the divine Self knows itself. The divine Self is not this self now engaged in the act of intellection. On the other hand, this self that proceeds from infinite Intellect, in which it eternally is as prior nonmanifestation, and that was not born on any day, is *in principle* the divine Self, or God. Our temporal "I" is not our primary or principial *I*. We all have what Eckhart affirms as that eternal *I*, "our truest *I*," and that eternal *I* is God.

"GOD IS NEITHER THIS NOR THAT"

First of all, the divine Self, or God, is not this self engaged in the act of intellection or in any other act, and any such identification is a complete aberration of the doctrine Eckhart expounds. The divine Self is not this self inasmuch as the divine Self is not this, not that.[24] Identically God, the Principle of all actuality and possibility, the divine Self is not an essence to be grasped by human intellection.

The all-pervading significance of the unrestricted isness of all-inclusive knowledge which God is, is not to be this or that, but simply *to be*. If essence is in any way regarded as virtually distinct from the isness that God is, then it follows that God is without essence. If God is virtually without essence, he is no virtual "whatness."

The only answer, then, to the question "What is God?" is, as Eckhart says: "God is!" or rather "God is nothing."[25] And in saying this he simply asserts that "God is no-thing, not this, not that." By stressing the unconditioned isness that God is and the isness of all that is known and knowable,

he never for an instant doubts the reality of God or the relational reality of himself and all contingent beings. In fact he
tells us that if we exclude essence absolutely from isness we
are then left with no intelligible relation with God or with
beings proportionate to us.[26] Those who assert that God is
absolutely without essence and thus conclude that God
is nothingness and mean that nothing is, are, he says, "contradictory and involved in a thorough abuse of intelligence." For there is then no way of knowing anything
whatsoever, not even oneself as a knower.[27] When, speaking
in the name of pure metaphysics, Eckhart says that God is
without essence, he means that God is the Reality and Principle whose essence is simply *to be*. God, then, is That whose
Knowledge or Godhead, being unrestricted, is transcendent
of all essence, unconditioned by any "what" as well as by
every mode of general or particular determination. "The
Principle itself is always pure [i.e. supradeterminate] Intellect in which there is no reality other than superessential,
unconditioned Knowledge."[28]

The will to know must never cease. "The intellect must
press in; it is not content with goodness or wisdom, nor with
truth nor yet with 'God' [as objective essence]. It is no more
content with 'God' than with a tree or a stone. It must never
rest until it gets into the Principle from which truth and
goodness proceed and takes them *in principle*, the fount of
truth and goodness where they are before they spring forth
in manifestation."[29] In his Latin Commentary on the Mo-
saic "I am who I am,"[30] Eckhart precisely points out what he
has stated over and over again in other works. "When God
says: "I am who I am," he teaches us that the subject "I am" is
identical with the predicate, the second "I am," that the
denomination is that which is denominated, the essence is
the isness, the *quiditas* is the *anitas*. . . . Here there is self-sufficiency itself. . . . Such self-sufficiency is proper to God
alone. In everything short of God [that is, universal mani-
festation] essence itself is not self-sufficient [or self-explana-
tory]. . . . There is [in all individuality] real distinction between substance and potency, isness and operation."[31]

All created beings have a whatness really distinct from

their own isness, which they have from God,[32] and this is why they are individuals and comprehensible. Not so with God, the divine Selfhood, whose essence or whatness is his isness and "in whom [that is, in principle] all beings are God." This axial principial truth the self knows when it is now absorbed in timeless intellection, for therein the act of intellection is known as a direct reflection of and hence an immediate participation in the divine essence, which is indistinct from God the ultimate Principle.

For the human knower this also means that the individual self and all individual manifestation proceed from God in his creative act as contingent knowables. Contingent because God does not cause any of the infinite possibilities known to him to become actually manifest out of necessity, inasmuch as his will is not necessarily obliged to affirm any one of them.[33] "God does not know any 'why' differentiated from himself." His will is uncaused, since it is identically all-inclusive isness. Hence *why* God manifests himself in universal being is unanswerable, because it is not a metaphysical question. But all that is manifested is, from the consideration of the human self, willed by God in his infinite goodness and so could not be a "better" manifestation.[34] Only God can truly manifest being, which is to say that God does not *have* isness but is all-inclusive and all-possible isness itself. Thus willed by God all manifest beings are known to exist in virtue of their own ends, that is, to actualize their own isnesses, which they have from God.[35]

Though these individuals or contingent manifestations, are nothing in themselves, that is, apart from unrestricted isness, and are as nothing in comparison with the unmanifested reality of God, they, comprising the entire universe of being, are real in having their own isness from God.[36] And this is the only way the human knower can intelligently affirm himself and all known and knowable beings, for the essence he and they have is only from being of this or that genus or species. The very isness of every individual being, which it has directly from God as his manifestation, is that which is most immediate in it.[37] The isness of any knowable is at once the manifestation of the Principle,

the ground whereby it is knowable, and the existential dynamism in virtue of which everything else in the knowable,
comprising its structure and essence, is its potentiality.

In other words, God's innermost presence and operation
in every manifest being is not of the order of essence, structure, or substance but of the immediate order of isness, and
to be realized principially. Moreover his presence is innermost, not only as long as individual beings are sustained in
intelligible manifestation, but also as their ultimate end. For
in being created and sustained in their proper isness by the
infinite isness that God is, they are directed to their ultimate
end as well as to their own proper ends, and their ultimate
end is God himself. After all, "the end is universally the
same as the Principle."[38] Without freedom being effaced, the
entire universe of manifestation is, then, in the direction of
emergence toward a consciousness of the union of the manifest being with unmanifest isness.

THIS SACRED UNIVERSE

With Eckhart we can now reasonably affirm that "the
entire created order is sacred," inasmuch as it and all individual beings that comprise it are directly involved in the assimilation of all things to God, the Principle. Intelligence
under the sway of the unlimited will to know assures us of
this fact. The profane is only the result of an unsuccess in
willing to know and a failure in willing to decide intelligently. It is the result of an unsuccess in intelligence and
being; it is a contraction of awareness.[39] Insofar as the unlimited will to know is arrested by any attempt merely to stop
and gaze at manifest being rather than participate in it, then
this world must obviously appear as profane and evil.

The very arrest of the dynamic will to know is a contraction of awareness, and out of this contraction spring opinions such as the following: Since God operates in all beings
as the efficacious cause of everything in universal manifestation, then he must be responsible for all evil, injustice, and
moral and organic failure. But an unsuccess in intending
and participating in God makes for an inability to understand in truth. And Eckhart says that it essentially makes for

an inability to understand that in evil, as in all failures in knowing and being, there is no being or knowable to comprehend. Since evil is not a being, and hence is not an intelligible, it can only be considered as a privation of or an unsuccess in being and the will to know.

"All things [or all individual manifestation] applies only to being. Sin, however, and evil in general are not being [but 'a failure in being and thus are not intelligible']. Consequently they are not caused by God but are without God. . . . For evil things *are* not [are without isness], neither are they made [caused or bestowed with a reason for existing], because they have not been effected nor are they effects but rather defects of some kind of being."[40] As a failure or unsuccess, sin and evil acts are simply the consequences of the irrational. The "primary sin," from which all sinful and evil acts result, is nothing other than a failure of the will to know without attachment and restriction.

But why does failure and hence privation in being occur? Here again our question is nonmetaphysical, because what cannot be in knowable dependence on anything else cannot have a cause or reason, and so God cannot in any way whatsoever be the cause or reason of a failure in knowledge or of its consequences in evil. From the standpoint of the human knower the freedom in God's creative act permits failures and evil, but God can never be correctly regarded as reasonably responsible for them. From the direct standpoint of Divine Knowledge there is really no failure and hence no real evil, for in the Principle and in terms of principial knowledge there is only unrestricted and perfectly unconditioned isness.[41] Any principial recognition of evil or defect in being and knowability is only oblique.

Though from the consideration of the divine Selfhood all manifestation is, in a sense, equivalent,[42] this is not so in terms of individuality. For "the creature has but one reflection, that of not being the other," and "where there is otherness there is difference in participation in being."[43] From the consideration of the human self all that which substantially is not God, that is, all individual manifestation as such, contains a necessary condition of not being nothing by being a knowable and hence a participation in all-pervasive being. On this point Eckhart is simply following through with the teachings of Aquinas and the Pseudo-Dionysius.[44]

To the degree that an individual modality is restricted by materiality, it is less an actual participation in being, since materiality, or potentiality, is the limitation of actuality. Conversely, the less an individual modality is restricted by its materiality, the more it actually participates in being. And if it is wholly unrestricted, that is, a pure intellectual structure, then its participation is total. Thus the very fact of more or less participation in being reveals a hierarchical universe of superiors and inferiors in which the higher, more qualitative beings should act upon the lower and the redeveloped be for the developed.[45]

So true is this in terms of manifestation, says Eckhart, that an abuse of this law of nature, which is a reflection of the eternal law, by any attempt to distort the hierarchy or to project a policy of egalitarianism into it, is an unsuccess in knowing and being. As long as anyone is in any way considering the time-space world of individual manifestation, even in terms of making life "better" for human beings, egalitarianism is out of the question. Nothing less than actual intelligence and the good will inherent in intelligence merit the affirmation of superiority over all other modalities of being.[46] The abuse of this law of nature is a contraction of awareness and intelligence, the consequence of which is more evil, not only in oneself but throughout the entire intraindividual domain.

The Principle in which God creates or manifests individual beings is God himself, "who is without beginning or end." "Each being in the sacred hierarchy of the created universe strives, inasmuch as it is, to cooperate in the assimilation of all things to God."[47] Eternally preordained in God prior to their "beginning in time," they are never outside God. They are only regarded as outside if we, under the influence of secular philosophy that unintelligently posits a principle of separation as fundamental, part them from God, separated from whom there is strictly nothing. In truth "earth has no escape from heaven. Flee it up or flee it down, heaven invades it, energizes it, makes it sacred."[48]

The universe of contingent beings is not destined to strict nothingness, because strict nothingness cannot be a final cause. Inasmuch as "strict nothingness cannot be the end of any operation,"[49] no contingent being "naturally strives to cease totally to be." Though as contingent structures some of them—that is, those composed of structure and materiality—do decompose and as particular compositions do die, there is a cessation neither of isness nor of potentiality. Intellectual structures are ever potential, not to nothingness but only to other immaterial structures. And material structures are such that their materiality is timeless and their structures are forever in the potentiality of matter from which they can always be developed. Though corruptible as particular composite entities, there is never a total annihilation, since their composite elements are indestructible. In other words, "in universal manifestation there is no potentiality because of which it is possible that beings strive naturally toward absolute nothingness."[50]

To be sacred is to have isness, to be a manifestation of the nonindividualized divine Self. Thus the entire universe of individual manifestation is sacred in its participality. Not striving toward nothingness, it and all individual beings in it ceaselessly strive toward assimilation to and ultimately identity in knowledge with the divine Self. The innermost presence of unlimited isness in the ground of each contingent being makes for the assimilation; the all-inclusiveness of the unrestricted act of knowledge, which is the ultimate term of all striving, makes for the identification. Participating in the divine Self, the entire universe of individuality, as manifestation of its Principle which is the Self, is never other than the Self. For in the divine Self "there is nothing whatsoever that is manifestly possible except that directly known to the infinite Selfhood."[51] In this universe of individuality only the failure in striving to know, or the contraction of awareness with its evil consequences, is profane, is not a manifestation of the divine Self and is impossible of being a manifestation. All else is sacred, and is sacred because in primal truth it is not other than the divine Self—God.

As already pointed out, it is in the infinite goodness that God is that he wills this manifest universe, and wills it as inseparable from himself and hence as sacred in its participality. But Eckhart also makes it very clear that God's infinite goodness is also "our certitude that God cannot leave the questing intellect without an answer to its inescapable question regarding evil and the intellect's failure in striving to know and unite with its source."[52] The all-inclusiveness of that goodness means that God would not be God if he could not communicate himself directly to man and bestow on him all that is necessary in order to attain the fullness of God, or knowledge through identity in God, to which he is called. To deny this possibility to God is to deny the all-possibility that he is, and whatever we consequently consider "God" is something less than true God.[53]

That God *has* perfectly communicated himself to man is fully evident to Eckhart.[54] It is fully evident in the sense that the intellect, when presented with that divine revelation and when urged on by the detached will to know, can find no valid reasons for not accepting it. It is also fully evident in the sense that the intellect then realizes that nothing is wanting when it is truly accepted in well grounded faith.

For Eckhart that perfect communication is Jesus Christ, who divinely and unconditionally affirms himself as infinitely more than just a voice or a prophet, infinitely more than a human intellect graced by unitive knowledge. He is God himself revealed in as well as to the entire manifested order. He is the eternal Word made flesh, the God-Man who uniquely discloses the very nature of God and the mode of Divine Knowledge. Thus, "God completely gives himself to all with all that he is. For it would be foolish to rely on and expect only half a communication from God."[55]

But the birth of the Word is not restricted to history. Being the Word of all-possibility its birth may also, and no less essentially for us, take place in the very ground of the intellective soul. "Here in time we celebrate a holiday

[Christmas] because the eternal birth which God the Father effects unceasingly in eternity is the same birth he effected here in time, in human nature. . . . But what benefit is that to me if it does not also occur in me? What is all-important is that it should happen in me."[56]

When "the birth" does "happen" in the ground of the soul the intellect may then realize the knowledge of God and of all things through identity. Then it may realize its principial identity with the Word, that is, with unrestricted Intellect itself. Then it may also realize that "the birth of the Word" is only an external expression of the eternal truth that the intellect has never really been outside or other than God. Then, with Eckhart, the intellect can say: "I am that Son and not other," or "my innermost Self is God."

DETACHED INTELLECTUALITY

From what has been said thus far it should be quite clear that the student disciplined exclusively in modern philosophy and its secular modes of education is ill prepared for a ready understanding of Eckhart's teaching. Even the person "well learned" in medieval thought must recognize how inadequately he is qualified as long as he grants priority to external modes of thought over the principial mode. In other words, the student of Eckhart must acknowledge sources of knowledge that are truer than reason. This in no sense implies a reaction against reason, which could only mean an irrational reliance upon feeling, but a transcendence of reason from within by an intellectual realization of unitive knowledge.

It is indisputable that since Eckhart's time there has been a progressive confusion of intellect with mere reason. In some academic quarters today, indeed, the term "intellectualist" is derisively used to designate a person steeped in erudition and analytical reasoning, the implication being that feeling and emotion are more trustworthy. Such a confusion was foreign to those schooled in the tradition of Christian intellectuality, as were Aquinas and Eckhart, who properly understood reason and will as distinct faculties issuing forth from intellect. For them, as we have noted, it is the higher intellect that makes for direct knowledge in contrast to the indirect knowledge of reasoning. It does this because intellect is realized as an immediate reflection of unconditioned, all-inclusive Intellect itself. And since the reflection is immediate the transposition into pure Intellect, which is knowledge of all that is through identity, becomes possible.

In a Latin Commentary Eckhart says: "While the standpoint of approach to pure and eternal Intellect necessarily implies the intervention of an element drawn from the human order of sensitive attachment, the standpoint of knowledge as it were in divinis is purely intellectual."[57] Though this statement would be sufficiently clear to men and women educated in the tradition of Gregory of Nyssa, Augustine, and Aquinas, to most people in our present age it might appear to describe the truly intellectual standpoint inadequately. Both science and philosophy, as pursued in our age, have pretensions toward intellectuality. But if this claim is not admitted as well founded by the qualified student of Eckhart, it is because a basic difference separates all speculations of this kind from detached intellectuality.

The detached intellectuality of which Eckhart speaks is fundamentally the knowledge of principles belonging to the all-inclusive order. Moreover, they alone can validly lay claim to the term of "principles." This does not furnish us with a definition of pure Intellect; in fact a definition in this case would be inaccurate by the very fact that one tried to make it.[58] Only that which is restricted is capable of definition, whereas pure, superessential Intellect is by its very nature unrestricted. Nor does the distinction between the All-inclusive and the naturally exclusive human orders indicate any opposition between them. Indeed, no such opposition is really conceivable, precisely because apart from the all-inclusiveness and all-possibility of Intellect itself, there is nothing.

"Truth," says Aquinas, "is unconditionally one in the divine Intellect, but from it many truths flow into the human mind, as one face may be mirrored with variety."[59] Moreover, "truth cannot contradict itself." Fully understanding these statements, Eckhart can then say that "as eternal truths cannot contradict temporal truths, so intellect cannot contradict reason."[60] And rational knowledge has importance for Eckhart primarily as an ancillary means for the formulation and external expression of truths that lie beyond its range. Eternal truths can only be apprehended in the ground of intellect where the intention is the direct consideration of that which does not pertain to the individual order of contingency. Were it not that many contemporary philosophers have used the term "intuition" to designate a purely instinctive or vital operation, which is really beneath reason and not above it, there would be no hesitation in applying this term to intellect.

Generally speaking it must be admitted that most modern philosophers and, indeed, practically all our educators have ignored the higher intellect. Aristotle[61] affirms the intellect as intuitive, because for him it is that in us which possesses a direct and immediate knowledge of truth. Aristotle also said that "intellect is truer than science."[62] which means that it is more true than the reason that constructs the sciences. And when Eckhart says that "nothing is more true than detached intellection grounded in pure Intellect itself,"[63] he means that it is indefectable from the fact that its knowledge is immediate and because, not being really distinct from its object, it is knowledge through identity.

If Eckhart was able to affirm the essential basis of intellectual certainty in this respect, it is because the tradition to which he belonged, and which remains irrefutable, neither ignored the higher function of intellect nor confounded it with something inferior. Indeed, those in the tradition granted the intellect its rightful "noble place" and acknowledged it as the ground from which rational modes of knowledge spring forth. Thus they were able to affirm that error can only enter in with the use of reason.[64] Moreover, since all rational expression is bound to be limited and imperfect, error is inevitable in its form. No matter how precise one tries to make the expression, what is left out is always greater than what is kept in. But the unavoidable error in reason's expression is slight when compared to the gross error that results from the expression of mere feeling or the vital functions. Whereas the former error contains nothing positive as such and simply amounts to an incomplete formulation of integral truth, the latter error is entirely positive, springing as it does from irrationality.

These remarks perhaps show how difficult it is for the contemporary student, considering the type of philosophical influence and schooling he has undergone, to understand that he does not have to choose between reason and feeling. Perhaps they also show how difficult it is for him to understand that the distinction between the all-inclusive order of pure Intellect and the individual order of human speculation does not essentially concern things themselves, but the standpoint from which they are considered. He may readily acknowledge that the same thing can be studied and understood by different sciences under different aspects. Man can be studied and understood biologically, psychologically, sociologically, and philosophically. The same student may even admit that man can be studied and understood theologically in either negative or positive modes. But how prepared is he for an appreciation of Eckhart's claim?

With a tradition to back him up Eckhart insists that man and the entire order of universal manifestation can also, by a suitable transposition, be understood principially—that is, an understanding that is as it were from the standpoint of pure Intellect with which detached intellection is coincident. In fact he insists that such an understanding is far truer than any other, inasmuch as it is in Truth itself and is Divine Knowledge. If the "suitable transposition" is actualized only by God himself, through his Self-revelation and our acceptance of it, it is because the reflected intellect of its own nature and power cannot transcend itself.[65]

After all, a consideration of all that is in principial mode, or in terms of "the possible intellect as it were fully actualized," is out of the question for the intellect illuminated by the reflected light of natural intellection alone."[66] It is made operative only by the direct light of the Word of God, which discloses all that the full actualization of the "possible intellect" entails, that is, pure Intellect itself. Because of that disclosure it is possible for man truly and wisely to consider all things principially and, by uncreated grace, ultimately to realize that knowledge wholly in God. This is the very essence of detached intellectuality, for when intellectual detachment from time, space, and all individuality and universal being is attained, there are no longer any real distinctions. Eckhart never lets us forget that "ultimately the only Knower is God himself."

This wholly supranatural or purely metaphysical domain does not have for its direct context those things which the diverse human ways of knowing have as yet failed to uncover by reason of their present state of incomplete development. Its essential context is rather that which, by its very nature, lies infinitely beyond the range of any special way of human knowing. And to say that it "lies infinitely beyond" is to say that it is the all-inclusive content of knowledge *in* God, in comparison with which knowledge *about* things or even *about* God is external. Indeed, the field of every external mode of knowledge can, insofar as it is capable of it, be extended indefinitely without ever discovering unrestricted Intellect. "Oh, if only the soul's eye were opened by God so that it could contemplate the Truth!"[67] One is either awakened to it by transcendent act or one is not.

Whereas the domain of multiple external ways of knowing are restricted by the contingent, the accidental, and the variable, the domain of pure Intellect is withdrawn from the entire time-space continuun. Where pure Intellect is concerned, all that can change with time and place is the more or less external forms of exposition that it may assume and the degrees of awakening to it to be found among humans. As for pure Intellect itself, it entirely remains immutable and essentially the same inasmuch as its "object" is identically itself, apart from which there is nothing. And since no external modes give us direct access to it, pure Intellect can only be studied in terms of detached intellection, the supranatural can only be studied metaphysically or "eternal wise."[68] That is, it can only be studied and understood from a standpoint detached from all notions of history, evolution, progress, and individuality.

Thus it becomes possible to distinguish integral knowledge from discursive or scientific knowledge, and affirm the primacy of the former. The first is immediately derived from pure Intellect, which has the All-inclusive for its domain; the second pertains to reason, which has only manifest restricted reality for its domain. There should be no confusion between them. And if Eckhart is able to speak with confidence in terms of Divine Knowledge or from the standpoint of knowledge in God, as it were, it is because intellect, as the immediate reflection of unconditioned, pure Intellect itself, is inverted into God by uncreated act. And this is simply another way of saying that the possibility of the inversion is made actual by the birth of the Word in the ground of the intellective soul.

Eckhart's consistent teaching on detached intellectuality obviously indicates why he cannot be counted with those among the faithful who insist that they must before all else be agents for healing social injustice. He affirmed not only that "action without contemplation in God is meaningless," but also that the social injustices over which so many people busy themselves are, after all, "in no way directly solvable."[69] He goes on to say that activists who think that problems pertaining to the purpose of human life are solvable by material means alone, or by human action alone, or even that man's determination to solve them is most pleasing to God's intrinsic will, are misled. The idea that social or political change can satisfy man's intellectual or spiritual needs is perhaps the "greatest deception" to which man is susceptible. This in no sense means that society is to be ignored; detached intellectuality does not mean indifference.[70] Eckhart simply knows that Christians who are merely content to adopt the activist habits of the secular world will lose the opportunity they have of realizing that true charity which springs from Divine Knowledge and "holds together that which is eternally bound."[71] Whatever social good is ever accomplished can only be the result of men and women who, in their intellectual ground, understand that there is something far more important to be actualized than just trying to save this world.

If the foregoing remarks and considerations make some sense, then the reader should now be in a better position to understand the essential aspects of the doctrine of Divine Knowledge that Eckhart expounds. There will be occasions when it will be necessary to refer again to several of these issues, though in the context of setting forth the fundamentals of that doctrine rather than in a preparatory context for an understanding of it. We must now assume that there is no longer any major reason for delaying a straightforward presentation of the essentials in Eckhart's teaching.

At this point, then, we must turn from a consideration of the manifest or created universe to the fullness of God. In itself the universe, including man, is implenitude and indeed insignificant in its becoming or nonbeing, yet directed to acquire that fullness. And we must admit that difficult as it has been to raise ourselves to a consideration of God and necessary as it has been to follow through with the negative way in order to apprehend him, it will be no less difficult to understand all things principially and as it were from within God.

Part II

The Doctrine

I

God and the Human Self

In expounding the doctrine of Divine Knowledge Meister Echkart repeatedly reminds us that "the essential property of intelligence is to apprehend all individual beings, or things, in their principles." Moreover, "what we know we must know in its principle; we can never actually know anything in truth until we know it in its principle. And until we realize it in the supreme [unconditioned] Principle, there is no pure understanding of it."[1] Unless we raise ourselves to this principial mode of intellection his exposition of Divine Knowledge cannot be fully grasped.

For Eckhart this understanding, which refolds the notion of identity in knowledge, implies more than a theoretical consent to it. It admits of consequences in terms of decision and actual realization that remain unsuspected by those whose insight into reality does not transcend the cognition of structure, individuality, and substantial being. Though this manner of knowing is quite foreign to those whose education is dominated by modern philosophy or even by most academic philosophy, regardless of place and time, it nevertheless is the pre-eminent way of knowing—pre-eminent because it is constituted as it were in that supreme Principle which is in no way contained by any particular individual being, by any other individual being, or even by the totality of individual beings.

The doctrine of Divine Knowledge, in the name of which Eckhart speaks and as it pertains to the human being, therefore demands from the very start the requisite of clarifying the fundamental and real distinction between God and the individual self. Inasmuch as the individual self, or human knower, is a created manifestation, God is its Principle.[2] Indeed, God is the primordial and immediate Principle,

whereas the individual self is only one among many manifestations of the Principle. God is the unrestricted Knower
and hence the infinite Personality and Reality, not only of
all that is actually manifest but also of all that is non-mani-
fest, that is, of all-possibility. Thus one may metaphysically employ the terms "Personality" and "individuality" for
God and the human self respectively; with, however, a basic
reservation that Eckhart notes must be kept in mind. For
God in his Godhead denotes that which is the source of the
infinite Personality that he is.[3]

It should be clearly understood that the use of the term
"God" does not here imply any identity of intention with
certain philosophers, ancient or modern, who may have
used this term in a nonmetaphysical sense. "God," says
Eckhart, "is not something drawn from or included in the
totality of things . . . he transcends all things . . . all things
are in him. He is reconditioned pure isness, or unrestricted
knowledge. . . . God is the Principle and end of all
things."[4]

The intelligibility of God as the first and immediate Principle of all actual and possible reality pertains strictly to
supranatural or detached intellectual knowledge, which is
principial in manner. It is never to be confused with a mere
logical or mathematical understanding of abstract principles, for God is nonabstract as well as nonindividual.
Indeed, from what could he be abstracted or individualized?
God is to be acknowledged as the "Selfhood of all selves,"
the "Subject of all subjects," the "Reality of all realities," the
"Principle of all true principles and of all manifestation."

The distinction between God and the human self is, in
other words, the distinction between All-inclusiveness[5] and
individuality, inasmuch as individuality means nothing more
nor less than a being undivided in itself yet divided from
each and every other being. "God is the transcendent and
timeless Principle of which all individual beings, including the human being, are only contingent images or reflections."[6] As with all reflections, which are simply modifications of their principle, they can in no way affect the
principle.[7] Thus God is never individualized. "To know

pure isness I must know it as subsisting in itself, that is, in God, not parcelled out in creatures."[8]

As utterly transcendent, infinite, and all-possibility, God's isness, which is God himself, is beyond all differentiation, for "apart from isness there is strictly nothing."[9] Inasmuch as he must always be apprehended under the aspect of eternity and changelessness, which are the necessary attributes of unconditioned isness, God can never become differentiated or individualized. God, then, is in no way susceptible of any particularization or individualization that would cause him to be other than himself.

Changeless and unrestricted in himself and thus uncontained, God simply manifests or renders intelligible certain multiple possibilities that he contains within himself. In the purely metaphysical sense, and hence void of any notion of succession, this is a relational progression from the Principle to the principiate.[10] The progression is only relational and is not a differentiated act at all except when considered in terms of the manifest order of creation and the individual self. Therefore his eternal and infinite isness, which is identically unrestricted knowledge itself, is in no way affected by the progression. In other words, there can be only perfect similitude, so that even what is virtual in terms of mere human comprehension is nevertheless to be realized in the "eternal now."[11]

PRINCIPAL MANIFESTATION

Our consideration of manifestation is, of course, always from a participative knowing situated in manifestation. Manifestation is the "showing forth in being" of the Principle, that is, of God who in himself is unmanifested.[11] And our participative knowing in being is already a manifestation and hence a modification of God's knowing, yet by that very fact a participation in the Principle. It follows, then, that any "knowing" based on adopting a stance whereby one mentally gazes at or beholds manifest being as something "out there" and separated from one's self can at best be only a pretended knowledge.[12] It is actually a contraction of intelligence.

Universal manifestation is never to be confused with "emanation" in any Plotinian or Neo-Platonic sense. Such an assertion of emanation is erroneous because it restricts the all-possibility of God. It is primarily an outcome of an attempt to behold manifestation in a separatist and essentialist mode. It is restricted by an intent to gaze upon some sublime Essence and therefore asserts the incorrect conclusion that all things arise necessarily out of the substance of God's being. Not so, says Eckhart, for whom manifestation is nothing other than an "issuing forth from God or the reflection of himself according to the exigencies of his unrestricted will,"[13] which is "identically his isness." And unlimited isness in itself[14] is without real distinction and transcends the entire order of ontological knowing, which is limited by being constituted in individuality and the determination of substantive being,"[15] or at best distinctive isness in its relation to our apprehension.[16]

Manifestation itself, and all the ways of manifestation, be they in terms of creativity, formless generation, or revelation and incarnation, none of which are contradictory to the all-possibility of unconditioned Godhead, are a consideration from the individual and just human way of knowing. "The Godhead [God undifferentiated and indistinct *in se*], with whom all manifestation is identical in principle, is fundamentally nonmanifested. . . . God [*Deus ad extra*] and Godhead are [intellectually] distinct as earth and heaven. . . . God and Godhead are distinguished by working and not working. God manifests and remains unmanifest. *Gott wirt unt entwirt.*"[17] That is, God manifests himself in being, or actualizes certain possibilities, yet in himself, in the "divine desert" or "prior nothing," he remains all-possibility and unmanifest isness.

The principial or purely intellectual apprehension of all manifestation as being the reflection, in various stages and ways, of the Principle in no way obviates, but includes, the created and uncreated orders. For creation is simply a determination of how the Principle actually "shows itself forth" in individual and contingent manifestation while in itself remaining wholly transcendent and unaffected thereby.[18] It is perhaps better to say that the term "creation" designates how God does not show himself forth. That is, it is not something apart from God that enters into his creative act, for apart from God there is strictly nothing; yet it does not involve a substantial emanation of God. In other words, "God creates neither out of something other than himself nor out of something actual in himself, but simply out of prior nothing."[19]

Here it is necessary to note that when individual manifestation is considered in terms of God's creative act, we must discriminate between what Eckhart designates as "strict nothing" and "prior nothing." Apart from God, the Principle, there is strictly nothing.[20] And "strict nothing" means contradiction, nonpossibility, the total absence of actual or possible being. Examples of "strict nothing" are statements such as "the fruits of a barren tree," "separate from pure isness is something," "there are two infinites," and so forth. Unreality in the absolute sense is synonymous with "strict nothing." Strict unreality is the outcome of contradiction or nonisness, and we correctly designate it as absurd. That which rigorously excludes all unreality, all contradiction, all impossibility, is, then, the primary isness or Reality innermost in all manifestation, regardless of its degrees or modalities of existence. That Reality is God. It is All-possibility, the All-inclusive. It is the Truth of all relational truths. As infinite Truth God neither deceives nor is deceived; as infinite Reality he excludes only "strict nothing." Whatever is not sustained in the unconditioned Principle is clearly strict nothing.[21]

Not to be confused with "strict nothing," there is "prior nothing" or "pre-existing possibility."[22] The possibility of manifest being is not something, is not actual. Metaphysically speaking it is "prior or antecedent nothing." Now such a possibility is not "strict nothing," inasmuch as it contains no contradiction, does not presuppose something actual but only the possibility for manifestation or the "mayhap" of creation within all-possibility. Once the possibility is actualized, the 'prior nothing' of what was possible is metaphysically reconsidered with reference to the actuality that is regarded as having "filled the place," analogically speaking, of that possibility. "It should be noted that all things in the universe were not strictly nothing prior to the foundation of the world, but had a certain possible being." [23]

Creation, therefore, and all individual manifestation, must be considered as being out of "prior nothing" or "the possibility of manifestation," and not out of "strict nothing." [24] God alone, the Principle, is fully self-sufficient and self-explanatory by metaphysical necessity. Since he excludes only "strict nothing," he is the Principle of all that is manifest and nonmanifest, of all actual and possible being. Thus all that is manifest and nonmanifest is, in *principle*, God. God is not the manifested, but principially (*tamquam in principio*) the manifested is God.

"All that we consider here externally in multiplicity is there [in God] wholly within and identical. . . . Yesterday evening I was thinking that all likeness here is identity in the Father, the Principle. . . . The teaching from nature [philosophy] that God is known by likeness [analogy], by this or by that, impresses me as being rather insignificant. After all, God is neither this nor that. . . . There in the Principle all grass-blades, wood, and stone, all things are identical. This is the highest of all considerations, and I have fooled myself with lesser considerations." [25]

When we rightly consider manifestation it may be affirmed that God issues certain multiple possibilities forth into being from his infinite content of all-possibility through many ways of realization. For the integral human knower these amount to so many distinct modalities of being. Yet of these many modalities, one alone, limited by the specific conditions that define it, constitutes the determination of the individual human being. The human being's essential affirmation of himself as a knower really distinct from all other knowers and from all nonknowing beings conforms to that determination.

God is therefore the Principle by which all modalities of intelligibility are, each in its own way. This, of course, must be understood not only of all the created modifications of being and even of uncreated manifestations, but also of the unmanifested which comprises all-possibility. But God derives his intelligibility, his isness and knowledge, from himself alone. He is in fact the self-subsisting and unrestricted act of comprehension, knowing all about all, for in his perfect and indivisible unity he neither has nor can have any principle other than himself. "He is the Principle without principle."[26]

GOD AS PURE SPIRIT

When we consider God in relation to all contingent beings and particularly to the human being, then God is pure Spirit, or the infinite Personality. In fact we must affirm it of him as the Principle of all conditions of knowledge and isness, manifest and nonmanifest. Infinite Personality is a direct affirmation of the principle Eckhart calls Intellect–as–such, or pure Spirit.[27] This term "Spirit" must, however, be understood as having nothing in common with modern philosophical uses of the word, whereby it is designated as a correlation of "matter." We must never forget that Eckhart is premodern, and that modern philosophy, in this as in other respects, has been consciously or unconsciously greatly influenced by Cartesian dualism.

Eckhart metaphysically as well as theologically affirms that "God is infinite Personality, or pure Spirit." In doing this he is simply saying that it is always possible, when considering God in relation to contingent beings, to speak of God "qualified." This is so because God *in se* is the immediate source of all quality, whereas there is no possible question of God "quantified."[28]

If quality, considered as the content of pure Spirit, is not exclusively confined to the world of individual manifestation, it is because it is susceptible of a transposition that renders its significance all-inclusive. Since in the all-inclusive order essence is identically isness, there is nothing remarkable in this. But in any such transposition quality ceases to be the correlative of quantity which, by definition, is restricted to materiality and the lowest possible degree of individual manifestation.

It is very important, therefore, that the affirmation of

pure Spirit must never be considered in terms of "spirit" as opposed to "matter." If we insist that the two terms are meaningless except in reference to one another, we depart from both genuine theology and sound philosophy, and radically from an understanding of the doctrine Eckhart and his traditional teachers expound. For to understand "spirit" in this way is the result of stopping to "take a mental look" at being rather than participating in it. It promotes demiurgic conceptions of God and the substitution of "a Being" or "a Knower" for the nonindividualized, unconditioned, and indivisible Intellect that God is.

Eckhart's *materia* is not by any means the same as "matter" as conceived by modern physicists, just as his understanding of *forma*, or structure, has little if anything in common with our modern idea of "form." For Eckhart the material aspect of individual manifestation, including the integral human self, is primarily its quantitative aspect. Though "pure quantity," or *materia prima*, in its complete indistinction is unrealizable, it is the principle of individuation. He also affirms that a realizable quantity is never without some quality; that in all individual manifestation materia and forma are inseparable as potency and act, essence and existence, are inseparable.[29] Thus it must be insisted that materia, which signifies quantity can never unite, that all attempts to establish "uniformity" are downward tendencies toward quantity and are never to be confused with unification, which is an upward tendency toward quality and pure Spirit in which all being is eternally united.

The metaphysics, or detached intellectuality, to which Eckhart attains is not only under the sway of an unlimited will to know. In fact it principially constitutes itself in a mode of knowledge that is quite beyond that which presents us with the oppositions of the type existing between "spiritualism" vs. "materialism," "mentalism" vs. "mechanism," "idealism" vs. "pragmatism," and "essentialism" vs. "existentialism."[30] These contraries, and all those of this type, are based on particular attitudes of mind which, by definition, are prejudiced from the start. "Prejudiced" because they constitute themselves, not in a participatory mode of knowledge, which permits distinctions only, but in a "beholding" of reality that necessarily insists on separation, a separation between the beholder and that which is beheld. And that is another matter altogether, for distinction within the unity of being must in no way be confounded with separation from it.

Cognition established on the basis of separation, no matter how "spiritual," "ideal," or "existential" it may be, is nothing other than pseudometaphysics, for the simple reason that it is situated as it were outside reality (isness), apart from which there is strictly nothing. Rather than transcend the order of the manifest self, or individuality, it results in a greater restriction within that order. Moreover, pure metaphysics is not called upon to concern itself with the more or less misdirected and usually artificial questions that such oppositions based on an idea of separation raise—except, that is, to correct and reframe them.

Being identical with God, pure Spirit permeates all beings which are, as it were, God's likenesses or modalities of existence in the manifestation of himself. Hence all beings constitute, analogically speaking, the "environment" of pure Spirit, whether they be knowing or nonknowing beings—that is, beings whose integral structure is wholly intellectual, wholly corporeal, or the composite of intellectuality and corporeality, as in the case of human beings. For these distinctions indicate only different modalities in manifestation and make no difference whatsoever in respect of God, the unconditioned and unmanifested Principle. As the Principle of all that is, and regardless of any condition or modality of existence, God remains ever the same throughout the multiple degrees of existence as well as in principial non-manifestation.

In relation to any manifest being, pure Spirit transcends all real distinction and individualization. Thus it is identical with God. Inasmuch as "there are no real distinctions or otherness in God,"[31] he is not therefore really distinct from pure Spirit, nor does he ever really become other from it in any way, even when we consider it "particularly" in relation to ourselves as human beings. God cannot be other than himself; thus he cannot be affected by any manner of our consideration of him any more than by any other contingency.

It must always be remembered that we depart from the direct consideration of God to the extent that we make this distinction between God and individuality. And we make this distinction only in order to consider his reflection in the human self or in some other modality of existence. When we directly consider God all modalities of manifestation are really nondiversified and are to be known in the "eternal now" in the same principial manner. Thus pure Spirit is the divine Selfhood, and principially the self is the Selfhood, or as Eckhart also says: "My truest *I* is God."[32] Principial knowledge, he reminds us, is the realization that "there is only *one* First Person, *one* true *I am*," and that it is in the lack of this knowledge that we think, speak, and act in terms of self-centeredness. Then we think, speak, and act as though we were really disassociated from God.

The Extended Order of the Human Self

It is the self, or human individuality as distinguished from but not separated from God, that presently concerns us, and the reflection that we are now considering determines what Eckhart calls "the very ground of the self." If separated from its principle, that is, from God, it can only have the appearance of strict unreality. Thus separated it is meaningless, illusory, nothingness. Why? Because it is from its Principle that it derives all its reality, and it has this reality only through the participation of its own isness in the unrestricted isness that God is.[33] Which is to say that it is identified with God, not substantially, of course, but principially. Separated from the Principle there is only nothing; distinguished within the issuing forth of the Principle there is nothing really other than the Principle.

Pure Spirit, Intellect itself, Personality, belong essentially to the order of the All-inclusive. Thus they cannot correctly be considered from any way of knowing except that of detached intellection which is entirely constituted in the All-inclusive. Inasmuch as God is the All-inclusive, apart from which there is strictly nothing, then detached intellection, or pure metaphysics, is grounded in God. Most modern philosophers in particular, however, are in the habit of confounding the all-inclusive order with that which actually pertains only to the order of the self or individuality. Perhaps it is better to say that since they are quite unfamiliar with genuine participative ontology, which may lead to metaphysics, they are wholly unacquainted with the possibility of principial knowledge. Because they lack insight into the real order of the All-inclusive and All-possibility, then that to which they designate God is usually the realm of the general, which correctly understood is simply an extension of the self. For the general is nothing more nor less than the realm of individual ideas or limited acts of comprehension. We are thus reminded of the idealists and rationalists.

Some confound their understanding much further, such as certain empiricist philosophers who cannot even affirm the general. That with which they delegate God or the All-inclusive, if at all, is the mere collective, which pertains correctly to the order of particularity. Thus by means of those successive degredations they end by reducing all reality to the modality of sensate awareness, which they then are inclined to assert as the only knowledge possible. Because oversight has replaced insight, because there have been repeated failures in sustaining an unlimited will to know—the term of which is all-inclusive isness, or unrestricted knowledge itself—the intellectual range of most modern philosophers does not extend beyond the particular and general orders. Yet they endeavor to impose on everyone else the restrictions that are the result of their own inability and unwillingness, whether inborn or acquired through an overemphasized analytical form of education.

Nevertheless the true student of Eckhart cannot fail to acknowledge that these same philosophers have made worthy contributions to the unity of man's intellectual quest. They have raised important questions that the seeking intellect cannot shun, and we can be sure that comparatively new questions will be raised by men and women in future ages. Since no true philosophical principle should be affirmed to the exclusion of other principles equally true, and since these manifest principles must ultimately be considered in the light of the all-inclusive Principle, which God in his Godhead is, then many of the questions philosophers naturally ask may have to be reframed and brought into conformity with the objective of the unlimited will to know. Though the various restricted standpoints with which many thinkers enclose themselves must be recognized and acknowledged for what they are, the student of Eckhart at the same time must realize that intellectual pride or snobbery can never be a factor in genuine principial knowledge. For, as Eckhart insists, "it is not by human effort alone that it is ever actualized." In its actualization there is not only the realization that "no one possibility within All-possibility can ever be considered dispensable," but also the recognition that every detached striving toward true knowledge "signifies its own need of inversion" into "pure Intellect which does not seek."

Eckhart continues with this theme by clarifying his position with these statements: "Everything short of God is this or that being[34] [that is, individual manifestation], not pure isness.[35] Pure isness is proper to God alone." "Although the manifestation in analogical relations derives from the Principle, it is nevertheless below the Principle, not with it. Moreover, it is other in nature [being individual] and so is not in itself the Principle. Yet insofar as it is in the Principle it is not other, is identical with God." "God is pure subsistence in himself, in whom there is neither this nor that, for whatever is in God is God." "All things [or modalities of manifestation] come from God. He [as their Principle] is in all things and all things are in him."[36]

In order to correct any misunderstanding and at the same time acknowledge the essential distinctions requisite for an apprehension of Divine Knowledge, which Eckhart endeavors to expound metaphysically, the following should be carefully noted. Universal ideas and concepts, which belong not to the order of the All-inclusive but to the realm of generality, are, along with proportionate analogy, necessary for human thought and communication. By reason of the fact that they have a real foundation in things they are still restricted to the manifest order of individuality, which is nothing but a reflection of the All-inclusive. It is the complete inversion of the reflection that is required in pure metaphysics. The world of manifestation must be inverted, for it, including ourselves in manifestation, is already "upside down."

Real distinction is always from that modality of manifestation which is the human self. The fundamental and real distinction, then, is between God and the self, between the all-inclusive, all-possible Principle and individuality. This distinction must never be regarded in terms of correlation, for the individual self as such, being nullified in respect to God, cannot in any way be opposed to him. An image is never a correlative with its source.

"An individual structure or image," says Eckhart. "is not of itself nor is it for itself; rather it stems directly from that whose reflection it is and it is due to this alone that it exists at all. It does not stem from nor pertain to that which is apart from that of which it is a reflection. An image derives its being directly from that whose reflection it is, having one being with it and is the same being [in principle]. I am here speaking of matters which do not belong exclusively in the schools; one may well propound them more properly from the pulpit."[37] Since man, an intellectual being, is an image of God, then he should live, continues Eckhart, "just as the image is here said to do—even so it behooves you to live. Be his and pertaining wholly to him [God], not to your own and pertaining to yourself nor indeed to anything or anyone."

In God there is no other and individuality is not and never becomes an other, though from the reflective condition of individuality God is really distinct and completely transcendent. On this point, which is most essential, Eckhart is simply stressing what Aquinas makes very clear when he says: "In God there is no real relation to creatures [individual manifestation], but in creatures there is a real relation to God."[38]

The distinction, then, whereby God is distinct from individuality must be of another order than the distinction of individual beings among themselves. For Eckhart, as for Aquinas, the principle of plurality is *non diversio, sed divisio,* that is to say, not separation, but distinction. God infinitely transcends any otherness, and because he is infinitely transcendent he is also, in his infinity, not an other.[39] As long as the following twofold truth, pointed out by Aquinas and given special emphasis by Eckhart, is granted priority, there should be far less difficulty in apprehending the Meister's exposition: "Apart from God there is strictly nothing and that which is in God is God."

Extending from individuality, however, there is the further distinction between the general concept and the particular. Whereas the former applies itself to a whole class, or genus, of being, the latter does so only to a part of a class. Extending now from the particular realm is still the further distinction between the collective concept, which is applicable to all members of a particular group, and the single concept, which is applicable to one single object considered in isolation. But generality and particularity are oppositions as extensions of the self, and the same with collectivity and singularity as further extensions of the self through particularity.

"Reason can never comprehend God in the ocean of his unfathomableness." "All that the mind can conceive, that is not God."[40] Eckhart never ceases to stress this truth. Fully recognizing that a concept is the content of an act of conceiving and that an idea is the content of an act of comprehension, he correctly affirms that the human self can have neither concept nor idea of God, since the concepts and ideas enjoyed by the human self are already limited by individuality. Only God, the unlimited act of comprehension, realizes the idea of all-possible knowledge, which is God himself.

But the individual knower may certainly have a notion of God inasmuch as a notion, or primary intention, is the content of the unlimited will to know.[41] And that content is all-possibility, the knowledge of all about all. Restricted as they are within the manifestation of individuality, any concept or idea attained by the human self, no matter how universal or exalted, is never a concept or idea of God. And the same with "isness," which is in no way conceivable or subject to human comprehension, though it is that without which true concepts and ideas are impossible.

To acknowledge God's all-inclusive isness in terms of the most general of ideas is an assurity that it is not God one comprehends. In fact a general idea grants us no more knowledge of God than a particular, collective, or single idea of God, since all are restricted by individuality. In other words, they are restricted by "this" or "that," and based, in one degree or another, on individualizing God, who is indivisible. "For God is not this, not that."[42] God is not an individualized actuality or any one possibility. "God is all-possibility and all-inclusive." Thus the unlimited will to know has furnished the intellect with a genuine notion of God.

The correlation of opposites can only arise within the extension of the individual self. And as God and individuality are not correlatives, so the nonmanifested is not correlative to the manifested.[43] Furthermore, though one might at first surmise that the All-inclusive and the unmanifested should perfectly coincide, thus leaving the manifested wholly to the order of individuality, this would not be correct. Indeed, the nonmanifested is identical with the All-inclusive, and metaphysically it is the All-inclusive that is supremely essential. But there are certain modalities of manifestation that are totally without structure, such as the transcendentals—truth, goodness, beauty, unity, and so forth—and all processions from the Principle, which are structureless and hence by that very fact transcendent to the self. Thus the distinction between God and the self obliges us to assign structureless manifestation to God, for in comparison with the self and all conditions of individuality, structureless manifestation is not susceptible of individualization.

This explains why Eckhart cautions us always to remember that all that is manifested, even in the order of transcendence, is necessarily conditioned by its own determination. The All-inclusive in itself consists not only of the nonmanifested but also of structureless manifestation, that is, of all that transcends the order of the self and contingency. In other words, uncreated and noncontingent essences, inasmuch as they are structureless manifestations of God, pertain exclusively to the transcendent order.

However, the order of individuality encompasses all degrees of structural manifestation. That is to say it comprises all conditions or modalities of contingency in which beings are invested with structures. For what constitutes individuality and essentially qualifies itself is precisely the presence of structure (*forma*) among the limited modalities of existence which define and determine that given condition and which are contained in the designation "*this* or *that* being." Thus we speak of "*this* atom," "*that* tree," "*this* man," "*that* star," "*this* universe," and so forth. On the other hand, when we refer to structureless manifestation we correctly say "Truth," "Unity," "Goodness," and so forth.[44]

With Eckhart we may therefore conclude: The un-manifested and all structureless manifestation pertain to God and the uncreated, all-inclusive order. Structural manifestation, which includes all intellectual structure and also material structure (corporeality), pertain to individuality or the created order.[45]

This last distinction within structural manifestation requires an explanation. The material modality, or corporeality, is, for the human being, simply organic existence itself, to which he belongs by only one of his conditions, that is, his physical, chemical, and sensory constituents, and not in his integrality. The intellectual modality includes the extra-organic conditions of the human being and of all other individual conditions of manifest selfhood or of every other being in the condition of contingency, inasmuch as the isness of every being is identically the intelligible.[46] Following Aquinas, Eckhart never lets us forget that isness is simply all that is known and all that is to be known.

It follows, then, that intellectuality and materiality are not really commensurate. Materiality designates only a minor part of one of the conditions that constitute structural manifestation, while intellectuality includes all the remainder of contingent being as well as the primary intention of all-inclusive and all-possible isness. Thus we must acknowledge that the human being, considered in its integrality, is an intrinsic composite of certain limited possibilities that constitute its organic modality and also an indefinite multitude of possibilities that, going quite beyond quantity and materiality, constitute the intellectual and qualitative modality. Nevertheless, all these possibilities together designate but one condition of manifestation, that is, contingent, individual existence.

THE DELUSIVE REALITY OF THE HUMAN

From all that we have gathered in the preceding section from Eckhart's teaching we are obliged to conclude that the human self is both much more and much less than most philosophers in our age generally think. Much more because they tend to regard it as constituting little if anything other than materiality or corporeality, which actually comprises only a minute portion of the human being's possibilities; much less because this human self, far from constituting the whole of being, is but one condition of being among a multitude of other conditions that are all limited by contingency.

Furthermore, the sum total of all these modalities of being, says Eckhart, is "as naught to God who alone is unrestricted isness."[47] Why? Because only God is noncontingent, eternal, and unconditioned, and also because there is nothing else that can be considered as ultimately Real. All the rest is certainly real to the human self, but it, including the human self, is real only in a contingent manner. Its reality is wholly dependent upon God the Principle; it is real only to the degree that it reflects him in some manner. Indeed, "the intellective soul which clings to multiplicity [or contingency] withdraws from God. And the more and more closely it clings, the less it really is."[48]

As the image reflected in the mirror derives all its reality from that which it reflects and can have no existence apart from it, so it is with all manifestation. "I take a bowl of water and place a mirror in it and set it in the sun. The sun sends forth its light rays both from the ground of the sun it-

self and from the disc, and thereby loses nothing. The reflection of the mirror in the sun is, in the sun itself, sun; yet
the mirror is what it is. Thus it is with God. God is in the
soul [the intellectual structure] with his nature, with his isness, and with his Godhead, and yet he is not the soul. The
soul's reflection is, in God, God, and yet the soul is what it
is. There where God's utterance is God, God is not the creature, the creature is God."[49]

But this contingent and lesser reality "is mutable and
therefore delusive" in relation to ultimate reality, as the
image is mutable and delusive in relation to its object. On
the other hand, if we should attempt in any way to separate
it from the Principle, for instance by some manner of mentally gazing at being rather than participating in it, then it
would become unintelligible; it would become a strict and
simple nothing, a total privation of being. In other words,
contingency is not strict illusion. The unnecessary is rather
the structural measure and means essential to the manifestation of individuality. In this sense, it is the experiential
world of differentiated being—"by which we may be either
enlightened or deluded" according to whether the will to
know is in the direction of the supreme Principle or in misdirection. Thus "in comparison with God the world is [not
illusory but] delusive, bearing the shadow of unreality." [50]

We must therefore acknowledge, says Eckhart, that all contingent being is at once real in one sense and delusively unreal
in another. It is real according to our participative ontology
and substantial way of knowing, which is always in terms of
individual manifestation. It is relatively unreal, and therefore
delusive, according to principial knowledge, which is always
grounded in the All-inclusive, in God himself. This is one of
the essential insights requisite for an understanding of the
doctrine Eckhart unfolds. However, it is one that most modern philosophers in particular have failed to attain. Having
distorted ontology by failing to acknowledge the intelligibility
of being, and hence by an incapacity to rise above mere particularity and generality to the All-inclusive, they have shut
themselves off from any possibility of principial knowledge.

Another point that must be remembered is that a principial relation, not being a simple relation of ontological substances, can admit identity in principle while affirming the transcendence and all-inclusiveness of the Principle. Such a relation is neither convertible nor reversible, and every suggestion of an identity of the Principle with manifestation, or God with the human self, is cut off at the root. The principial relation is not only essentially necessary on the part of the restricted realities, which owe their very actuality to the Principle, but has to be understood metaphysically as an eternal inalienable relation. This understanding of the relation between the restricted and the All-inclusive, or the self and God, is one in which the transcendence of God is maintained while fully recognizing the eternal relation which constitutes the principial bond between the limited, individual, and qualified reality of the self and the infinite reality that God is. And this notwithstanding God's independence, immutability, and transcendent all-inclusiveness.[51]

Such an understanding, true as far as it goes, nonetheless falls short of Divine Knowledge, which constitutes the purity of detached intellection. The unlimited will to know has to be regenerated and sustained by transcendent act itself. It must go beyond to a final consideration in which, while never disallowing the lesser reality and dependence of the universe of contingent manifestation, "God alone is apprehended as Reality." By identity through knowledge God is apprehended to be the true all-inclusive reality—necessary, transcendent, and indivisible. In regard to such an apprehension all manifestation is rigorously naught if considered in any separatist mode. Because of its intrinsic limitation and entitative dependence, the manifest reality can never stand metaphysical comparison with the infinity of the supreme Principle, which contains all actuality and possibility principially. For this reason Eckhart regards all creation and everything in individual manifestation as serving its purpose as a requisite springboard and support to this highest consideration, that is, Divine Knowledge. Otherwise, he insists, the entire created universe, including the self, is nothing.[52]

To those whose cognitional horizon is grossly limited by

their education in modern philosophy, it must be pointed
out that what Eckhart designates as the All-inclusive and individuality, or God and the self, are in no sense what they
call categories. Eckhart reminds us that categories in the
original Aristotelian meaning of the word are nothing but
the most general of all genera.[53] In fact "all ten categories
are denied of God." Thus they still belong to the individual
order of which they at best denote the limits of conceptualization in terms of the human self. And the foremost of
these categories is substance—*a* being that has existence in
itself by virtue of itself.[54] It is far more correct to compare
with the All-inclusive, or God in himself, what Aquinas designates as "transcendentals," inasmuch as they really do transcend all genera, including the categories.[55] However,
though these transcendentals belong to the order of the All-
inclusive, it would be a gross error to think that they constitute the pure reality of the All-inclusive or even that they are
the most important consideration in pure metaphysics.

Unity, truth, goodness, and so forth, which are convertible with being, are certainly coextensive with the being of
God. But they do not transcend that being, and it is at that
being that the ontology in which they are thus constituted
stops short. Substantial being (*ens*) is never a simple notion,
inasmuch as it comprises the notions of existence and subsistence: it ever remains a manifestation of the unrestricted
and unmanifested Principle. "God is above being. . . . But if I
say that God is not *a* being and that he is above being, I do
not by so doing deny isness to God. On the contrary I
enhance it in him."[56]

Although ontology is the "threshold" to metaphysics, it
does not constitute metaphysics in its purity. Consequently
that which is beyond substantial being is metaphysically
more important than the being *of* God. In other words, it is
God as the unrestricted isness of Divine Knowledge itself
that must be acknowledged as the ultimate Principle of all
that is nonmanifest and manifest.

The Negation of Negations Is Divine Affirmation

Following Eckhart we are now obliged, by our unlimited will
to know, to consider that which is "beyond" the being of

God, or more precisely that which transcends any approach whatsoever. The Meister has already made it clear that when considering God in himself there is nothing to be regarded as external to him.

If detached intellection or pure metaphysics, in terms of which Eckhart expounds the doctrine of Divine Knowledge, is not to be confounded with ontology, neither is it to be identified with any contingent form of mysticism. Insofar as mysticism, even in its noble aspects, is a condition of higher awareness within the standpoint of individuality or some extension thereof, it is always rooted in the self and from the self toward the other. In its approach toward the other it regards the other as susceptible not of intelligibility but only of some incommensurable "experience." Thus situated *in via* it designates anything other than or beyond the knowing self as mystical.

Indeed from the condition of individual. manifestation principial knowledge may *appear* as mystical. But this is only because that condition, as well as all conditions of manifestation, are not transcended by a metaphysical or supra-individual consideration that is wholly constituted as it were *in patria*, or within the supreme Principle. Eckhart reminds us that "*in patria* there is no otherness." "It is proper to God and to everything divine, insofar as they are divine, to be within, to be innermost." But "to be within, to be innermost," is not to be in the self in any way. It is "to be as it were transcendently in God." Be *there* [in God] and you will know; seek to be there and there you will find."[57]

The determination of genuine mysticism, which is essentially theological and basically a mysticism of "being," is never to be degraded, since it is a corrective challenge to mental determinations enclosed in the modality of general ideas. But mystical experience must always be recognized as a determination that is restricted, nonetheless, to a condition of *exstasis* differentiated from the *instasis* of God. Thus it indicates a final unsuccess in transcending the most subtle modalities of manifestation by a principial knowledge that renders the self and all manifestation as such naught. It should be pointed out that a few who have been labeled "mystics," but who never acknowledged themselves as such or stopped short at the consideration of some determined mystical state, were actually genuine metaphysicians.[58]

When God himself is acknowledged as the all-inclusive Principle there is nothing that can principially be affirmed as mystical. For God is the unlimited act of comprehension, the knower of all about all, both actual and possible. And since in God there is no otherness, then there is, in principle, no other that could be considered as mystical. God is no more a mystic than he is an ontologist, and the orientation of pure metaphysics, which is as it were in God, is a principial transcendence of all individual selfhood and every contingent state thereof. "In God, God is the only Selfhood, the only Subject, the only Knower who in knowing all about all is unrestricted knowledge itself."[59]

Eckhart asks, "What is meant by object?" And he answers: "Man is confronted by two objects: one is otherness—not I; there is also the pure Self—the truest I. The first is *becoming*, all that has come into existence; such things breed otherness and pass away. . . . The other object is to realize one's truest Self, to be identified with all perfection, with that most precious treasure—one's first Principle [and only ultimate Subject].. . . . He who realizes this is really perfect in the sense that he is wholly without otherness in eternity." But "as long as we find ourselves in an approach toward God, we do not yet realize God."[60]

It is true that many considerations intrinsic to pure metaphysics can also apply from the theological standpoint. Though the latter normally stays within all that is implied in the determination of Being and Personality, its entire order is rendered valid and meaningful only when that which is understood as "negative theology" is considered as its ground and only if that ground is not forgotten, that is, when only attributes that are negative in structure can rightly be designated of God. If practically the whole theological framework of Aquinas is admitted by Eckhart, it is because that lofty endeavor is thoroughly grounded in "negative theology," as expounded particularly by Dionysius the Pseudo-Areopagite. And, according to Eckhart, those who fail to acknowledge this fact fail properly to understand the teachings of Aquinas.

If, theologically speaking, anything pertaining to unconditioned God must be expressed in a negative form, it is
because in thought and language every distinct affirmation
is necessarily particular and determinate. Every determination is the affirmation of something that excludes something else and that therefore restricts that which is so affirmed. "Every determination is a restriction," says Eckhart,
"a negation."[61] Hence it is the negation of a determination
(or negation) that makes possible a true insight, and the
seemingly negative terms are, in their real sense, truly affirmative. Thus the term "infinite" expresses in reality a negation of all limit. It therefore indicates total affirmation,
which includes all particular affirmations, but which is not
any one affirmation to the exclusion of others, precisely
because it implies them all equally and nondistinctively. It is
in this way that "Infinite," "Unconditioned," and "All-inclusive"
are directly convertible, like also "All-possibility," which contains strictly all possibilities.[62]

Everything that can be expressed by means of an affirmative form belongs of necessity to the realm of *distinctive* isness, since "isness is the first determination"[63]—that from
which all other determinations proceed. But in the unconditioned, all-inclusive order we are beyond distinctive "isness"
because we are beyond all determination, even principial.
In itself, then, the All-inclusive is neither just manifested nor
just unmanifested, at least so long as one only considers the
unmanifested as the immediate principle of the manifested.
Rather it is the Principle of both and therefore transcendently non-manifested in its immutability and its impossibility of being designated by any positive attribution
whatsoever.

Thus "Godhead in itself, identically the, All-inclusive," is
"comprehensible by nothing other than itself," that is,
Divine Knowledge. "Neither speech nor thought can ever
attain it, and this explains why no man can fathom or
describe it."[64] It transcends all that is known distinctively and
all that is not. It is beyond all individuality, one with undifferentiated isness in itself, which is the affirmation of its
unrestricted knowledge. It is that which is not manifested
but by which speech and thought and everything else is

manifested. It is not that which is considered as "this" individual Being or "that" distinctive Being, but is God in himself, wholly undifferentiated and without distinction.

A distinct and certain knowledge is possible in respect of
every being capable of becoming an object of knowledge,
but it is not possible in the unique instance of God-in-himself who transcends distinctive isness and cannot be such an
object. He in himself is the infinite Knower, and as such
knows all about all in the unlimited act of comprehension
that he is and that is identical with All-possibility. But God
cannot make himself the distinct object of his own knowledge, inasmuch as in his eternal and immutable identity he
cannot cease *to be* himself all-knowing in order to become an
all-known, which would be another "God." Nor can it strictly
be affirmed that God-in-himself is able to become a *proper*
object for any being distinct from himself, since the knowledge of all knowing beings, considered relationally to God,
is nothing more nor less than a participation in his infinite
knowledge.

Thus it is that while "negative theology" closely approximates Divine Knowledge insofar as it indicates Godhead as
its Principle, it falls short of finally constituting us wholly
within the supreme Principle. That there are further considerations in Divine Knowledge that lie beyond the content
of "negative theology" is clear, inasmuch as this content is
restricted to the simple denials of certain multiple possibilities of individual determination. But the content of Divine
Knowledge is manifest and unmanifest All-possibility, as
already explained. It is the person who, by uncreated grace,
realizes "I know God, yet I do not know him" that Eckhart
refers to as being blessed with "unknowing knowledge," [65]
and who is truly saved by being liberated from all that is not
in function of Divine Knowledge.

Liberation, or the final state of the knowing being, is the
ultimate toward which the unlimited will to know tends.
Liberation differs from all human or posthuman states that
that being may have traversed in order to realize it, inasmuch as it is the realization of the ultimate and unconditioned state. All other states, no matter how elevated or

"mystical," are still conditioned. That is to say they are subject to certain conditions that define them, making them what they are and qualifying them as distinctive states or degrees of clarification of our knowledge of all-inclusive God. This pertains to structureless as well as to structured states—even to the degree of distinctive isness. Although distinctive isness transcends all existence, it still implies a determination that though principial is nevertheless a subtle limitation.

It is certainly through pure isness that all things in every mode of universal being subsist, and in this sense infinite isness subsists through itself. It determines all the states of which it is the principle and it is only determined by itself.[66] Yet "to determine oneself is after all to be determined and therefore in some respect limited," so that the ultimate all-inclusive Principle is truly infinite "unknowing, Divine Knowledge" of which pure isness is eternally in function. Thus, doctrines that stop short at isness, even when understood to be infinite, retain a subtle degree of incompleteness from the standpoint of pure metaphysics. The result, of course, is that "the actual realization of knowledge *in divinis* [that is, in principial mode] is neglected." As often happens with those who expound such doctrines, profound as indeed they are in comparison with the superficiality of most philosophy, there is exhibited an embarrassing tendency to deny, or at least neglect, that which actually lies beyond their domain. And it is "that which actually lies beyond" that is, for Eckhart, precisely the most important consideration of all.

The attainment of higher states, mystical or otherwise, is thus only a preparation for Divine Knowledge and a partial consequence of the seeking intellect. Though this result may appear immense in comparison with the workaday state of human individuality, it nevertheless must be said that in itself it amounts to little in relation to the ultimate state. It is not Divine Knowledge, which neither seeks nor determines any otherness. "The purification of *our* notion of God is incommensurable with the unrestricted reality of Divine Knowledge wherein all otherness is naught." "The finite [while becoming indefinite through the extension of which it is capable, that is, through the development of its own possibilities] always remains as nothing in comparison with the Infinite." [67]

Therefore the consequence of a higher mystical state is of value only by way of preparation for that immediate union, or transcendent identity. In other words, it is still only a means and not an end. To mistake it for the end, as many students of Eckhart do, is to perpetuate a delusion. For Eckhart makes it very clear that all states in question, up to and including distinctive isness, are in themselves delusive, or "as nothing," in the sense in which the term "delusive" has already been explained. "In any state of knowledge where some degree of distinction is retained, it is impossible for unrestricted knowledge itself to be fully in act." [68] Beyond the determination of pure isness one cannot speak of distinctions of any kind, not even of relational or principial distinctions. Yet in that final transcendence there is no confusion or obscurity whatsoever, for "*there* [in Divine Knowledge] all is without otherness and without distinction." [69]

We have no way of knowing whether Eckhart the man ever attained any experiential realization of a mystical state. Never does he dwell on "mystical experience" or speak in the name of "mystical states." Nor does he ever consider himself a mystic. In fact he recognizes that the determination of mystical or negative theology is, after all, no more than a necessary corrective, within the condition of individuality, to the realm of general or particular theological ideas and concepts. It simply designates a "negative way" in reference to a "positive way" of cognition. But this relationship is dissolved in the purely metaphysical consideration of Divine Knowledge, for in the Principle all individual concepts and ideas are already naught. Hence a "negation of a negation is transcendently acknowledged as God's affirmation of himself." [70]

Genuine ontology, like sound theology, points to pure metaphysics or detached intellection, but it does not constitute it. For ways of knowing directed toward God, whether by so to speak "going straight toward" or "backing toward"

God, whether by ontology or theology, must be inverted. They are not the same as principial knowledge which, by reason of that inversion, is constituted as it were wholly within God in whom there is no direction. There all is direct, or directionless. "That which in God is transcendently direct [*in recto*, i.e. without direction] is direction in man, because man is indirect [*in obliquo*]. . . God's isness in itself is not really either an end by which [*terminus ad quo*] or an end to which [*terminus ad quem*]"[71] It is wholly direct (i.e. directionless) and has never not been; it is in him the Selfhood of all manifestation and all individuality. Indeed, where else could it be?

2

The Word

If we now consider the order of Divine Knowledge, which is all-inclusive God in his Godhead, we must understand that while principial knowledge is as it were fully constituted in this order, no insight into it is possible for the human knower unless it is revealed to him. As the human self cannot comprehend the nature of pure transcendence, "so it cannot understand the mode of knowledge in God unless God speaks it in the ground of the intellective soul."[1]

The principial mode of knowledge, which is essential in pure metaphysics, is not to be confused in any way with a mode of knowledge in terms of contingent principles or causes within the order of individuality. For the human knower the "mental word," or comprehension, by which his intellect understands something other than itself, derives from the other, represents it, and hence is really distinct from the intellect and is not the intellect's being.[2] The comprehension in the individual intellect has only a mental reality and is not identical with the psychological state and activity of the intellect. But in unrestricted Intellect isness and act are identical and thus the Word, or Comprehension, is within both the isness and the knowing of that Intellect. In God, to be and to know are identical. The Word of God is coessential with him. The Word of God in God is God in every respect, is identically the Principle, and whatever may be predicated of God may also be predicated of the eternal Word.[3]

When the intellective soul is "silent" and not intruded upon by desires other than the will to know as it were *in divinis,* then Christ speaks "in the temple, that is, in the soul." And "What does the Lord Jesus say? He says that he is 'he who is.' What is he then? He is the Word of the Father. In this Word the Father affirms himself, and all the divine nature and everything that God is, just as he knows it; and he knows it as it is. Being perfect in knowledge and in all-possibility,[4] he is also perfect in utterance. When he speaks the Word he speaks himself and all things in another Person, and gives him the same nature as he has himself. In this Word he expresses all rational creatures, making them like the Word." Christ "reveals himself and everything that the Father has spoken in him, according to the manner in which the soul [of each human knower] is receptive of it. . . . He reveals himself in the soul in boundless wisdom, which is himself. . . . When this wisdom [Divine Knowledge) is united to the soul . . . then God is known through God in the soul. In this way the soul knows itself and all things through this wisdom; and through God it knows this wisdom, and through this wisdom it knows the glory of the Father in his fruitful all-possibility, and it also knows essential isness in strict unity and without any difference."[5]

Without the revelation of the Word a true metaphysical insight into this divine mode of knowledge would, of course, be impossible, and Eckhart is insistent on this point. A genuine understanding of the principial mode, which is constituted as it were within Godhead, is an understanding of truth that is beyond the potentiality of human cognition, restricted as that cognition is to individuality. Insight into this truth is a possibility only by way of transcendent act, never by way of potentiality.[6] Yet the revelation of the Word *is* that transcendent act as assented to by the intellect when moved by the detached will to know. It discloses that "the Word is the comprehension or principiate of the all-inclusive Principle and that it is identical with the Principle, that is, with the unrestricted knowledge which God is."[7]

"Where individuality ends, there God begins. God wants nothing more of you than for you to go out of yourself and all individuality and let God be God within. The most insignificant individual structure that takes form in you is as big as God. How is that? It completely obstructs God. Once the structure appears, God and all his Godhead disappear. Once the structure is transcended, God enters."[8]

The Triune Godhead

The revelation of the Word to the human knower is, for Eckhart, pre-eminently the revelation of the transcendent mode of Divine Knowledge. Without that revelation this mode of knowledge would inevitably be confused with individualized knowing, or mental activity in the realm of existential causes, the rational categories, or general and particular concepts.[9] The divine mode (or "modeless mode") of knowing disclosed by the communication of the Word is the Trinity of the Godhead. Formally presented to the human knower it is this: Although God is nondual and uncompounded in his limitless being, he is nevertheless God the Father, God the Son, and God the Holy Spirit, and these are not three Gods, but one God. Precisely herein is to be discovered all that is essential in principial knowledge once the form in which it is presented has been inverted.

Eckhart tells us that as far as the theological enunciation of the doctrine of the Trinity goes, it has its orientation in being in the sense that "being" and "essence" are identical and affirmed as infinite. There is nothing unreasonable in this; it is certainly cogent theology and Eckhart himself frequently speaks within such a formal framework. This framework, necessary for the human knower, is nonetheless of the order of individuality and hence restricted to enunciation in terms of the categories of substance and relation. So he reminds us that no concept is adequate to the simplicity of "being", inasmuch as we need to combine concepts of existence and subsistence in order to affirm at once its simplicity and reality. And of course we have no concepts that are not grounded in being as divided by potentiality and actuality.

With Pseudo-Dionysius Eckhart will speak in terms of "super-being", but he will not say so much that the subtlety of the analogical transposition is assisted by this approach as that it suggests another mode of knowledge in which the same things may not be said in quite the same words. "Another mode," because what is at issue is not merely the deploying and tying up again of concepts to express the doctrine of processions, relations, notions, and so forth. What is primarily at issue is apprehending as it were the Trinity *within* the Godhead, apprehending reality as an "eternal and immutable going out and coming in: out of Godhead into being and from being into Godhead."[10] And this is true of each of the divine Persons as well as in the order of their proceeding.

As already stressed, Eckhart understands first and foremost God as the All-inclusive, the All-possibility. If he goes on to identify Being with. God,[11] he does not by this negate the all-inclusiveness of God. On the contrary, he simply makes an identification of Being with the All-inclusive, which is another matter altogether. We do not deny "the All-inclusive as such" when we affirm an ontological aspect of it. But Eckhart would have us understand that to acknowledge the all-inclusiveness and transcendence of God is thus to imply that which is "beyond Being"—in other words, that of which "Being" is an affirmation. Ultimately, of course, Being is ineffable, not merely because it is one of God's names but because it is presupposed by every attempt to define it.

Now all intellectuality depends on the preconceptual light of the intellect, which is the effulgent *instasis* in which that which proceeds returns. Though the affirmation of Being is necessarily and invariably a diminution of preconceptual intellection, it is true insofar as it is open to pure intellection, false insofar as it is shut off from it and substituted for it. Eckhart certainly realized that strictly speaking the *esse* (isness) of St. Thomas Aquinas goes beyond "Being"—really, though the unawareness of most Thomists of the law of inverse analogy in principial knowledge leads to a rather crude clamping down to the level of *ens*. Some have indeed spoken of "divine reality" *(res divinia)* which they, like Cajetan, insist is "neither purely absolute nor purely relative but super-Being."[12] But if its use is less affirmative than "Being," it is only because it conveys that which is "beyond." Affirmation is positive and, so to speak, blind to *That* which transcends it.

We finally have to admit that *That* which is beyond affirmation is indicated by a step back from the total and positive affirmation of Being. There is no other way. Eckhart's repeated reference to the law of inverse analogy applies here and helps to explain why such terms as "infinite," "unconditioned," "unrestricted," "all-possibility," "all-inclusive" are used. There is no implication whatever of limitation, confusion, or potentiality. He will say that the only answer, if an answer must be given, as to what *That* is that Being is not, is that *That* is not a "what " but ultimately and principially every "what" is *That*.[13]

"As the drop poured into the ocean is the ocean, not the ocean the drop, so the soul [the manifest intellect] drawn into God is God, not God the soul. Then the soul loses name and virtue but not isness and the will to know. There the soul is in God as God is in himself."[14] "The self *in* God is God. . . . As God is indistinct in himself according to his nature, though truly and in a special sense [from the standpoint of individuality] distinct from all things, so the self *in* God is indistinct from all—for in him all things *are* [he being all-inclusive]—and yet distinct from all things."[15]

If the transcendent identity of the self with God appears baffling to the discursory light of reason, it is because reason seeks to penetrate within. Nevertheless it is evident within. Pure metaphysical intellection is knowledge *within;* to say that it "penetrates within" is already an externalization. Principial knowledge does not deny the object from outside the triune Godhead; it transcends it within. And there within, knowledge is identity with the Principle and in the identity Eckhart discerns the threefold nature of Godhead: Principle, Principiate, Recession, the three being precisely identity. "All possibility," he says, "is in the Father, likeness is in the Son, nondiversity is in the Holy Spirit."[16] Thus the three-in-one expresses expansively all-possibility and reductively identity; in the Recession, or "negation of negation," the Holy Spirit abolishes that which is not Godhead and transforms everything into it. And this is essentially the threefold nature of principial Knowledge. "Thus it is for us," continues Eckhart, "to expire all diversity as the Holy Spirit expires it eternally."[17]

It is in this order of Divine Knowledge that the root of Eckhart's language is primarily grounded, an order that enables him to stress that what is negation in terms of Being is affirmation in terms of Godhead, which is supra-Being.[18] Were his apprehension of Being the same as that of philosophers who understand it as it were from "outside" the Trinity, certainly much of what he says would be invalid. But his understanding is situated as it were *within;* it is grounded in the Principle itself. "The eye [or principial intellection, which is wholly contemplative] wherein I see God is the same eye wherein God sees me; my eye and God's eye are one eye, one vision, one knowing, one love."[19]

In other words, God's eye, the unrestricted Intellect, "is the Subject of all reality." God manifests his multiple aspects in reality through the eternal affirmation of himself, and this is presupposed in the affirmation of the eternal Word. In pure intellection, the intellective identification of the object with the subject, God is the Subject—and love is realized by metaphysical necessity through the act of negating self as such, of returning to its own Principle, the divine Selfhood.

Thus. to apprehend the Trinity within Godhead is the most significant way of saying—and it must be repeated in order to avoid confusion—that principial knowledge is as it were the mode of knowing in God, and not to realize that God alone knows in this mode is to consider one's proper self as God.[20] Eckhart never for an instant considers his proper self to be God. It is the inverse of this that is implied when he says: "My innermost Self is God," or "My truest I is God." The proper self is nothing and as such is negated, for the ultimate love of the Holy Spirit negates all that is bound by time, sense, individuality, and differentiation, all that is not the Godhead.

THE GROUND OF THE INTELLECTIVE SOUL

If the unlimited will to know is not quenched by other intruding desires, the human knower will assent to the revelation of the Word, which is the God-communicated answer to the inescapable problem of contracted awareness and human evil. The act of faith in the Word is not believing something that the intellect denies—it is the choice of the highest meaning of metaphysical truth accessible to intelligence when that intelligence is not restricted by any particular observation, individualized inquiry, or selfish motivation.

But the reasonable assent of faith involves more than an objective belief in the Word; it involves faith seeking understanding. Yet faith seeking understanding, says Eckhart, involves more than considerations *about* the Word; it involves considerations that are as it were wholly *within* the Word, and ultimately a realization of awareness and love that is not other than the knowledge and love that God is. Therefore "Come up higher, my friend,"[21] assume the nobler place within [the Word in principial knowledge]. I will make of two one. "Friend, come up higher," is the twofold speech between God and the soul, which is consummated by "One God, Father of all. . . ."[22] Grace constitutes the soul in God [principially] where it has never been without.[23] As long as we think we are outside God, as long as we think *about* the Word, then "go up higher," says Eckhart. "It is better to know *in* God than to believe God."[24]

In a Latin Commentary on the verse "Put on the Lord Jesus Christ"[25] Eckhart says: "God assumed our clothing so that he might truly, properly, and naturally be man and that man might be God in Christ. But the nature assumed by God is common to all men without distinction of more or less. Therefore it is granted to every man to become the son of God. . . . And so we have "put on"—expressed by the passive form of the verb, not the active as though the action were an external one, emanating from an external source, but as though it occurred passively and from wholly within. For the word *induitio* (putting on) takes its name from the fact that it is within *(intus)*."[26] And Eckhart has already explained that *within* means *in* God, not in our inner self.

As God is infinite truth, so he is all-possible goodness. Hence "God's Godhead consists in the full communication of himself to whatever is receptive of him; were he not to communicate himself he would not be God."[27] So long as the intellect is under the sway of the unlimited will to know,

the all-possible goodness that God is cannot leave the intellect without the answer to its unresolved questions.
Moreover, that answer must necessarily transcend the mode
of all theologically and ontologically "correct" answers.

As has been noted, the Word is never to be considered as
distinct from God. The Word is identically God in every respect; it is unrestricted Intellect, the divine Selfhood; it is
indistinct from the all-possibility and isness that God is. The
identity of the Word with God is, indeed, the primordial
identification. Knowledge of this identity is brought about
by the communication and is actually realized by contemplation. It is realized through the direct and principal union
of the intellect with all-inclusive God wherein intellect and
the Word are identified in the Principle.

Despite the various interpretations, each more opinion-
ated than the last, which psychologists and heterodox theologians have suggested, the proper meaning of the Christian
revelation is the unique communication of the all-inclusive
order to the order of individuality. This communication
unites individual manifestation with *its* Principle, and the
proper meaning of contemplation is also union. When
accepted by reasonable faith, the revelation of the Word
unites the structural intellect with the structureless manifestation of that communication "as intellect is united with
Intellect-as-such"; "as the letter is united with the spirit of
the letter"; as "the just man is united with justice." But
"union is identity." [28] And contemplation is a knowing and
actual realization in that union in principial mode.

This unitive knowledge in terms of transcendent identity
is not, strictly speaking, an attainment; it is not acquired. It
is not constituted in any potentiality whatsoever; it is not an
achievement or production of a nonpre-existing intellection. "It is only by way of *act* that [this] knowledge is effected, and that act can be nothing other than transcendent
act." [29] In other words, the transcendent act, or uncreated
grace, effects the knowledge that the union really is, even
though that union is only virtually to be fully realized in
"the fullness of time," that is, beyond time. [30] Thus the intellect is made effectively aware "in its ground" of what ac-

tually is from all eternity and what it may otherwise not know theoretically. And this involvement in grace necessitates nothing less than the inversion of created grace into uncreated grace.

"There is the manifested word [which is all individuality], namely the angels [pure intellectual structures], men, and all creatures [animate and inanimate]. There is a second word, thought out [the mental word] . . . that I form within myself. But more, there is the Word which is neither manifested nor thought out, but is eternally in God who utters it. It proceeds eternally from the Father and it is in him. . . . The intellect works eternally within God [in principial knowledge]. The more subtle and the more spiritual a thing is, the more powerful it works within. The more powerful and delicate the intellect is, the more its knowledge is united with it and the more its knowledge becomes one with it. . . . God's blessedness depends on the inward working of the intellect, in which the Word dwells."[31] Moreover, "The prophet says: 'God spoke one [Word] and I heard two.'[32] That is to say, God eternally speaks only once. His Word is only one. In this Word he speaks his Son and the Holy Spirit and all creatures, and yet there is only one Word in God. But the prophet says 'I heard two'; that is to say, I [this human self] hear God [the uncreated order] *and* the creatures [the order of manifested universal being]."[33] From the standpoint of our mere human mode of knowing there is God *and* universal being, including the self; from the standpoint of the principial mode, there is only all-inclusive God, or non-twoness.

It is only in respect of the individual intellect that one can speak of this unitive knowledge and virtual realization. Hence it is understandable why Eckhart says that "the Word dwells in the very ground of the intellective soul," though in truest reality "it is the inverse of this that is so." Not only is the Word innermostly present by its creative and sustaining isness, but pre-eminently as principle of the active intellect, for "the principle descends in its entirety and with all its properties into the things originated."[34] This is actually true of every human being, and not only of one who is united or saved—these two words designating the same thing considered under different aspects, the first in relation to the Principle, the second in relation to conditioned existence. The Word is there in the ground of the intellective soul as Principle of the human being whether or not the will to know it and realize it is fully actuated.[35]

In the context of Eckhart's teaching this very ground is considered as corresponding analogously with the fundament out of which the modalities of the individual are manifested. It must not be confused with any substance or integral structure within or without the human knower, but clearly determined only as that wherein the Principle manifests the materiality and intellectuality of the human knower as being one integral self. This self is capable of indefinite extension in its own sphere, which occupies, moreover, but one degree of existence. Yet the material modality, which is a composition of physical, chemical, and sensory elements, constitutes only a very small portion of this self. The ground of the self is, then, to be considered not only as the proximate source of life for the human knower but also in a far higher sense as the direct and immediate "seat" of the Word, or of Intellect-in-itself, and hence of that wherein the unity is actual.

Many interpreters and translators of Eckhart have unfortunately been influenced by some modern form of an essentialist mode of philosophy, as well as by spurious or incomplete texts. But contrary to what they have said, "the *ground* of the intellective soul" is not the essence of the soul with its various faculties and operations. Rather that ground is, in Eckhart's own words, "its very isness," which is the direct manifestation of unrestricted isness itself. If Eckhart sometimes speaks of this ground of the intellect as a "power," it is not only because "isness is dynamic in itself," or because it is "the fundament of possibility and the drive toward unrestricted knowledge." It is primarily because it is that in which the Word, or pure Intellect, "innermostly dwells," and which "is closer to me than I am to my own self."[36]

The Word is in the ground of the soul with all its meaning and all-possibility. "The uncreated Word is in the created ground." In fact it is "in all creatures insofar as they have isness, and yet it is above them. And it is the same in all creatures as it is above them." [37] This is simply saying that from the consideration of the human knower one must always refer to the Word, which is God in every respect, as transcendent-immanent. Only the transcendent can be immanent and that which is immanent must be transcendent, the two terms being inseparable. "When I say the innermost I mean the transcendent and when I say the transcendent I mean the innermost." [38] In Divine Knowledge, however, the two terms are inadmissible, since apart from God there is strictly nothing and within God there is only God, as Eckhart has explained.

"The Word itself has no why or wherefore, but is itself the why of all things." [39] Nor is the Word a mediator between God and the ground of the intellective soul, for the simple reason that "the Word is God in every respect." The ground of the intellect is the direct manifestation of the Principle. It is not that God manifests the Word, which then in turn manifests the individual intellect. [40] The eternal triunity of the Father, Son, and Holy Spirit is totally within the unmanifested, all-inclusive order, and it is "the Trinity in consort, or God in himself, which creates, sustains, and transforms universal being." [41] "All beings are *from* the Father because in him they have effective being, *through* the Son they have it formally, and *in* the Holy Spirit they are as in their final end [which is God]." [42]

In other words, "it is not due to any imperfection in God that he operates only on what is present, and immediately, and not by intermediary or at a distance, as the more perfect creatures seem to act. For no creature can exist without God, no matter how far it seems to be from him [that is, how low it may be in the hierarchy of participation in being]. Furthermore, there is no intermediary between him and creatures. . . . God does not work on anything outside himself inasmuch as there is nothing apart from himself [God being the All-inclusive]. It is because of the sublime perfection of God [who is without any lack] . . . that God does not work by a medium or at a distance or on anything other than himself." [43]

The Word does not really dwell in or operate in anything outside itself, because there is no outside. But from the standpoint of the human knower, whose intellect is a "seeking intellect" and hence as such not "Intellect which does not seek," [44] that which is to be found is correctly regarded as really distinct from it and "dwelling within the ground of the seeking intellect." This is a perfectly valid mode of reference for the human knower "who hears two," because his standpoint is in the order of individuality from which the Word can only be affirmed as transcendent-immanent. The Word is Intellect-as-such, or "Intellect which does not seek," because it knows and is all-possibility.

But where is the Word to be found? "It is to be found only within. That which dwells innermostly in the soul is wholly within; it dwells there in the soul, in the intellect, and it does not go out [or seek] and does not look at anything [because apart from itself there is nothing and in perfectly knowing itself it knows everything about everything). *There* in the ground all the faculties of the soul are equally noble [for the ground is their proximate and unitive source]." [45]

Now the faculties of the soul, which comprise its essence, are to be distinguished from the ground, or isness, of the soul "from which they spring forth and in which they are rooted." Reason, memory, will do not act by means of the intellect's ground inasmuch as all the faculties of the intellect are inoperative in the ground, activity in terms of individuality ceases there. There "only God is, in the truest sense, *in act,*" for "the ground of the soul is accessible only to God." [46] Hence that which is known and virtually to be realized there is *oneness,* or nonduality. The faculties pertain to creatures; the ground of the soul does not. [47] For the ground is "the holy of holies"; it is "where union with the Word is effected by the operation of the Holy Spirit." The end of the intellect is the realization of oneness with the Word, and when this realization is actualized in the ground then all is known principially—"*gleichwie* [48] in the Word." It is there and only there that the transposition to principial knowledge is effected.

The Word must never be confused or identified with the ground of the soul. The more faithful we are to Eckhart's teaching the more abundantly clear it becomes that the Word is not the ground of the soul in any sense whatsoever. Eckhart insists that the tempting but erroneous doctrine of "substantial deification," or the identifying of God with the soul, must always be shunned. Indeed, as long as one re-stricts the intellect by some form of idealism or pseudomys-tical outlook one remains really ignorant of the principial mode of pure metaphysics and the essential truth that "the Word is God, and God is not this, not that." It is precisely the interest in the exaltation of the self, both in its outward and inner aspects, that Eckhart insists "must go if the ground of the soul is to be understood as that in which the Word dwells."[49]

The intellective soul is the informing principle of the body and when considered more especially under its vital aspect it is the form of individual existence specifically de-termining the human condition. But the Word is not the soul; nor is it the ground of the soul.[50] The ground of the soul is an individual manifestation and though principially that ground cannot be considered as other than its Princi-ple, which is the Word, the Word is not and never can be manifested individuality.[51] And while the soul characterizes itself as principle of life in the realm of individual existence and therefore in delusive manner, it is, from the standpoint of *in divinis*, identical with the Word. For the Word, be it never forgotten, is unconditioned Godhead, the ultimate and all-inclusive Principle, which contains all manifestation and all-possibility within itself.

PRINCIPIALLY I AM THE SON

If it has been necessary to emphasize repeatedly the non-identity of the Word with the ground of the soul, it is because it is an understanding fundamental for Eckhart. Nonetheless the identity of that ground with the Word, which is a principial identity and another matter altogether, is so because analogy is here applied in an inverse manner—as we have previously noted, and shall reserve for more extensive consideration in a subsequent chapter. In our present context it need only be stated that as an image of an object is reflection in relation to that object, then that which is first or immediate in the principial mode of knowledge is, from our human, *in via*, and contingent way of knowing, last and ultimate. "As long as we are on the way we are not there."[52]

The ground of the human knower is also referred to by Eckhart as the center, the heart, the temple, the citadel of the soul. These terms are traditional and are meant to designate the ineffable being of the intellect itself. They are, of course, to be taken analogously and not as a strict indication. Between the two there is only a correspondence and the analogy is perfectly valid, even though many people are undoubtedly led by their habit of thought to ignore the profound reasons for it. Obviously the "ground" referred to by Eckhart must be regarded symbolically, for any conception of "localization" is wholly inappropriate once the consideration of the corporeal world as such has been overcome; that is to say, once mere experience has been transcended by comprehension, questioning, reflection, and judgment in an act of knowing. For all the modalities pertaining to intellectuality are not subject to time-space conditions.

The intellect, as Eckhart has already explained, "considers all things above here and now"—and in this context "*now* means time and *here* means place."[53] "True understanding is where there is no 'here' or 'now,'" and the unlimited will to know "receives nowhere but in detached intellection [in the ground of the intellect] where there is neither 'here' nor 'now.'"[54] Necessary as names for the soul sometimes are, the soul itself is really without name. No name is adequate, and "these names do not reach the ground of the soul. God who is without name [in his unmanifested Selfhood] is ineffable, and the soul in its ground is ineffable, just as he is."[55]

It goes without saying, then, that the ground of the soul is not merely the vital center that is the principle of all sensory knowledge, as might be supposed by those who restrict themselves to the most external meaning of the "self" as it is related to corporeal reality. The ground does in fact play the part of a principle in the world of corporeal reality, but "only in a relative sense," inasmuch as the world of "corporeality is eminently potential to intellection and spirituality."[56] Hence it is precisely this corporeal determination that has to be transposed. Were the human self a pure intellectual structure,[57] it would not require "the Word made flesh." But inasmuch as the human being is composite of corporeality and intellectuality in his integral structure, he can never dispense with the Incarnation. In fact it is in the context of "a requisite support for the transposition" that "Jesus Christ is indispensable," in the same way that the very ground of the human being is to be considered as the principle of life. But if nothing more than the ground as the principle of life were to be considered, then there would be nothing more to seek.

The will to know transcends the will to live, and the detached, unlimited will to know seeks its own ultimate principle in the ground of the intellect. "There God is apprehended as *oneness.*" The faculty of reason can apprehend only distinct aspects of God, but "the Word is in itself *one* [or not-two], and the faculties [of the soul] know him only in part."[58] "Only in the ground of the soul is God known as he is," for there in the apprehension of God's unity "the intellect knows as it were within the Trinity and without otherness." It is there in terms of unity that "understanding as in principle is effected," and "there only *one* is heard."[59]

Appropriate here is an analogy from mathematics; only because mathematics is wholly an abstract realm within the order of individuality. The geometrical point is quantitatively nothing and does not occupy any space. Yet the point is the principle by which space in its totality is produced, inasmuch as space is nothing other than the development of its intrinsic possibilities. Again, following Eckhart, if one considers unity as situated in the series of the multiplicity of numbers, it is the smallest, yet it is the greatest in principle because it virtually contains them all and produces the entire series by the individual repetition of itself. The principle of unity is not the actual series; it transcends it, though without the principle there would be no series."

From our contingent, or *in via,* manner of knowing we must then also say that so long as union is not actually realized, the Word is only virtually in the intellective soul. This is why Eckhart validly designates the Word dwelling in the ground of the soul as a germ, a spark, or a birth. The intellective soul and the totality of individual manifestation exist through "the birth of the Word alone," and have no reality except through participation in it. Completely transcending all existence, the Word is the Principle of universal being and intelligibility.

Thus when Eckhart says: "God granted us in this world the possibility to become sons of God, even only-begotten sons, or rather the only-begotten Son [the Word] in order that we may live [or know] in him,"[61] he is clearly designating the transposition, by transcendent act,[62] to a principial mode of knowledge which is as it were within the Word. "The Father begets his Son as himself in eternity. 'The Word was with God and God was the Word.'[63] The Word was the same as God and in the same nature. I will say more: He has begotten him in my soul. Not only is my soul with him but my soul is the same as he is [principially], and he is in it. The Father begets the Word in the soul in the same way he begets him in eternity [without intermission, God not being subject to time or development], and not otherwise. . . . He begets me as his Son and the same Son . . . not only does he beget me as his Son, but he begets me as himself, and himself as me, and me as his being and his nature [for apart from God there is nothing]. In the innermost spring [the Principle] I well forth in the Holy Spirit. There is one knowing and one act [isness] *there* [in God]. All that God does is *one;* thus he begets me as his Son without diversity."[64]

"The Father begets his Son in eternal knowledge and thus the Father begets his Son in the soul just as in his own nature. . . . Once I was asked what the Father does in heaven [*in patria,* the all-inclusive order]. I said that he begets his own Son, and that this act is so pleasing to him and suffices him so well that he never does anything else than beget his Son and from both proceed the Holy Spirit. *There* in principle[65] where the Father begets his Son I am that Son and not other. Indeed we are here [*in via*, in our contingent and ontological mode of knowing as human knowers] diverse in our humanity, but *there I* am that Son and not other."[66]

Efforts on the part of interpreters of Eckhart's teaching who struggle endlessly somehow to squeeze statements like these—and they are numerous—into the framework of cognition restricted to individual manifestation, and thus within the categories of substance and relations, are entirely fruitless. Rather than being insights into pure metaphysics, in the name of which Eckhart speaks, their understandings are gross oversights and evince an ignorance of the principial mode of knowledge which he rightly insists is essential for a true understanding of reality.

This is the case of those who endeavor to "exonerate" Eckhart within the framework of ontological cognition, as well as those who "condemn" him for not always speaking within the terms of that ontological mode to which they have attached strict priority. But Eckhart is simply reminding us of what he says Christ came to remind us: The order of individuality, or knowledge and reality *in via*, is reflection and hence relational to the all-inclusive order, or knowledge and reality *in patria*. Principial knowledge is pre-eminent and is, in fact, by definition prior to all other modes. If it is ever actually to be realized, we must, by ceaselessly accepting God's grace, cultivate the habit of understanding as it were from the standpoint of God; that is to say from the standpoint of the full actualization of the *intellectus possibilis*. And if this means becoming "sober on Divine Knowledge," then so be it.

Thoroughly engrossed in individual manifestation and captivated by general and particular concepts of reality, we have "forgotten our true origin and principle," "fallen from oneness with the eternal Word." Eckhart makes clear that the First Cause of Aristotle is not God himself, rather it is only the *ratio* of the being of things and, for Aristotle, that *ratio* is pure Being.[67] We are rarely, if ever, tempted to question the reality of the sensible world; it is the very foundation of our philosophy, and before denying the world of experience as the alpha and omega of reality we would gladly sacrifice anything. And when we occasionally confront aspects of reality that do not properly fit into our philosophical structure, we endeavor to force them in somehow. Or since we tell ourselves that wisdom is also humility, we confess our human weakness. But much like Aristotle, we will never surrender the priority of being, experience, the absolute reality of the time-space continuum, and the rationality of the general categories of thought. In order to make intelligible that which we refuse to deny, we will consequently affirm an active Creator, a Supreme Being, even though our minds spin in trying to reconcile the creation with the immutability, perfection, and self-sufficiency of that individualized Being.

We at times even accept Christ as the Reconcilor of our difficulties, but we still insist on understanding the reconciliation and the revealed Trinity of the Godhead only in terms of substance and relations, and as it were from "outside." But Christ, says Eckhart, is the one "who tells us to turn within," and "that can only be in God," not into our puffed-up existential selves. Eckhart says that to accept Christ fully is to cease to be primarily concerned with the reconciliation of the difficulties confronted in our world of manifest individuality as though that were all important. Christ is before all else the "Reminder." [68] He reminds us of the truth that has been "forgotten" and hidden from our conscious and subconscious minds, but that is ever present in our super-consciousness, in the ground of the soul.

"The nature of a word," says Eckhart, "is to reveal what is hidden." In revealing the forgotten and hidden truth, Christ the eternal Word reminds us of true principial knowledge, wherein "all things are in God and that which is in God is God." "The blessedness Christ brought us was already our own," but we contracted our awareness, failed in willing, got intoxicated on individuality and then thoroughly inebriated on whatever the imaginative mind could concoct in order to escape from the ensuing boredom of individuality. "Our Lord Christ reminds us that our being and our life are eternal in divine oneness," that the "truest reality of all things is to be found not in created reality but in the Word."[69]

The "birth of the Word" is also the "speaking of the Word in the ground of intellect." Christ reminds us that "the heavenly Father speaks his Word and speaks it eternally . . . and in the Word he completely expresses his divine nature, and all creatures. . . . The Word lies hidden in the soul in such a way that one [distracted by desires other than the will to know] does not know it or hear it. . . . There [in the ground] God speaks in the soul and expresses himself completely in the soul. There the Father begets his Son, and he has great joy in the Word and has, moreover, such great bliss that he never ceases to speak eternally the Word that is beyond time."[70]

"Why has God become man? That I might be born again [in the realization of Divine Knowledge] as God himself. That is why God died [in the Crucifixion]—that I might die to the whole world [of individuality] and to all created things [or universal being]. It is in this sense that we should understand our Lord when he says: 'All I have heard from my Father I have made known to you.' [71] What does the Son hear from the Father? The Father can only beget; the Son can only be begotten. All that the Father contains and is, the incommensurability of his divine isness and nature, he brings forth once and for all in his only-begotten Son [there being no hind-thought nor forethought in God].[72] This the Son 'hears' from the Father; this he makes known to us, in order that we may realize [principially] that we are the same Son."[73]

We, of course, are not and never shall become Christ or God substantially, not even in the beatific vision.[74] To think that possible is "obviously absurd." Ontologically speaking "nobody as such is God, no created rational being as such is or becomes God"; individuality as such is not and never becomes the All-inclusive. But "there where my self and all things are known only *in* God, then I and all things are simply God."[75]

Eckhart is here again speaking not in the name of knowledge constituted in the relational order of substantial being, but in the name of knowledge constituted in the principial order of God and as one in whom grace is as it were perfectly operative. Thus in the transposition, or inversion, of the sense of "being" from one of substance and relation to one of all-inclusiveness and all-possibility, that is to say "isness itself in Divine Knowledge," his statements are perfectly valid. They also unfold that truth to which all other true statements are related, regardless of the modality of manifestation from which they spring.[76]

THE DIVINE SPARK

The "birth of the Word," the "birth of the Son," is a theme to which Eckhart frequently returns. To say that the Word is ceaselessly "being born" in the ground of intellect, and that union exists only virtually prior to its actual realization in Divine Knowledge, is to say that this is an understanding only from the consideration of the human knower. But "that whereby the soul expresses God does not in any way affect God's intrinsic reality."[77] Actually "the Word is in no way affected by any contingency," inasmuch as the Word is pure Intellect itself, essentially unconditioned and identical with the unrestricted and necessary isness that God is. "The Word is entirely immutable in its eternal actuality," and thus is totally without the potentiality of "being born."

Here it is especially important to understand the difference between potentiality and possibility. Potentiality designates "a capacity for a certain development"; "it presupposes a possible actualization."[78] As sense experience on the part of the human knower presupposes the possibility of an actual comprehension which in turn presupposes the possibility of an actual judgment, so sense experience is potential to an act of knowing. Potentiality can only be applied to individual manifestation, to becoming, to "being born." However, when considered principially in the all-inclusive order, as it must eventually be considered, "possibility is devoid of all potentiality" and is never "being born." There is, in other words, no potentiality in the all-possibility or the isness that God is and apart from which there is strictly nothing.

But to the human self all possibilities that transcend him *seem* to be potential. Insofar as he regards himself as differentiated from the Word he supposes his own intellection and being to be derived from himself. Thus whatever he attains is nothing but a reflection and not those possibilities themselves. Although this is only a delusion, we may say that for the self these possibilities always remain apparently potential. Why? Simply because it is not as a manifested being or as just a human knower that he can attain them, but only by and within the Word, the divine Selfhood. And once they are actually realized in the Word, then there is no longer any human self, individuality, universal being, or otherness to comprehend.[79]

The transcendence of the human self is a "dying to the self"; it is a vault beyond individuality, or rather the inversion of all reflection. But at this point of considering the transcendence it must be acknowledged that even while asserting the entire order of individuality as delusive, we must recognize that degree of being which pertains to it and which it has within its own order. When we consider the knowing self in any way it can only be in virtue of its real dependence upon the unrestricted act of knowledge itself. But the orientation of this dependence is primarily in the vertical line of detached intellection, so to speak, rather than that of the existential causation. And this is so whether or not we are aware of it. In other words, the sole Principle of the human self's reality, and insofar as he is virtually or effectively an integrated knowing being, is the Word. Metaphysically all reality must ultimately and therefore principially be considered as not in any way other than the Principle, or all-possible Reality itself.

Eckhart's description of the ground of the soul as the "place" of the Word's "birth" is, as we have found, fully justified. Moreover, the Word, considered in this manner as dwelling within the human knower, is also identified with

unmanifested isness, because the Word is innermostly present in the self as the sustaining act of its very being. Though
we are dealing with the integral human self, and not merely
with individuality limited to its materiality or corporeal
modality, one can consider the Word in like manner in
every other condition of individual being.[80]

The Meister frequently resorts to the scriptural (and perennial) symbolism of "light" to designate the Word. The
eternal Word as innermostly present in the ground of the
soul is the "effulgence" or "spark of the soul" *(scintilla animae).* This terminology is used by Eckhart on several occasions to express directly and principially what cannot be
expressed by indirect reason. "'Spark' in this context means
'principle' or 'in principle',," says Eckhart. The "spark must
always be referred to fire, of which it has the same nature"; it
is not the soul or ground of the soul that is fire, analogically
speaking, but God, and "the soul on fire is sparked by the
fire of God."[81]

Here again many interpreters of Eckhart, especially pseu-
dotheologians and pantheistic mystics without any apprecia-
ble understanding of metaphysics, have wrongly identified
the "divine spark" with the soul itself or the ground of the
soul. But "it is *in* the ground where the spark shines." The
spark is not the ground of the soul, is "not a part of the
soul"; "the spark is not this, not that." "The spark is of Intellect-as-such [the Word], is not other than a spark of the
divine nature, a divine light, a ray, an imprint of divinity."
Also "the exalted spark wherein we realize Divine Knowledge, that spark never parts from God, nor is there anything
between."[82]

Eckhart explains the "exalted spark" with an example
from nature: "When fire ignites the wood the spark has the
nature of the fire and is one with pure fire. . . . The father
of the spark is the fire . . . the spark of the fire lights and kin-
dles the wood [analogously the ground of the soul], it
makes the wood fire and unlike itself . . . and makes the
wood more and more one with itself, the fire. Yet neither
warmth nor heat nor likeness will ever calm or silence or
satisfy the fire or the wood until the fire begets itself in the

wood and gives the wood its own nature and its own being, so that *it* is all one fire."[83] Thus the "spark in the soul" is the *fünklein Gottes*, the spark of God in the soul; it is also "uncreated grace."

"Many times have I spoken of that uncreated and uncreatable Light or *fünklein* that is in the [ground of the] soul. It is this Light that I so often refer to in all my sermons. It is this Light that discloses God unveiled and unmanifested as he is in himself; indeed, it discloses him in his act of Self-affirmation. Thus I can most truly say that this Light is indeed one with God rather than one with my soul-powers, which are nonetheless one with it in its isness . . . Thus I say: If one turns from self and from all individuality, then insofar as you do this thus far are you identified with and blessed by the spark in the soul, which is never affected by time or space. This spark negates all individuality and affirms nothing but God unveiled as he is in himself. Not enough for it to disclose the Father, or the Son or the Holy Spirit or even the three Persons together, so far as they stand in their own properties. I swear that it is not enough for this Light to disclose even the unity of the processions of the divine nature. Indeed I will say more, and this may sound surprising; I say by eternal truth that it is not enough for this Light to disclose the impartable, immutable divine Being, which neither gives nor takes; it will rather disclose that from which this Being comes; it will penetrate directly into its unconditioned Principle, into the silent desert, in which no distinction ever enters, neither Father, nor Son, nor Holy Spirit. Only there in the Innermost, where no individualized one (or other) abides, is the Light fulfilled, and it is more within [the Principle] than it is in itself. For the Principle is purely unmanifested and wholly immutable and unaffected in itself; but from this immutable Principle are all things manifested."[84]

"Though we are God's sons, we do not realize it yet." Present in the ground of the soul this "spark of pure Intellect never dies . . . though it may flare up and set the soul on fire in any moment. . . . How are we God's sons? By realizing oneness with him [through principial identification with the spark]. But any knowledge of this, that we are

the Son of God, must be by understanding the distinction
between *extasis* and *instasis* knowledge [that is, knowledge
without and knowledge within the Principle]. . . . Not that
this *instasis* knowledge is the soul itself, but it is constituted
in the spark of the soul as in the Principle[85] of the soul, the
soul's intellectual Principle, the Principle wherein a man is
born God's Son eternally. . .for this knowledge is without
time, without place, and without "here" and "now." In this
Principle all things are one and all things are together all in
all identified."[86]

"How is one the Son of God, or how can one realize that
he is the Son, inasmuch as God is not like any individual?. . .
When I realize myself in nothing and nothing in me, when I
cast out everything in me, then I can be transposed into the
naked isness of God, and that is the pure principial isness.
All likeness must be abolished if the transposition into God
and identity with him is to be effected. . . . Thus is one transposed into God and is the Son of God. That nothing in God
be concealed from me, there must appear in me no likeness, no structure, or image, for no structure or image can
show us the Godhead or God's isness. So long as knowledge
of structure or likeness remains in you, you are never one
with God."[87]

"To separate soul and body[88] is bad enough, but for the
soul to be divorced from God, that is a far worse matter."[89]
"As the soul is the principle of the body, so God is the principle of the soul." "When the spark of Intellect-as-such is carried right into God in himself, then the man [born eternally
as God's son] really lives and knows." "The spark in the soul
is the light of divinity [the Word] which is always intrinsic to
God."[90] Moreover, the spark in the soul, or the "in-shining
light," is also the "synderesis"[91]—a "binding" and hence the
principle of intellectual conscience which directly unites
the conscience to itself and directs the conscience to "tend
heavily and ceaselessly toward understanding the Good." It
is by virtue of the synderesis that the ground of conscience
is united to the Good and to Justice, as it is by virtue of the
spark that the ground of the soul is united to Divine
Knowledge.

If the Word is represented as "impartable Light," it is

because Light symbolizes Divine Knowledge. It is the source of all other light which is but its reflection, since no relational knowledge, no matter how remote or indirect, is possible except by participation in the Light which is the *act* of unrestricted comprehension. As the uncreated Principiate of the nonmanifested and all-inclusive Principle, the Word is identically that Principle in isness and knowledge. In the direct light of this Divine Knowledge all things are in perfect oneness and unrestricted simultaneity. For principially there cannot be anything but identity and an "eternal now," inasmuch as Divine Knowledge excludes all otherness and immutability excludes all succession.

  If, however, we choose to speak of "the spark of the soul" as synonymous with the natural light of the soul, with created grace, with the ground of the intellect, then we must, as Eckhart insists, say that it "is an image of the divine nature and so created by God."[92] Then, of course, we consider the "spark" individually in terms of each distinct intellective soul. Even so, the spark of the soul, especially when regarded as the dynamic unlimited and detached will to know, is in this context that which urges the seeking intellect on toward oneness with its ultimate term, that is, the Intellect that does not seek and of which the seeking intellect is a reflection.

  But this is not the light or spark of which Eckhart essentially speaks, and he is usually misunderstood on this point. When considered correctly the spark in the soul is "neither created nor creatable." "There is a somewhat (call it spark, light, principle or whatever) in the soul that is so intrinsic to God that it is *one* with him. . . . It has nothing whatever in common with anything that is created." "It is pure Intellect itself." "It is uncreated grace."[93] "The spark is *oneness* itself," which "the intellect apprehends in its ground" and as a transcendental is intrinsic to God. It is not a structured manifestation but a manifestation that is "structureless as *oneness* is structureless and wholly within God," and hence pertains entirely to the order of the All-inclusive.

  "As long as anything created can make a distinct impression on the soul, then the soul is unsatisfied. . . . There is that in the soul which transcends its created nature. . . . It has nothing in common with anything. Anything created is nothing, but to *that* [the spark] everything created or manifested in time is alien and remote. It is Oneness in itself, taking nothing from outside itself."[94] "*If* man were wholly of this nature, he would be wholly uncreated and uncreatable."[95] He would have no direct awareness of individuality, "but man, as man, is greatly conscious of self." "There is a power or principle immanent in the soul of which I have already spoken: *if* the whole soul were as it is, it would be uncreated and uncreatable, but this is not so."[96] The individual soul is a created manifestation and is not its own principle.

WITHIN THE WORD

Save for the divine spark "the ground of the soul is dark, for the active light of reason does not shine there, but only outward in things." But when, by sustaining the unlimited will to know, we turn within, into the ground or isness of the soul, only the Word is known, and the known and knower are one. Therein "God makes us to know him, so his knowing is mine and as his mode of knowing."[97]

But in this unitive knowledge we are no longer conscious of our proper selves. We are "identified as it were with the spark" or principle, and "my knowing is really God's knowing." There within pure metaphysical knowledge is prior to and so detached from the created order of manifestation. After all, the doctrine of creation *ex nihilo* is simply a unique way of enunciating, for the human knower, the evident universal manifestation and its relation to the Principle. A "unique way" because, from the standpoint of individuality, it is indispensable in that it cannot be enclosed in a system of general or particular ideas. As an open doctrine and free from conceptualization, it prepares for and points to the principial mode "wherein all that is known is nothing other than the uncreated and uncreatable Word in whom there is no otherness or real distinction."[98]

From all this we can therefore say that the spark of the soul is the indwelling Word, born in, speaking to, or glow-

ing in the ground, the very isness of the intellect. From the
consideration of the organism it is the principle of life, and
from the consideration of the intellective soul it is the principle of all its operations. Still we have not gone beyond the
order of individual possibilities to that of infinite possibility.
To get there these operations must cease. We must turn
within, into the ground of the soul where, by inversion,
identity with the divine spark is effected. And it is uncreated
grace alone, or the spark itself, that effects the transposition
to principial knowledge—a knowledge that is as it were
wholly constituted within the Word.

Thus from the standpoint of detached intellection all is
understood as though from the summit of all-possibility,
which is identically God in his unconditioned Selfhood. Any
other *Weltanschauung* is by definition delusive. As "innate in
the soul" the unlimited will to know ever seeks and is dis-
content with any *Weltanschauung* that the scientific or philosophical mind may attain. "In its first issuing forth [in the
ground of the soul] it [the unlimited will to know] does not
stop at God insofar as he is good, nor does it rest with God
insofar as he is the truth. It goes on searching for the Principle and seeks God in his identity [or nonduality] and in his
desert [as unmanifest]. It seeks God in his wilderness and in
his own isness. Hence it does not rest satisfied [with God as
Goodness, Truth, Unity, or Being], but it seeks further to
find God in his Godhead and in the very Selfhood of his nature [as the isness of Divine Knowledge itself]. Now it is said
that no union is greater than that of the three Persons in
God. Apart from this, it is said that there is no closer union
than that of the soul with God. There [in this union] the
soul is embraced by identity. In the first touch [knowing]
with which God knows the soul and still knows it as uncreated [metaphysically prior to manifestation], the soul is as
noble as God himself is [for it is one with him in his participatory essence]. God knows it as he knows himself." [99]

Thus in truest reality it is not the Word who is innermost
in or who dwells in the manifested soul; rather it is "the soul
who dwells in God and is God." "My body is more in my
soul than my soul is in my body. My body and my soul are

more in God than they are in themselves." [100] Metaphysically prior to individual manifestation, all is in the Principle. "All things come from God. He is in all things, yet pre-eminently all things are in him," and "that which is in God is God." Moreover, "the reflection of the soul in God is God himself." The soul "dwells in the Principle, in the stream and source of the Godhead" and "*there* there is no one other than divine Selfhood, not even my knowing self," for *there* "I is proper to none but to God himself in his identity." [101]

Though the searching knower may theoretically understand this metaphysical truth and the pre-eminence of principial knowledge, effective awareness of it becomes actual only when, by uncreated grace, union is realized. This actual awareness implies a freedom from all the limitations that constitute the self as such and that, in a more general way, condition all individual manifestation. Not an escape into some subconscious or subjective state, which is a further enclosure within a still more limited modality of the self, this freedom is by way of transcendence and attainable by full acceptance of the transcendent act itself.

When it is said of the Word that it is in a certain sense indwelling in the human being, indeed in all manifested beings, this means that the knower has adopted the consideration of individual manifestation. Nevertheless this is nothing more than a concession from the standpoint of Divine Knowledge inasmuch as it is an application in terms of reflection and therefore delusive. For such an application is an extraction from the *instasis* of the all-inclusive Reality into the *exstasis* of its manifestation in individuality and universal being, even though the self is regarded as a participant in being. To get into the Word and understand that one has never been without, this application has to be inverted and "when fully within the Word, the inversion is total." [102]

3

The Primal Distinction

We are now obliged to undertake an intricate consideration in the doctrine that Eckhart expounds. To bypass it would no doubt lead to confusion, if not a simplification of a teaching that is anything but simple. In fact Eckhart warns us that the desire for simplification, which runs parallel to the desire for uniformity, is a divergence from the desire for unification. After all, "everything that is not strict impossibility has its place in divine all-possibility," which "negates the exclusiveness of any one simple possibility." [1]

If it has been made sufficiently clear that principial knowledge, as affirmed by Eckhart, is as it were knowledge *in* God, then it should not be difficult to understand that it is grounded in all-possibility, all-inclusiveness, and indistinction. Our natural human or individualized modes of knowledge, which are at best to be regarded in terms of approach toward God and hence as external to him, start as they must from the standpoint of the human knower and objective being. Inversely, the principial mode of Divine Knowledge—once the revelation of the Word is fully accepted—starts within God and then proceeds to understand all things from the standpoint of divine *instasis.*

This knowledge by identity, which is the principial mode, pre-eminently acknowledges neither the "mystery" of pure isness nor the "mystery" of Divine Knowledge, but their identity. Whatever intellectual distinctions that may, for the sake of a clearer understanding of manifest reality, be made principially are within and therefore from Divine Knowledge itself. Thus, to speak, as Eckhart does, of isness as not really but only intellectually distinguished from Divine Knowledge is to speak of that which is in function of pure Intellect.

It has already been noted that isness-in-itself is, as Eckhart says, "all-inclusive One without a second, without distinction, not this, not that." And "isness-in-itself is identically unrestricted knowledge," [2] which is another way of saying that pure Intellect is the Reality of all realities. It is also another way of saying that the all-inclusive Principle, which the terms pure Intellect or Godhead indicate, is not restricted by any essence or by any determination of "isness." We must here recall that for Eckhart isness primarily signifies knowability and infinite isness in itself signifies nothing other than "unrestricted knowability." Now inasmuch as unrestricted knowability directly demands the necessary reality of the infinite Subject who immediately knows all that is or is knowable, then Divine Knowledge or Godhead is that Knower's unrestricted knowledge and hence is beyond all distinctions or determinations regardless of kind or mode. It is in this sense that Eckhart wisely says that isness is always in function of knowledge.

At this point, however, it is no doubt wise to consider isness, not in itself, but in relation to manifestation. Without this important consideration, which we are now about to undertake, it would be difficult, if not impossible, to understand that "isness can be regarded under distinct aspects while it remains indivisible in truest reality."[3] Yet once we consider manifestation in any way, even principially, we are already in the sphere of relations.

THE EXISTENTIAL HIERARCHY

Inasmuch as all manifestation issues forth from God, it may be correct to say that the isness that God is enters into a certain relation with another principle. Though such a relation is not really present in terms of the supreme aspect of isness itself, since it is wholly indivisible and there cannot be any principle other than the ultimate "Principle without principle,"[4] nevertheless it is there intellectually. Thus in the consideration of manifestation the relational principle into which we are introduced is *"essence, the undifferentiated original quiddity or whatness."* While isness is eternally in act, or rather *is* pure act, essence is in a sense regarded as passive. And "though both are identical in truest reality, in God [where there is no potentiality], and remain hidden [unmanifested] in themselves, these two are the primordial principles of all that issues forth." "Essence is an intellectual division within isness." Moreover, "for all created [or individual] beings, act and potency are divisions of isness. Isness is the first act, the first distinction [once manifestation is considered], though in God in himself there is no distinction."[5]

In truest reality the unmanifested and undifferentiated triunity of the Godhead in itself transcends the distinction of isness and essence, inasmuch as the "eternal [and non-successive] generation of the Word is God's intrinsic and necessary affirmation of himself."[6] Nevertheless, insofar as the Trinity is distinctively rendered knowable in revelation, it is the direct issuance of the union of these complementary principles, isness and essence. And this is also true of all structureless manifestation, which belongs not to the order of individuality but to the order of the All-inclusive. In terms of unmanifested Godhead, or God "not in his divine works but in himself," the Word is the primordial identity or Self-affirmation of all-possibility. Thus it is extolled above all manifest realities, structureless as well as structured. It is indivisible Reality itself, for "while isness is the Word, it is in function of Knowledge itself whereby God speaks [himself] and speaks all things."[7] And "in saying that there is that in God [that is, in unconditioned knowledge of all-possibility] of which isness is the determination, I do not thereby deny him isness, but exhalt it in him [above the relational distinction of isness and essence]." "Isness is God. And isness suffices itself and all things. God is therefore the Principle of all."[8]

But once intelligibility is considered in any state of manifestation, isness must be understood in relation to essence. For "it is only through the intellectual essence that God brings things into being."[9]

Now that which produces the integral development of the human being is also the union of these intellectual principles, isness and essence, and that applies likewise in relation to each self. The same may be said of all other manifest conditions in individuality, for though we are here primarily concerned with the human condition, it must be remembered that it is but one among many conditions. "Material beings are one and yet not one, since they are composites of form and matter [and their whatness is really distinct from their isness]. Immaterial beings, such as those endowed with intellect, are one and yet not one, because their isness and essence are not identical, or rather because isness and understanding are not identical [in them but really distinct]. They are therefore composites of isness and intellect."[10] Thus, "in every created being isness and essence are really distinct, the former being derived from something else [that is, the union of unrestricted isness and essence] and the latter not being derived from anything as such."[11]

But the consideration of each composite self as distinct from other composite selves is not the only one to be made within manifest reality. If we now consider the entire order formed by a determinate degree of existence in which the human being unfolds itself and which includes all the beings that develop their corresponding possibilities of manifestation in it, then for this realm unrestricted isness is the divine will. "The divine will is identified with pure isness" in that it is an aspect or expression of God himself when regarded as "Almighty Authority of his entire province of universal being."[12] This *will* is also identified as the "eternal law" which is reflected in each modality of individual existence as the "natural law" and holds true identically in the macrocosm of all creation and in the microcosm of the particular self. As a reflection the natural law is clearly that each creature "simply operates according to its own nature, or essence." Yet the very diversity of natures, in their more and less participations in being, presupposes their inequality in the hierarchy of universal existence. Hence it is also the natural law that "the inferior is never equal to the superior" and "inferiors must by their very nature be led by superiors."[13]

If the human being, in harmony with the divine will and

the natural law, is to lead lower beings and benefit from them, he must do so under the sway of the unlimited will to know, not the will to power. At the same time he must allow himself to be led by intellects purer than his own who point to pure Intellect itself, or God. The divine will as reflected in the natural law "negates any duality between man and Nature." The divine will asserts the commandment: "Do unto others as you would that they should do unto you." A perennial commandment, says Eckhart, which applies not only to our relations with our fellow men but "to our relations with beasts, plants, and inanimate things." Otherwise the beasts, plants, and inanimate things will do as irrationally unto men as man has done unto them, for "instead of bringing tribute to man they will bring retribution upon him." [14] Thus the relation of isness and essence in the really distinct order of individuality and all modalities thereof is a reflection of the original relation of unrestricted isness and essence in the supreme Principle. Essence is always and in all conditions "relationally dependent" on isness.

Ignorance of this basic dependent relation largely accounts for the aberrations of the natural hierarchy of individual manifestation that man, both singly and collectively, commits. The hierarchical relationship holds within each species as well as between species. While "human nature is wholly present in every rational creature," it is manifested there in "remarkably diverse ways according to the inherent qualities of each." It is "the qualitative essence intrinsically related to the created isness of each being" that determines its "superiority over inferiors and its inferiority to superiors." To think otherwise is to think that human persons—or even all creatures—are all alike and differ among themselves "only numerically." [15] "Though liberty is in the will, it depends on reason and intellect." [16] But egalitarianism is without intellectual foundation. Hierarchy will always prevail in the created order, and unless we acknowledge and sustain it according to natural law we will reap its completely aberrated form, the summit of which will be occupied by a being whose roots will "spring from the bottom of the pit of Hell."

Though all this is true in terms of universal manifestation, it is not so in God or when God in himself is our primary consideration. In God there is no hierarchy for the simple reason that there is no real otherness in him, and hence nothing that could be affirmed as inferior or superior. "As in God in their primal issuing forth from God, all things are equivalent." Once manifested, however, "inequality is the natural order of all beings."[17]

NONDUALITY

We must not forget that the metaphysical determination of the complementary principles of isness and essence has nothing whatever to do with any "dualistic" conception. It is, in particular, wholly incommensurable with that type of dualism, such as mind and matter, so prevalent in modern philosophy, the origin of which is really imputable to Cartesianism and the subsequent horrors of which are found in the closed systems of Hegel and Feuerbach. Nor should we forget that the distinction of isness and essence in ultimate reality, primordial as it is in comparison with all other distinctions, is nonetheless an intellectual distinction only and therefore purely relational. For, to repeat, the distinction "does not have reality but is only understood. So where isness is not understanding, there is never unity. But only in God are isness and understanding identical."[18]

Moreover, "essence refers to isness . . . and the relation, as it is intelligibly distinguished in God, does not pertain to the unconditioned isness that God is [in himself] but to the mutual relations [of isness and essence to one another in the consideration of manifestation)."[19] "The distinction between isness and essence is intellectual and [they are] taken as One [in reality]. It is only when the One is not kept within itself that it receives and confers distinction."[20] Now, "the One is not kept within itself" as soon as we consider manifestation in any degree.

Again Eckhart reminds us that "God speaks the One, but we understand two." The distinction of isness as the determination of the All-inclusive in relation to manifestation is the first of all distinctions. It is the distinction in which the relationship of isness and essence is immediate, and it is from this relationship that all other qualitative distinctions directly or indirectly derive. Hence one must never regard this distinction of isness and essense as the affirmation of any strict irreducibility, for in the Principle itself the distinction is nonexistent. It is only in relation to the manifestation of which it is the Principle that all-inclusive isness distinguishes itself into isness and essence. And this without its intrinsic identity being thereby affected, inasmuch as "God cannot be disturbed by any distinction or multiplicity." [21] In this sense, and from the very fact that it is metaphysical, the doctrine that Eckhart, following Aquinas, expounds is fundamentally the perennial "doctrine of nonduality."

In a Latin exposition on the theme "God is One," [22] Eckhart says that "all things are in the One by virtue of its being One, for all multitude is One [in principle], and is in and through the One. . . . The One refers, properly speaking, to what is all-inclusive and perfect in itself and for that reason lacks nothing. . . . The One refers by its essence to pure isness itself [and hence is not to be confused with the 'One' of Plotinus, which is devoid of all-possible isness]. For essence, too, is always single and therefore it is appropriate to union and the act of isness by virtue of its unity. . . . [The One] is one isness with isness itself. . . . By virtue of being One, God is primal and supreme. Hence, though the One descends through essence into all things [as manifested reflection] and into every single thing, it always remains One and unifies things that are divided." [23]

But Eckhart takes great pains to deny that the One that God is should ever be considered as identical with any essentialized "one" or with this or that individualized "one." The One is God; indeed the fulfillment, the plenitude, of the Godhead is Oneness. [24] The "One without another" is transcendence; it is not the "one" of a series, since every series is finite. "God is One without the essence of one and number"; is "without all number and supranumber." For "the One is the negation of negations [and therefore unique]." [25] Moreover, "when God is called "One," the "One" does not refer to the genus of number nor does it impart something to God. Thus it does not itself give rise to any series." [26] Now a series indicates the division of one or one multiplying itself, making two, and so on indefinitely. But "isness in itself is indivisible, nor does it multiply itself and nothing is added to it." Indeed, "people think that they have more if they have things together with God, than if they had God without things. But this is wrong, for all things added to God are not more than God alone." [27]

It should here be repeated that the very consideration of manifestation, even principially, necessitates the intellectual distinction of isness and essence. And insofar as individuality is considered, the distinction between God and the self is real for the human knower. Nonetheless, "real distinctions are not separations," and "in itself isness is indivisible, is not-twoness." "Not-twoness" is simply the principial way of affirming that "isness itself is beyond all limitations and manifest determinations, even that of oneness," [28] and in order to affirm its transcendence of all duality as beyond any doubt, unconditioned isness must be considered as "not-two." As Eckhart says: "In truest reality there is no duality." [29]

The finite and the infinite are certainly not to be considered as separate, for that would exclude the finite from the infinite and thus limit the infinite, which is absurd. Nor is the infinite to be considered as identical with the finite, for that would make the infinite finite, which is contradictory. Rather the finite and the infinite are related as not-two, thereby involving neither contradiction nor compromise. Upon reflection it is found that this is the only position which, if properly understood, "allows the finite full scope to have its being in the infinite without loss of meaning to both." Thus we can better understand why, in principle or in terms of the transcendent One, which is non-twoness, "the finite is the infinite." [30]

It should be clear, then, that the doctrine of nonduality, which is at the very core of pure metaphysics, is not to be confounded with what modern philosophers ascribe as "monism." Regardless of the form in which monism may be clothed, it always remains a philosophical conception within the category of substance, implying a pure substantial immanentism and not an apprehension within the principial order wherein such a determination is out of the question. Nor has the doctrine of nonduality anything in common with "pantheism," for when properly understood "pantheism" necessarily indicates a naturalism that is basically non-metaphysical, inasmuch as metaphysics means precisely that mode of knowledge which in every respect is *supra totius naturae*. Thus the doctrine, in the name of which Eckhart speaks, has no connection with either Hegelianism or Spinozism, with any derivatives of these philosophical conceptions or with any similar outlooks, regardless of place or time.

While "monotheism," on the other hand, is essentially the doctrine of nonduality, metaphysically speaking,[31] Eckhart at times intentionally speaks, as we have noticed, in terms of nonduality. He does so because he wants to remain free of the formalism which the rational faculty attaches to "monotheism;" that is, he does not want us ever to confuse "mono" with the distinct "one" of number, series, distinction, and otherness. For "mono" actually means "not-two," "not-of-a-series," inasmuch as it in itself is indivisible, all-inclusive, and beyond distinctions. The inversion of the determinate "one" is the unmanifested and supradeterminate One of which Eckhart speaks; it is "not-two" and "not-two is the negation of a negation."

If the metaphysics of Aquinas has appeared "dualistic" to those who have failed to understand it, it is because their apprehension of it stops short at the consideration of the distinction of isness and essence. But Eckhart correctly understood that this first "duality," being intellectual only, does not in any way affect God or prevent metaphysics from admitting as possible all that transcends this distinction.

As Aquinas himself points out: "One [as indicating God *in se*] signifies not only that which is non-twoness, but also that which is perfect [or without defect]." Whereas "unity as the principle of number is contrasted with numerical multitude, unity as convertible with isness is contrasted with the kind of multiplicity that designates defect." Therefore "taken as a principle of number, oneness is not to be predicated of God." "Inasmuch as there is no composition of quantitative parts in God, for he is not a body; nor a composition of matter and form; nor are his nature and complete substantiality distinct; nor his essence and isness; nor is there a composition of genus and difference; nor of subject and accidents, it is clear that God is altogether unconditioned and in no wise composite." After all, "God is the primal reality, strictly speaking, and no part of a whole can be that," inasmuch as in "the unity of the primal reality, which includes all that is actual and possible, there is no twoness or division." Indeed "to know God as it were in himself is not to call on a multitude of words (to name or determine God); for then our knowledge is unconditioned as his knowledge is unconditioned." [32]

Unfortunately this insight was not fully appreciated by many followers of Aquinas, and what occurs in the enclosed conceptions to which most modern philosophers are especially attached is directly contrary to this metaphysical insight.

ISNESS AND WHATNESS

Having called attention to the metaphysical significance of "nonduality," to which Eckhart attaches great importance, we should now return to further considerations of isness and essence. Isness has to be considered prior to essence because there is no way whereby essence, which is the substratum or supporting principle of all manifestation, can be endowed with voluntary act. It is necessary, then, to clarify more precisely the significance of essence, or whatness. For essence, or quiddity, means nothing more nor less than "what makes a being what it is."

In itself "essence is purely non-act, or non-isness" in the sense that it, as Eckhart says, "contains every kind of affirmation, yet is never capable of affirming itself." In other words, "essence by itself can never be an efficacious cause." [33]

Essence is nonefficacious in itself and thus, being a distinction from isness and "inferior to act," it "requires the act," or rather "the influence of isness." And in order to stress this point Eckhart reminds us, as did Augustine, that "essence [*essentia*] even derives its name from *esse* [isness]" and being thus derivative is intellectually inferior and necessitates the impact of isness in order that there is real production.[34]

In explaining this point further Eckhart says: "For it is in accordance with the reality of the intellectually higher (which is isness) to influence essence, just as it is natural for the lower (which is essence) to receive such influence."[35] In other words, essence must receive the affirmation of itself from isness in order that production may be actualized. All manifestation certainly issues forth from divine essence, of which there are so many modifications, but without the innermost presence of the immediate impact of isness, these "productions" would be naught in every respect and strictly without reality.

The philosophical view according to which essence is wholly self-sufficient as the principle of all manifestation can only be the result of an entirely misdirected way of thinking. Arising out of stopping to "take a mental look" at reality, rather than knowing participation in it, such a view absolves itself from isness. It becomes enclosed in concepts or absolute ideas that are mistaken for concrete reality, and hence fails to understand the significance of efficacy. Yet this is a typical manner of much modern philosophy, and largely explains its divorce from genuine ontology and therefore its inability to attain even a slight insight into Divine Knowledge.

Though the principial mode of knowledge transcends ontology, a requisite understanding of ontology—not a textbook learning about it—on the part of the human knower is presupposed. Eckhart never initiates a rebuke against ontology or intellectuality. On the contrary, he is in full agreement with Aquinas in insisting that insofar as we are "on the way" the "concept" is not only inevitable but perfectly valid. After all, it is the concrete reality that is known in conceptual knowledge, and it is the principle of being, according to which we make abstraction, and not what we abstract, that is significant. What he does stress, however, is that knowing *in via* reflects pure knowledge *in patria* and as such signifies an individualized principle in comparison with the all-inclusive Principle.[36] Since the *extasis* of all reality is from its principle, the intellect's approximation to Divine Knowledge [its Principle] is nothing other than an inversion of *extasis* into *instasis*. And the inversion is made requisite only in grace because the order of "distinct reality has been extracted from the Godhead, the Principle."[37] Any rebuke that Eckhart initiates is only one against antiontology or pseudointellectuality, which takes abstract representations for the presence of concrete reality, considers essence as self-subsisting, and turns ideas in idols.

In order to preclude any possible misinterpretation, it should be added that the sense in which essence is here taken by Eckhart is not that adopted by certain latter-day students of Aquinas. Under rationalistic influences they tend to regard it as prior to isness, and thus designate isness as though it were another "essence" and answerable to the question "What?" Not containing all-possibility, "essence," says Eckhart, "contains only the possibilities of manifestation." All-possibility is not essence; rather it is God wholly in himself, the Principle of both manifest and unmanifest possibilities. All-possibility is beyond the distinction of isness and essence, is that apart from which there is only contradiction or strict nothingness. "The distinction between isness and essence is referred back to the One [indivisible and all-inclusive Principle] where essence is identical with isness. When Oneness is no longer in oneself [as the only consideration] then division has crept in. To seek unity short of the isness that God is, is to delude oneself."[38]

In truest reality, and therefore in Principle, God is his all-possibility and all-inclusive identity. He transcends the distinction of essence and even the primal distinction of isness, which distinctions are necessarily made once isness is determined or once any aspect of the manifested principiate is considered. Being beyond all mental distinctions and determinations, God nonetheless "eternally affirms himself, or rather negates all negations, which is pure and infinite affirmation."[39]

When Eckhart says that *isness* is the first distinction, the consideration is in terms of manifestation wherein this first and highest determination signifies that God is not vague, indeterminate, or abstract. Nevertheless, distinctive isness is a negation from the standpoint of the unmanifest Principle. Hence essence as distinguished from isness, though a necessary intellectual determination when considering distinct reality, is also a negation from that transcendent and supreme standpoint. In other words, the distinction of essence from isness is subsequent upon the prior determination of isness, "purest and most simple of all possible determinations." If Eckhart apprehends God in his transcendence of this primal distinction and of all determinations, even the purest, as Divine Knowledge itself, it is not the essence principle as such that Divine Knowledge signifies. Rather it is simply *That* of which isness is in function; it is the primordial and necessary negation of all negations. For "Divine Knowledge in itself is neither a 'what' nor an 'is,'" insofar as "whatness" and "isness" can in any way be considered as positive. Godhead, or Divine Knowledge in itself, is neither a determination nor a distinction but "*That* in virtue of which all noncontradictory distinctions and determinations are possible,"[40] and "isness is the first of all."

Still, "essence in itself is undifferentiated"; it is not a composite of things. And while it is unmanifested and incomprehensible in itself, it nevertheless is the content of all production without itself being a production. Essence itself is not the manifested intellect. It is only "with us," as Eckhart says, inasmuch as "the undifferentiated essence itself is proper to God, the differentiated essence to the creature."[41] But the undifferentiated essence itself contains the differentiated, as the infinite contains the finite.

"When God created all creatures he had a prior-nothing or nonproduction that was unmanifested and that contained the *ratio* of all creatures. . . . This [essence] is so assimilated to God that it is a single, undifferentiated One, passively containing the *ratio* of all creatures, is structureless and super structure."[42] This is why Eckhart is able, in the same discourse, to answer both affirmatively and negatively the question: "If I am in principle the only Son whom the

Father has eternally begotten, have I eternally been Son? I say yes and no. Yes, Son inasmuch as the Father has eternally begotten me; not Son in terms of the unbegotten. 'In the Principle': here we are given to understand that we are the only Son whom the Father has eternally been begetting out of the concealed darkness of eternal nonmanifestation, and yet remaining within the supreme Principle of the primal manifestation, which is the fullness of all perfection. Here [in the Principle] I have eternally been at rest and asleep in the unmanifested comprehension of the eternal Father, wholly within and unspoken." [43]

Essence is the *ratio,* the reason or rationale of all production. It is the "seed" of all manifestation, "yet it is without seed," for if it had a seed it would not be a seed. As seed it is grounded in isness, and without this actuating or nourishing ground, there would be no production whatsoever. As "the divine, passive and participative principle distinguished [intellectually] from isness," essence is the dramatic "player" of all structures, and hence the source of all delusion insofar as it is separated from isness. Structure as such is unreal in that it is always, in the knowing course, nothing more than a comprehended potentiality to the act of affirmation that determines reality. Essence is purely intellectual, or spiritual, but when differentiated from its ground it also discloses an extrinsic delusive tendency toward *materia signata quantitate.* Thus separated it finally tends toward "prime matter, or the pure potentiality of things, whereby they are not yet entities and whereby we call those things that are not as though they were." [44]

Essence is unmanifested, is not a production. But all things, from pure intellectual structures to the powers of the intellective soul, to the individual awareness that promotes the notion of "self," and on down to the further determinations of all things, are productions of divine essence. They are also productive in their own modality of existence and in relation to those things which follow. On the other hand, while common sense and the faculties of sensation and motion, including the sensible elements, are productions of essence, they are not themselves productive. Inas-

much as all things are productions of essence "we have, ac-
cordingly, these considerations, namely: that the thing issuing is in the producer [essence under the influence of is-
ness]; that the thing is in essence as the offspring is in the
seed, as the word is in the speaker; and that it is in it as the
ratio in which and through which the product issues from
the producer. We must, however, realize that by the very fact
of a thing's issuing from something else it is distinguished
from it. . . . In this connection it should be noted that in
analogical relations the product is always inferior, less . . .
and unequal to the producer, whereas in principial relations
it is always one with it, not sharing the same nature but
receiving it in its totality from its principle, simply, integrally." [43] Principially because "in essence itself there is no
division or privation," for "division by its very nature is privation and nothing—no-thing, no being—exists by privation." [46]

Isness, however; is neither produced nor is it alone productive. That is, it is not productive in itself, inasmuch as the
complementary principle is required for production to be
manifested. Nevertheless, "isness is its own act, or rather it
is pure act itself, as actioniess actuality that fundamentally
determines everything that is produced through essence." [47]

Thus we have four basic divisions consequent upon the
primal distinction or determination of isness, or rather the
consideration of isness, not in itself, but in its relation to
manifestation. Here Eckhart is following John Scotus
Erigena, who explained: "There is that which creates but is
not created; that which is created and itself creates; that
which is created and does not create; and that which is neither created nor creating in itself. . . . But the first [essence]
. . . and the last [isness] . . . are one in divine reality [the
unrestricted act of knowledge], for it can be called creative
and uncreate, since being infinite [the all-inclusive
Principle], it cannot produce anything apart from itself and
likewise there is no possibility of it not being in itself and by
itself." [48]

It should also be noted that while necessarily without differentiation, divine essence is not only the *ratio* of all pro-

duction but contains indivisibly within itself the transcendentals of truth, goodness, and beauty which with unity "are interchangeable with being." [49] When actualized under the ordering influence of pure isness, these constitutive qualities unfold themselves for the human knower in the multiplicity of determinations and so are present in every individuality from the lowest to the highest in the hierarchy of participative reality. In divine essence these constitutive qualities are, of course, in perfect unity and principially coincide in the nonmanifested order of undifferentiation. But every manifestation or modification of essence signifies a break in the unity, and all beings, or participations in intelligibility, share in these qualities in different proportions.

In principial mode, of course, all is true, good, beautiful, and united. But for the human knower, whose standpoint is that of individual manifestation and therefore delusive, all things are not true, good, beautiful, and united. As "there is untruth in our truth," [50] so there is "a lack in our good, ugliness along with beauty, and diversity mixed with unity." Essence contains, therefore, "that which is conformity to isness," designating an expansive or upward qualitative tendency toward pure knowledge. It also contains "that which is divisible and obscure," representing a contraction or downward quantitative tendency toward ignorance. In other words, "essence has an ambiguous character," obviously, because it is already a distinction from isness and "division by its very nature is the way toward non-being." [51] But these aspects of essence are not orders of manifestation. They are simply conditions of existence, to which all manifested individual beings are subject, and which must not be confused with the special conditions that limit this or that mode of manifestation.

A further consideration of isness as related to manifestation discloses the fundamental realms between which all modes of manifestation are distributed. First, of course, is transcendent isness itself which, being immutable and infinite, pervades and sustains all manifest beings. But within the manifestation of individuality there is the recognition of what Eckhart designates as corruptible entity and incorruptible entity. Both are created and therefore contingent; one or the other, as indefinitely distributed among the multitude of beings, is the entity of each individuality. "God, the immutable isness, is the Principle of both and transcends the corruptible and incorruptible."[52]

The corruptible entity is the existential principle of all nonknowing beings, which are strictly a composite of materiality and structure and whose distinct existence is in fact transitory. The incorruptible entity is the existential principle of all knowing beings, the very ground of the intellective soul and of pure intellects.[53] Though the human being as such is perishable and decomposes, his one existential principle, which sustains his composite structure of corporeality and intellectuality, is not perishable.[54]

It is contradictory and fallacious to think that any individual being, including the human being, has more than one substantial isness. The isness of each person's integrality is the very ground of the intellective soul, which actualizes his essence as specifically rational and which is immaterial and indestructible. As previously noted, each human being is one self, but free to correctly acknowledge his integrality in the ground of the intellective soul or incorrectly regard himself as fragmented and separated from it. Not forgetting that infinite Personality, or pure Spirit, is an original determination of all-inclusive God, and as such really transcends the domain of individual manifestation, we are now able to understand why Eckhart affirms a personality for each human being and says that "when speaking of a human we mean a person."[55] It is the ground of the intellective soul, which is wholly spiritual, that establishes the personality of the human self, and "if separated from the ground the self can only be regarded as a naught, a non-entity."[56] "Though death [the decomposition of the human being] separates soul from body and man dies,"[57] the intellective soul, being a personality and having an incorruptible existential principle as its ground, "does not die."

When regarded as identical with the unrestricted isness of Knowledge itself, the infinite Personality is, so to speak, an intrinsic aspect of all-inclusive God, "as a ray is a portion of the light, the nature of which is present in each and every ray." In saying this, we must remember that God is, however, really without parts, inasmuch as he is in himself "strictly indivisible and without duality."[58] Thus the Personality, or pure Spirit, is in no way subject to individual personality, which is but its reflection, or to the conditions that determine the self. Even in its relations with the self, the Personality remains unaffected by any individual modifications, which are wholly contingent and not exigent to the Personality, inasmuch as they all proceed from divine essence, as from a single seed.

"The seed needs the influential ground, but the ground does not need the seed," and so "essence does not suffice in itself, rather is wanting and requires something other," that is, "the actuality of isness."[59] It is "from essence," which contains the possibilities of manifestation, that modifications are produced in the manifested domain "by the actualization of these possibilities." However, "since isness in itself alone directs the issuing forth of the possibilities of essence, it is the principle of all that is," and "nothing that is created adds to or takes away anything from isness."[60] It never enters itself into manifestation, which means that beings, insofar as they are considered individually, are really distinct from it, and nothing regarding their distinctive development can affect the immutability and identity of isness.

These remarks should help to explain why genuine ontology always emphasizes the unity of being even while describing it as multiple—despite the fact that ontology never attains to the all-inclusive isness that God is. As explained by Eckhart, ontology must assert no complete whole less than universal being. This is why it points to pure metaphysics, which recognizes universal being inversely and therefore as a manifestation of the superessential Principle in which the only "complete whole" to be considered is all-inclusive God. "All creatures can say 'I', for the word is common [to self and to all beings]; but the word *sum*, '*I am*', signifies that which is totally all-inclusive and it is denied of any creature."[61]

THE SIMPLE NOW OF ETERNITY

Eckhart has said, insofar as it can be said, that isness is the
primal distinction in knowledge once manifestation is considered in any respect, even principially. On this point, however, we could easily be misled if we did not acquire a further understanding of isness, an understanding that is essential in principial knowledge.

The Meister says that "since isness is primal and the Principle of all things, then all the works of God are new [that
is, always fresh and present, from the standpoint of the manifested individual]. For what is in the Principle and whose
end is always the Principle, will always be and always is. He
has produced everything in principle, because he himself is
the Principle. Again, he, in himself the Principle, has *always*
produced, that is, always *now*. . . . But God, pure isness itself;
is the Principle, the beginning and end. For prior to isness
nothing is, and after isness there is nothing, since isness is
the term of all becoming. Indeed, that which actually is, is
not able to become, as what is already a house, though it
become whitened, can no longer become a house. It is
through essence [which is identically his isness, the distinction being intellectual only] that the possibility of beings
[in his essence] receive actuality from the isness that God is,
and from him alone. Thus he has either produced nothing,
or he has produced all in himself as the Principle."[62]

"God has always produced, that is, always *now*," designating, of course, the *nunc simplex aeternitatis*[63] (the simple now
of eternity). "In eternity there is neither 'before' nor 'after.'
For this reason what occurred a thousand years ago and
what will happen a thousand years hence and what happens
now are all one in eternity. Therefore what God produced a
thousand years ago, what he will do in a thousand years, and
what he is doing now is nothing but one single act."[64]
Consequently "production is always in the Principle—so too
with us, if you do away with time, evening is morning—and
since it is always in the Principle, it is always now being produced. Either never or always, since the Principle, or 'in
Principle,' is always *now*."[65]

Any metaphysical exposition of Divine Knowledge is wanting if it does not focus on "the eternal now," and this is why
it is a recurrent theme in Eckhart's writings. It is in respect
of the *now* of eternity that he says that "the world [of mani-
festation] has been from eternity, for there never was a time
when the world was not or when the world did not yet exist."
There being no time, no "before" or "after," apart from time,
"God therefore produces the world in the principial *nunc
aeternitatis,* in which God is and which is God." [66] As principial knowledge is always as it were *in divinis,* so is it always as it
were in the *nunc aeternitatis.*

It is very important to be clear on this point, as Eckhart
cautions. "Indeed, creation and the very act of God is [prin-
cipially] the isness that is God, yet it does not follow from
this that if God created the world from eternity, the world as
such [in its distinct reality] therefore is from eternity. For in
the passive sense creation is not eternal, just as the thing created is not eternal." [67] When Eckhart uses the inferior term,
he will always speak of a double isness of the creature—in
God and in itself: "It is to be noted that all creatures pertain
to one isness in their principial source, namely in the Word
of God, and this is permanent and immutable, but the other
isness of things in their own proper nature they have in
themselves and from God." [68]

But to drive home the correct consideration of all manifestation he recalls from the writings of Isadorus that "people are always asking what God was doing before he created
the heavens and the earth, or whence there came to God
the new intention to produce creatures? And I answer: no
new intention ever arose in God [inasmuch as God transcends 'before' and 'after', 'old' and 'new'], for although
the creature does not exist there as it does here, it is from
eternity in God and in his Intellect." [69] As St. Augustine says:
"God does not know [or act] in a temporal manner and no
new knowledge [intention or act] arises in him." [70]

Consequent upon the same question, people ask whether
or not the procession of the Word and the production of
the world of manifestation are simultaneous. The formal
theological answer is properly that the former precedes the

latter, and Eckhart does not dispute this. But when we consider the distinction between *in via* and *in principio* modes of
knowledge, it must be understood that whereas the human
thinks in terms of succession and therefore affirms two different acts, "in God there are not two or many, but one single, immutable, and undivided act which is isness itself."
And this act is "wholly without time, multiplicity, and succession." and so we must understand that "in the one and
the same pure act [and intention] that God is, he begets his
Son coeternal with himself and also creates the world." [71]
Again Eckhart reminds us that "God has spoken once; twice
have I heard this." [72] After all, it is only the unwise, or the
antimetaphysician, who asks questions such as "What was
God doing" or "Where was he before manifestation," or
"When was there nothing else besides him?"—being ignorant of the truth that "God was where he now is, that is, in
himself and apart from whom there is nothing, for he is the
self-sufficing Selfhood." [73]

As long as the intellect "hears two," is actively knowing or
in the process of altering its consideration from one of time
to one of eternity, it is here on the way. "Were the intellect
always united to God in actuality it would not change. For
the *now* wherein God created first man and the *now* wherein
the last man disappears and the *now* wherein I speak, are the
same in God and not other than one *now*." [74]

THE REFLECTION UNRESTRICTED ISNESS

When considering the relation of the manifested world to
God we must pre-eminently regard it as a principial relation.
Thus it follows that the relation is a real one from the fact
that it implies no contradiction, for it is simply a relation of
restricted isness to unrestricted isness.

It must therefore be carefully understood that the dependent reality of universal manifestation "is a reflection."
However really related to God, it cannot without contradiction be confused with the nondependent and nonaf-
fected reality of the All-inclusive. "If anyone sees a stick
reflected in water, the stick appears to him to be crooked,
although it is quite straight. This is due to the fact that the

water is a coarser medium than air. Yet the stick is both straight and not crooked in itself and also in the eye of the man who sees it in the clarity of the air." [76] The analogy is quite clear: reality appears disordered, fluctuating, topsy-turvy when understood only from the indirect standpoint of manifestation, but when considered principially it is known as it truly is. Though the relation is real, there are not two separate realities, for in the Principle, the reflection is not really other.

In fact the reflection of the stick in water not only appears crooked but "may easily be mistaken for a serpent." When so regarded by the self in error, says Eckhart, it assumes a reality that is precarious and threatening. As long as the self does not know that it is a reflection of the stick, but takes it seriously for a serpent, he is confused, without confidence, and imprisoned in ignorance. If his ignorance is abolished by knowledge of the truth of the stick, a change at once comes into his attitude toward the reflection. His fear is banished and full confidence is gained, though there is no change in the image, which continues to be what it was. The reflection of the stick does not vanish when ignorance is abolished; it is the "serpent" that vanishes. As long as the human being does not know the real truth of all manifestation, "he is disturbed and terrified by the appearance of the world as an independent reality and the incomparable importance of himself." The result, of course, is that his whole approach to reality in every endeavor is grossly affected by this basic mistake or contraction of awareness.

When, however, "this ignorance is displaced by true knowledge," he understands that "the entire world, including himself," however real and significant, "is in no way independent, self-sufficient, or ultimately important. Rather it is completely dependent, contingent, and therefore delusive in its non-Reality inasmuch as it derives all its meaning, not from itself, but from all-inclusive isness which alone is Reality and in which the reflection is not an other." [76] To regard the reflection of the stick as a serpent is certainly the consequence of "passive ignorance." But a greater ignorance is that which is "positive" when, for example, the human being uses that type of "analytic reason," which is divorced from intellect and arbitrarily constituted in an idea of separation, as a means of establishing the "serpent" as all-inclusive reality. Metaphysics always respects reason, which is naturally constituted in the unity of being, but it has no respect for its exclusive use in a separatist mode.

Thus, "the Spirit of God moved upon the face of the waters." [77] Metaphysically understood by Eckhart, the "Spirit" corresponds to isness and the "waters" to essence. And the ground of the intellective soul is the reflection in the water, which reflection is likewise the ground or manifested isness possessed by all individual beings as multibly distributed. The primordial waters are the possibilities of manifestation, insofar as the latter constitute the actualizable aspects of substantial and universal being. Moreover, "essence is always an obediential potency to isness." [78] But there is another meaning to the same symbolism, which is unfolded when it is carried over beyond manifest being itself: the waters then represent "not essence but *all*-possibility, apprehended in principial manner." That is to say it embraces at the same time both the realms of manifestation and nonmanifestation in its all-inclusive reality, or God in himself. And the "Spirit of Godhead [the isness of Divine Knowledge itself] is identically all-possibility and beyond distinction." [79]

This last meaning is, of course, "the highest of all." At the degree directly below it, through the primal distinction of isness, which immediately involves its complement, we have essence, with which we have still only attained the "seed" of manifestation. Then, continuing downwards, the further basic degrees of manifestation may be considered, that is structureless and structured.

But without the primal distinction or determination of isness, all considerations of manifestation are meaningless, for "isness itself is the primal One, the unrestricted act of Divine Knowledge, which is in no way affected by anything whatsoever, for apart from it there is strictly nothing." [80]

4

The Inversion

Eckhart speaks primarily to those who are capable of sustaining a principial insight, and what he says is understood only by those who do.[1] In no sense, however, is the natural light of the intellect to be quenched. It must be granted its full range, and in this context Eckhart has no sympathy for any anti-intellectualist tendencies whatsoever. However, since "grace does not destroy nature but perfects it,"[2] the natural light of intellect must be perfectly united with the transcendent light of faith in the Word. Unless that union is effected, neither intellect nor faith alone can establish true principial knowledge.

For Eckhart the first chapter of Genesis and the Prologue of St. John are more "metaphysical," though obviously less dialectical, than a peripatetic ontology. Inasmuch as both the light of intellect and the light of faith are identical in their common source; inasmuch as "all truth, by whomsoever it be spoken [or known], is from God,"[3] there is a sense in which it may be said that the light of intellect derives its intelligibility from the light of true faith. Why? Because "Christ is Truth," and "believing in order to understand establishes us *in* him."[4] For the most part Eckhart's metaphysical writings are simply commentaries on those scriptural texts which disclose the eternal doctrine of Divine Knowledge, or knowledge that is wholly within the nondual, unconditioned Selfhood.

Pure metaphysical unity, or principial identity, cannot be stressed more emphatically than is done in the unrestricted divine doctrine of Christ as revealed especially in, for instance, the seventeenth chapter of St. John. This is why, according to Eckhart, we have to ground metaphysics in the doctrine of Christ if it is to be made pure and if we would truly understand it. The essential purpose and importance of that doctrine is "not to safeguard our intellectual insights but to perfect them." For "Christ is the incarnate Word of God, eternally knowing his personal relation to and real identity with his Father, the unmanifested Principle. He is intellectually prior to the manifestation of universal being; he is the ineffable Word of God, is strictly that, is supreme truth."

Without this ground metaphysics must always contain a certain defect, a lack of infallible certitude, and that certitude can only proceed from God. If the all-inclusive Reality that God is gives us a term for the principial relation of the manifested self to infinite Selfhood, the Word gives us the term for the essential relation of the trinitarian Son to the trinitarian Father and thus constitutes metaphysics in all-possibility, the very content of Divine Knowledge.

As already pointed out, the principial mode of knowledge is wholly in terms of divine Subjectivity, which must in no way be confused with the type of subjective knowledge so highly extolled by certain modern thinkers. It is not difficult to understand that this latter conception, which is presented to us as the be-all and end-all of knowledge, is a knowing that gives prominence to an individual point of view. Belonging to the thinking subject, or existential self, such knowledge emphasizes a dynamism in the human mind and claims to have no direct certitude of concretely real objects but sees them only as projections of sensations and ideas. Philosophically it is called "subjectivism." Immediately we think of the existential "lonely *angst*" of Kierkegaard on the one hand, or of the mentalist "cogito" of Descartes on the other, and our disciplined reflection, moved by an unlimited will to know, rightly makes us wary of such philosophical oversights.

When, however, Eckhart speaks in terms of principial Subjectivity, which is divine and infinite, he is considering, as he makes perfectly clear, "a mode of knowledge that is transcendent and pure." Belonging entirely to the order of the All-inclusive, "which excludes only contradiction and nothingness," this detached intellection is acknowledged as being necessarily beyond all distinctions that condition the knowledge of individuals, whether they be of sense or intelligibles. That is, it is beyond all things of which the distinction of subject and object is the fundamental pattern. "There [in this detached intellection as identified with the purely real Subject] is found all creatures constituted in the same clarity as they are constituted in God. . . . Thus the soul enters the Primal, the Principle, where God issues forth with his goodness [and truth, unity, and being] into all creatures. There it knows all things in God in the pure oneness in which they are in God."[6]

To speak with certitude in terms of the ultimately true *I*, or Self-identity, Eckhart says is to speak as one in whom grace is perfectly operative and as it were in virtue of that operation. And it is always necessary to repeat that it is as it were wholly *in* God, or *in patria*, that this standpoint is situated. Presupposed is Aquinas's "way of remotion," his *via negativa*, his "analogy of intention" as well as the employment of inverse analogy, the principle of which is Aquinas's formula that what the creature is *secundum quid*, God is *per se*. The consideration of ourselves and all other beings in terms of "that according to which" we and they primordially and ultimately are initiates an understanding immeasurably more real and to the point of truth than that of any specific determination or even any experience structured by our natural habits of mind.

INVERSE ANALOGY

Eckhart insists that detached intellection, which is direct knowledge, must never be confused with the indirect exercise of the rational faculty. But to affirm that it is suprarational is certainly not to regard it as irrational. Divine Knowledge never contradicts reason or active intelligence, never renders false or meaningless the order of genuine ontology just as the infinite never contradicts or falsifies the finite, or the divine the human. Rational knowledge has importance for Eckhart chiefly as the reminder that intellectuality reflects Divine Knowledge, and also as a necessary means for the formulation and external expression of

truths that reside beyond its province. Moreover, he rightly
insists that suprarational truths can be known in detached
intellection only insofar as the *instasis* of the individual intellect is apprehended as all-inclusive Intellect and hence
are known in terms of Knowledge-in-itself, which can only
be identified with God. It is precisely this inversion of the
exstasis to the *instasis* of knowledge that must be understood
if insight into the principial mode is to be gained.

Not belonging to the order of individual manifestation,
this knowledge, which is of uncreated grace and therefore
as it were *in* God, is necessarily indisputable and indistinguishable from Divine Knowledge itself, since it is immediate, direct. Thus it is that when Eckhart speaks in terms of
divine Selfhood and says "My truest *I* is God"; "I am the Son
and not other"; "It is true that there, where I am in principle, there are no distinctions"; or "While I stood in my
Principle I had no God,"[7] and so forth, he wants us always to
remember that these elliptic statements do not represent an
ontological opinion. They do not represent an individual or
mere human opinion at all, but the realization of the perfect simplicity and all-inclusiveness of primal truth in *That*
which, by the very realization, is divine and not other than
the transcendent Self. For as Aquinas makes clear, only in
God can the infinite capacity of the intellect rest in the subject without having to reach out to anything.[8]

"In God," says Eckhart, "there is nothing not God; in ourselves, however, we consider all things in an ascending scale,
from good to better and from better to best. But in God is
neither more nor less. He is just the simple, pure, essential
Truth."[9] It is in statements such as this that we are introduced into inverse analogy.

Now in the concrete order all analogous perfections
imply either a dependence upon the one principle or an ordering to the one end; also analogous perfections admit of
degrees of more or less that are essentially dependent upon
one another. Eckhart reminds us, however (since we invariably forget it), that the degrees of analogous perfections
that are essentially dependent upon each other are not literally degrees of "more or less." If we take the "more or less"

literally, what we would have would be fundamentally uni-
vocal, or what Aquinas calls "analogy according to being
only" and not "according to signification." It is not that God
is *more* perfect; there is no 'more or less' in the All-inclusive
and "perfection is not that which is made manifest," inasmuch as the manifested "contains an intrinsic lack." Rather
the impact of "proportional analogy" is on the proportion
itself.[10]

As the human self is to isness, so God is to isness. But
what is here signified is: As the human self is to individual
isness, so God is to unmanifested, all-inclusive isness.
Although the middle term "isness" is the same it does not
mean an identity but an analogy of proportions. On the
other hand it must also be said: As that which has not its sufficient reason (or principle) in itself is to that in which its
sufficient reason resides, so individual isness is to all-inclusive isness. So the self is to unrestricted Selfhood, and in this
sense "the creature *is* not, only God *is*."[11]

Thus Eckhart can principially say: "All creatures [as such]
are a mere nothing. I do not say that they are small or
something; they are a mere nothing. What is without pure
isness [as its sufficient reason in itself] really is not."[12]
Moreover, "In God creatures are identical in the One, they
are God in God. In themselves they are nothing."[13] The
same can be said of every transcendent perfection that has
its sense in manifested individuality according to its order
toward God, and this, of course, is the analogy of attribution. Apart from this order the individual as such is "pure
limit and unrelated negation," which is nothing in the sense
of a contradiction or an impossibility. And apart from the
order of attribution the analogy of proportionality would
be found to rely on a purely logical substitute for the notion
of isness.

Inverse analogy is *within* the order of uncreated grace,
within the order of the all-inclusive Knower. Analogy is
inverse as between the Principle and its manifest reflection.
And if Eckhart speaks confidently and vividly in these
terms, it is because what he says depends upon insights that,
with the traditional background that supports them, are

available to us primarily, if not solely, in the metaphysics of "the negation of negations." "Every creature contains an initial denial; the one denies it is the other; even an angel denies that it is another angel. But God contains the negation of negations, and he negates all otherness, for there is nothing apart from God. All creatures are in God; they are in his own Godhead, which means directly knowledge of all-possibility, as I said above. He is the Father of all divinity. I say *one* Godhead because *there* he is unmanifested, immutable, and unthought. Thus by negating something of God—though by negating, for instance, goodness of God I do not negate God—by negating of God something that I assert that he is not—even this negation must go. God is One, he is the negation of negations."[14] Hence the inversion must be complete.

The "inversion" expresses the discontinuity; "that which is inverted" expresses the analogous identity of an attribution, and therefore the analogy of attribution is fully presupposed. A focus of inverse analogy, which for all Christians is inexhaustible, is in the crowning with thorns, the ironies of the trial of Jesus, the crucifixion itself, and the resurrection. Or, with Eckhart, we may consider it in another way: by the very fact that our notions of transcendent perfections are obtained from what is in direction, or *in via*, their application to what is "wholly direct" or *in divinis*, involves a "reversal in a certain strict respect."[15] For example, "God's pure act is a rest more active than any striving" or "Divine Knowledge is unknowing knowledge without activity and the need of any object."[16] This "certain strict respect" is total so far as our consideration is focused on a mode of being and knowledge "in direction."

In the Principle, which is without direction and therefore direct, the Principle is not the manifested, but the manifested is the Principle. Inverse analogy is not univocity; it is "the apprehension of all things, so to speak, turned outside in"; it is totally within, and "that which is wholly within can only be in God, for he has not outside." "Therefore the shell must be broken if what is in is to come out; for if you want to know reality uncovered, all likenesses [analogies] have to be shattered. When the intellect finds the One [by the negation of negations], in which all is included, the intellect is inverted and is the One." [17]

When considering the relation of unconditioned isness to manifestation, Eckhart is in no disagreement with Aquinas, who says that the infinite isness is distinct, definite, and determinate. This because they rightly want to declare that God is not vague, indefinite, or indeterminate in our natural understanding of these terms, and also that God is in no sense a logical abstraction. As the individual is determinate in its limited way, so God is determinate in his ineffable, infinite way.

Yet in truth this mode of analogy, as noted in the preceding chapter, is concessive to a standpoint that is situated in the midst of the diversity and distinction of manifestation." This is not a standpoint adopted voluntarily but the participative standpoint of our very human condition. From our natural and rational way of knowing we strive to transcend that condition by means of analogies drawn from it. But at the same time we are obliged to admit that "nature cannot transcend nature," [19] and that the way in which any divine attribute is realized in God not only must remain incomprehensible but must involve a total inversion. For we, including all manifestation, are already inversions "as the reflection is the inversion of its principle." Such a striving is certainly justified so far as we acknowledge that only thus predicated of God are the divine attributes true. Whereas the rational intellect is, in the act of affirming, conforming itself to God; it nevertheless does not comprehend the content of what it affirms.

"Here on earth we grow in likeness, but there *in patria* we are bound in unity." [20] In other words, the striving of the rational faculty bears the impress of repose, affirmations their own negations, and analogy points to its own inversion. "An analogy is an 'outwork.' I do not see a thing unless it has some likeness to me, nor can I know a thing unless it is analogous to me. Yet God contains all things hidden in himself—not, however, this or that as distinct, but one in unity. The eye receives color, the ear senses tone and the tongue tastes. It is the case of like to like." But "the term of likeness in knowledge is unity," and "unity is identity." Thus, "in the 'inwork', or inversion of likeness, the intellect and God are one, there [in God) where we are the Son." [21] If "nothing unites as much as likeness," it is because 'likeness,' "which pertains solely to the order of participative being," signifies its complete inversion, which is identity in principle.

"I was once asked why one blade of grass is so unlike another. I said, it is more marvelous that they are so much alike. A Master says that the blades of grass are all different owing to the overflowing goodness of God which he pours out abundantly in all creatures the more to show his majesty. But I say it is more remarkable how much alike the blades of grass are, because just as all the angels are identical in their original Principle, so all the blades of grass are the same there and all things are identical there [where they are the inverse of their difference here]." [22]

The possibility of the inversion and its realizable truth is grounded in the primacy of knowledge, which is established "in the very reality of God who is Knowledge-in-itself, or the unrestricted act of Intellect-as-such," and also "in the basic nature of man, which is intellect." [23] On this point Eckhart stresses his agreement with two masters: with Aquinas, who clarified the notion of knowledge as being "essentially unitive," and with Aristotle, who explained why intellect has "the possibility of understanding all things." [24] Thus "knowledge and reason unite the soul with God. Reason falls into universal being, but knowledge runs ahead; it goes on and breaks through [the ontological objective] in order that the only-begotten Son of God may be born [or rather that Divine Knowledge may be realized]." [25]

THE PRIMACY OF KNOWLEDGE

Eckhart says: "I am not blessed because God is goodness [or truth, beauty, unity, or being]. Never should I desire God to bless me with his goodness, for that he cannot do. I am blessed only by the fact that God is *Knowledge* in itself and that I *know* it." [26]

Elsewhere Eckhart says that "knowledge is higher than life and nobler than being."[27] Indeed, knowledge is even higher than love, in the sense that "knowledge stands in itself [whereas love stands in knowledge]. For knowledge is better than love. . . . Knowledge is better inasmuch as it founds the love." But to prevent us from confusing this direct, contemplative knowledge with our mere human mode of indirect, discursive knowledge, he adds that "no distinct thought attaches to this knowledge, it stands wholly in itself, it is detached and apprehends God directly as unmanifest, as he is in himself."[28] Love is desirous of being, but, as previously explained "God [in himself] is that which necessarily transcends being." "The intellective soul that does not go out to consider things externally, comes home to stay in unconditioned pure Intellect. It desires not, nor does it have anxiety or concern. Knowledge is the basic principle and foundation of all being. Love, on the other hand, has no hold except in knowledge."[29]

Now this coming home to stay in unconditioned Knowledge signifies the transposition of knowledge *in via* into knowledge in God. Thus the intellect inverts itself, as it were, into its immediate Principle, pure Intellect itself. Then all is known as in Divine Knowledge wherein "understanding penetrates truth and goodness, casts itself into unrestricted isness and knows God without a name."[30]

To be without a name or beyond determination is to be that of which being is in function. And that can only be "supra-being and indeed supra-isness"; in other words, "ineffable, unconditioned Knowledge-in-itself"[31] "Knowledge-in-itself" is precisely that which is not and cannot be a name or distinct determination, rather it is *that* by which all acts of intelligence, names, and determinations are actualized and rendered functional. God certainly and infinitely is, but the intellectual primacy of knowledge must be maintained, as it has been throughout, for being is always in function of knowledge, and unrestricted isness is unrestricted knowability.

In raising this axial question in a renowned disputation in Paris, Eckhart the metaphysician, fully cognizant of un-

created grace as the requisite actualization of "inversion,"
had to assert once and for all the proposition most essential
to the doctrine. It is this: "God does not know because he is,
rather he is because he knows, in the sense that God is unrestricted knowledge and understanding, and knowledge is
the foundation of his isness. For as St. John says: 'In the
Principle was the Word [*Logos, Intellectus*], and the Word was
with God, and God was the Word.' The Evangelist did not
say: In the Principle was Being and God was Being." [32] In
other words, the supreme Principle is "Divine Knowledge in
the isness of itself," the unrestricted Knower of all about all.
"When we apprehend God in his Being we take him in his
threshold, for Being is the forechamber in which he dwells.
Where, then, is God in his temple wherein he shines in his
glory? Pure Intellect, or Knowledge-in-itself, is the temple of
God." [33]

"To ascend, therefore [by God's act which effects the
inversion] to Knowledge-in-itself is to be united to God. To
be united, to be *one* [and not two], is to be identical with
God [principially]. For God is One. All that which is except
Knowledge-in-itself is distinctive, is creaturely, is distinct
from God, [34] is not God in himself. For in God [the nonmanifested and unrestricted act of Divine Knowledge] there
is no other, no distinction, no division." [35]

Thus this principial understanding of God-as-Intellectus
becomes a new starting point in pure metaphysics. But
Eckhart will add that "if you want to designate Divine Knowledge as Isness, it is all right with me, only I insist all the same
that if there is that in God that you call isness, it pertains to
him through Knowledge." [36]

This is the very root of the doctrine Eckhart expounds,
that is, the metaphysical affirmation that the reflected light,
in its simple regenerate or baptized state of intellection,
"inworks" the inversion. Thus it understands first of all the
transcendent, immutable, supereminent Principle that is
ever present to it as *meaning*, in which it contemplates and
without which all individual realities are inconceivable, nonexistent. "Since God is supra-being and supra-isness [insofar
as being and isness are determinations or distinctions] he is

therefore the Principle of all being and isness. God transcends all number and qualification. For he is *one* without number, triune without trinity, good without quality." [37] It follows therefore that "the Principle itself is eternally pure Divine Knowledge in which there is nothing other than the unrestricted isness of understanding." "God is Knowledge-in-itself, and his isness is total understanding." *To be* is in function of Knowledge; Knowledge is not in function of anything. "Isness is God, but God is Knowledge-in-itself, the all-inclusive Reality." [38]

Such a consideration is, of course, beyond the distinction of isness and essence, and also beyond the relation of pure isness to manifestation. "As the point is never the line, so the Principle is never the principiate." [39] But if this consideration is effectively made, it is then, in the consideration, impossible to conceive of a being that is not a "knowing," for "knowledge is the basis and foundation of all being." [40] Intellection in this context of Divine Knowledge is not a mental activity, nor is it specifically human or angelic. But in this context a stone "knows" that it is not a plant, gold differs from silver by its "intellectual" particularity, and "this wood has an intellectual image in God; it is not merely intellectual, it is [principially] Intellect-as-such." [41]

The unerring "instinct" of animals is a lesser "intellect," and man's intellect may be called a higher "instinct," for "you must understand that all creatures are by nature endeavoring to attain this end: to be one with God. Heaven would cease revolving if they did not hunt and seek God, or oneness with God." [42] If the discursive faculty, caught as it is between instinct and intellect, is constantly in the process of nostalgic striving, it is because it, in a sense, contains a seductive simulation of Divine Knowledge.

"God is in all things by mode of intelligence and is more immediate in things than they are in themselves." Again: "God's making me to know is the same as my knowing [principially], so my knowing is his." [43] And while we can make no sense of an experience that is not a knowing, or not in function of knowledge, we have no doubt whatsoever in recognizing knowledge itself, which is not in function of

experience and which transcends experience. We know innately, in the immediacy of the unlimited and detached will
to know, that what we seek is knowledge. "Were God able to
turn away from knowledge [which is impossible], I would
cling to knowledge and let God go; but God is pure Knowledge-in-itself."[44]

Eckhart knows that whereas experience is what he precisely *cannot* directly desire, he cannot *not* desire knowledge,
and when he says that this must be an "unknowing knowledge" he simply underlines the fact. For "this unknowing
knowledge [by inversion] is wholly transformed knowledge,
not ignorance, which comes from lack of knowing; it is by
knowing that we get to this unknowing. Then we know with
divine knowing; then our unknowing is ennobled and
adorned with supranatural, pure metaphysical knowledge. . . .
Inasmuch as God is limitless in giving, so the intellective
soul is limitless in receiving; as God is all-possibility in act, so
the intellect is profoundly able to accept that act; thus its
inversion by God into God. God must act, the soul must suf-
fer [or receive that act] for God to know and love himself in
the soul and for the soul to know with his knowledge and
love with his love, and since the soul is far holier in him
than in itself, it follows that its holiness depends on his act
far more than on its own."[45] Moreover, "to know God in
principial mode, your knowledge must be inverted into
downright unknowing knowledge, to a forgetting of yourself
and all individuality."[46]

God, or unmanifested Knowledge-in-itself, may be called
"unknowing," but only in regard to individual manifestation.
Principially the human knowing process is already a negation. Hence, as previously noted, the negation of this negation is the infinite affirmation of Divine Knowledge, which
is supraindividual as Personality is supraindividual. The unconditioned Knower is sufficient unto himself by metaphysical necessity. Since he excludes only contradiction or strict
nothingness, he is the first and immediate Principle of all
reality, whether existing in fact or merely capable of existing, manifest and nonmanifest, actual and possible—that is,
purely principial. This is the principial starting point: the

divine Selfhood, the unrestricted isness of Knowledge-in-it-self. Thus Eckhart, in the name of Divine Knowledge, first understands the Principle and then proceeds to explain all manifestation, all distinction, and all being in function of *That* which is the All-inclusive, All-possibility, unconditioned Meaning in itself.

It should be clear that when Eckhart speaks of the priority of knowledge and affirms that isness is in function of knowledge, he is speaking in the intellectual order only. "In pure isness there is no place for opposites or correlations." [47] Isness and knowledge are in no sense opposed but are entirely identical in God himself, who "in knowing himself knows his infinite isness." It is the knowability of isness that must be insisted upon. 'To be' is to be knowable, and to be knowable, manifested or unmanifested, is to be in function of knowledge.

Nor has the doctrine of the priority of knowledge anything in common with what certain modern philosophers extol and call 'the necessity of thought', which is wholly inappropriate in metaphysics unless it directly involves the apprehension of the 'necessity' in the isness of things. For what would follow if it were a necessity of thought only? Then, while, for example, one could *think* that this tree is barren and is not barren, the tree itself might be barren or not be barren, and known to the knower as that. But to admit this is to admit that one can think this tree to have and not have, in identical time, place, and respect, the same character in the very act of asserting that one cannot think it; and this is self-contradictory.

If Eckhart also says that God is neither 'isness' nor 'non-isness', he wants not only to emphasize the priority of knowledge but also to indicate a correct consideration of Divine Knowledge itself, which, being eternal and infinite, transcends all determinations. God is not 'strict nothingness', nor is he in himself 'isness' as a first distinction. That is, he is not distinguishable from *That* of which all true determinations are in function; he is not *an* isness, not *a* God, for he is beyond all distinctions and indistinguishable in himself. No Aristotelian need be disturbed on this important point, because the principle of the excluded middle is not violated by the special sense in which Eckhart defines these terms. Moreover, Aristotelian thought does not consider the 'infinite' in the purely metaphysical sense of that which is All-possibility, excluding only strict nothingness, but in the sense of the merely indefinite. However, the metaphysics of Aquinas and Eckhart necessarily does, for the simple reason that in their case metaphysics is constituted in the revealed Word and the transcendent term of the detached and un-limited will to know.[48]

DISTINCTION AND IDENTITY

It follows from Eckhart's emphasis on the priority of knowl-edge that a basic point must constantly be stressed; in fact, without it there can be only a complete misunderstanding of *pure* metaphysics or *detached* intellection. It is this: All the principles and determinations about which we have previ-ously spoken, and which Eckhart describes as distinct, are certainly so when considered from the standpoint of indi-viduality. But they are so only from this standpoint, for in truest reality they merely constitute so many manifested modalities of all-inclusive God. Although contingent or rela-tional insofar as they are manifested, they serve as the expression of certain possibilities of God, that is, those, and only those, which are possibilities of manifestation.

Yet these possibilities, in principle and in truest reality, are indistinct from God. This is why Eckhart says they must primarily be considered *in* the unity and identity of God and no longer in relation to beings, not even the human being. And when they are so considered they are under-stood as being in truest reality God himself, who is without duality and apart from whom there is strictly nothing, ei-ther manifested or unmanifested. "For he who apprehends duality or who apprehends a distinction does not appre-hend God."[49]

Moreover, whatever leaves something apart from itself, even a possibility, cannot be the All-inclusive inasmuch as it is restricted by that which it excludes. Thus the universe of contingent manifestation is only distinguishable from God in a delusive way, while God is really transcendently distinct from all that he permeates. Why? Because we cannot apply to God any of the determinate attributes that pertain to the created universe and since universal contingency in its indefinite entirety is naught in relation to God's infinity.

Eckhart can therefore say that God is all-inclusive for the very reason that God is infinite. On the other hand, though all beings are in God and that which is in God is God, they are not 'in God' when considered from the standpoint of real distinction, or rather in their quality of being conditioned and relational entities. For their existence as such contains a degree of unreality, and so they are delusive.

"It is impossible ever to have two things completely equal in the universe or to have two things the same in every respect. For then they would no longer be two, nor would they stand in relation to one another. . . . We always find and confront diversity, difference in structure and the like, apart from the realm of Divine Knowledge. 'But thou are the same,' we are told in the Psalms.[50] For identity is unity. From what has been said one may consider how 'he who binds himself to God is one with him spiritually.'[51] For Intellect-as-such [or pure Spirit] pertains to God and 'God is One.' To the extent, therefore, that a being has intellect, to that extent it has God and the One, and to that extent it is [by inversion] *one* and not-two with God. . . . Hence God is never and nowhere as God save in Intellect."[52]

"An example[53] of all that we have been saying [concerning inversion and principial knowledge] may be found in the consideration of the just man, insofar as he is just, in relation to justice which begets him [and of which he is a manifestation]. Thus it is obvious that the just man as just is *in* justice. For how could he be just if he were outside justice, if he stood without, separated from justice? . . . The just man is the 'word' of justice, by means of which justice asserts and manifests itself. For if justice did not justify anyone, no one would know it; it would be known only to itself. . . The just man proceeding from and manifested by justice is distinguished from it by that very fact [that he is considered as manifested]. . . . Yet the just man is not differentiated from justice, since 'just' signifies justice alone.

"It is clear from this that the just man is the offspring and son of justice. He is called, and actually is, the son because he became diverse in person but not differentiated in nature, since otherwise justice would not manifest the just man. . . . In manifesting or justifying the just man, justice does not cease to be justice nor does it cease to be the principle of the just man. . . . The just man as just is what he is, wholly and completely, from and in justice itself as his principle. Furthermore, the just man, insofar as he is just, knows nothing, not even himself, save in justice. Indeed, how could he know himself as a just man apart from justice itself, which is in fact the principle of the just man? Manifest justice is the 'word' of justice in its principle. . . . But the just man *in* justice is no longer manifest justice, but is unmanifested justice itself. . . . Moreover, the just man *in* justice itself, his principle, by the very fact of being unmanifested, the principle without principle, is also light [or intellect] itself. For every single thing is light and is radiant in its primal principle.

"Or to consider the question from a different standpoint: it is always the case that the principle is the light of that which it originates, the superior the light of its inferior. Inversely, the thing originated and inferior, by the very fact that it is inferior and subsequent and as having its being from another, is in itself darkness [relationally speaking], the darkness of privation or negation; of privation, that is to say, in the realm of the transient and corporeal; of negation in the realm of the individual intellect. . . . For every created being as such is tainted with the shadow of nothingness . . . and therefore delusive. . . . For the just man, whom we are now discussing by way of example, considered in himself or for what he is in himself is not light. . . . The just man or that which is just, being dark in itself, does not shine. *In* justice, however, which is its principle, it does shine, and justice in turn shines in it, although by reason of its inferiority it as such does not comprehend justice itself.

'The light shines in darkness, and the darkness comprehended it not.'[54] It is clear that justice is present in its entirety in every just man. For half of justice is not justice. But
if it is entire in every just man, it is also entirely transcendent
to every just man and everything just."[55]

It has been thought important here to quote extensively
from this detailed exemplification of the requisite inversion
and as it arises for special comment in the Meister's Latin
exposition on the last Gospel. But it must not be forgotten
that this is, for Eckhart, "only one of many possible analogies." And so it must be realized that "justice in itself, as here
understood, is the negation of a negation"; it is the "transposition [or inversion] of the distinct attribute and comprehensible only in terms of Divine Knowledge."

That which is designated of individual beings and which
cannot apply to God is simply an expression of relationship.
Insofar as this relationship is delusive, all distinctions are
equally delusive, because one of its terms disappears when
brought into the presence of the other, nothing being able
to enter into correlation with God. The determination of
'justice' when brought into God disappears. So the intellective soul is really distinct from God, but when brought into
God and considered in Divine Knowledge, it as such vanishes. "Thus it is that whatever comes to God is inverted;
however insignificant it is, when brought into God, it turns
from itself. Take this, for instance: If I have wisdom, I am
not myself as such wisdom. I can gain wisdom, I can lose it.
But whatever is in God is God."[56]

It is the inversion that carries all things over into God, so
that it is only in principle that all things are God, and it is
also only God who constitutes their reality. "God is neither
anything nor all things, but in principle all things are
God."[57] It is precisely this that must always be remembered
if there is to be a proper understanding of the principial
knowledge that Eckhart constantly expounds.

It is, then, "silly to inquire whether God is or is not in this
or that being. God is in all beings and all possible beings as
their Principle. That is why God is acknowledged as all-
inclusive. That which wills certain possibilities to be beings is

not itself subject to the same laws as beings. That which wills beings to be limited is itself unlimited." As for manifestation: "God produces the succession of its modes, but he is not that succession. He is the Principle of all causes and effects, but he is not the causes and effects [which are particular and contingent]. He is the Principle of expansion and contraction, of birth and death, and of changes of state, but he himself neither expands nor contracts, nor does he change in any way. All being proceeds from him and is modified by and according to his will [which is identically his isness]. He is in all beings, sustaining them in reality; but he is not identical with them, being neither differentiated nor limited in any way. In primal Reality, however, all beings are in God and are God." [58]

The unity and identity of God are inviolable. No distinction arising in individual manifestation, such as the distinction between knower, knowing, and known, affects the unity and identity of God. It is as Primal that God in himself is the all-inclusive Principle and as nonprimal that the principiate is God. But it does not follow that God ceases in any way to be without duality, for the nonprimal is delusive insofar as the principiate is considered apart from the Principle.

Therefore, to speak of God the Son as polar to God the Father is wholly inappropriate, for such an expression not only ignores the Holy Spirit, which annihilates all polarity, but presupposes a comparison or a correlation that cannot possibly be. "Son" is delusive if separated from "Father." "If we are the Son, we must have the Father; no one can say he is a son unless he has a father, nor father unless he has a son." [39] The principiate is not other, never separated or apart from its Principle, although the Principle is primal. God is One as truest reality, without duality as supreme Principle. He is not diversified by any limitations from his modes of manifestation, structured as well as structureless. "He is the Word in every possible state and the Word in itself is God and indistinguishable from God." [60]

This explains why it can be said principially that God freely manifests himself in diverse ways in the indefinite multiplicity of intelligibles without any external means and without his unity and identity being thereby affected. In other words, although beings exist only in effect of his manifestation, it is not possible to say that God is really modified. This apparent difficulty, which plagues many interpreters of Eckhart, is resolved once we recall that we are now considering that which is well beyond the distinction of isness and essence, and that both isness and essence are already identical in all-inclusive Reality.[61]

When the notion of 'multiplicity in unity' is transposed beyond distinctions, it is no longer with determinate isness or essence that we are dealing, but with infinite all-possibility. "God is indivisible and without parts, but this is no objection to [this notion of] multiplicity in his Oneness."[62] It is not his immutable totality that issues forth in universal manifestation, nor is it any of his parts, for he has none. Rather it is simply, as Eckhart adds, "God himself as considered under the special aspect of distinctive determination."

If God can be so considered, it is because "God includes all-possibilities in himself without these possibilities being in any sense *parts* of his reality." To deny the possibility of considering God in terms of distinction, and therefore in terms of individual manifestation or as 'creative act', is to limit God, that is, to negate that possibility as being constituted in All-possibility. Neither his immutability nor his infinite isness is violated and no contradiction whatsoever is involved when a special distinction is considered and determined as real. Nonetheless, it is only one possibility within the all-possibility that God is. After all, "distinctions are made wholly within the unrestricted actuality of Knowledge-in-itself; separations are always without, and it is only when separation or partition from God is conceived that contradiction arises."[63]

"If the intellective soul would truly know God it must not consider anything in time, for as long as the soul is regarding anything in time or place, or anything external wise, it can never know God. . . . If the soul would truly know God it must have nothing in common with nothing. The knower of God knows that creatures in themselves are a nothing.

Compared one with another a creature appears fair and as something, but compared with God it is nothing." [64]

DIVINE NECESSITY

Since God contains all things and all-possibility in principle, he likewise may be considered as "omnipotent, capable of every act, though actionless, without any distinctive motive or objective end." [65] The inverse of the individual act, to which distinct motive and objective pertain, is that there is in God only his will, which is identically his infinite actuality, and which eternally wills only himself. Hence, as already noted, no motive or special end should be assigned to the determination of universal manifestation.

Considered in itself, the divine will is God and only to be regarded intellectually, and not really, as a distinct aspect of All-possibility. If it is differentiated from the Principle in order to be separately considered, it is then nothing but illusion, that is, unreal in its exclusively contingent sense. It is this that must not be forgotten if there is to be a proper understanding of what now follows:

"I will now say something I never said before. When God created the heavens, the earth and all creatures (in the *nunc aeternitatis),* God did no work. He had nothing to do; there was no activity in him. . . . God said: "Let us make a likeness—not thou Father, nor thou Son nor thou Holy Spirit, rather *we* the Holy Trinity in concert [which essentially signifies the knowledge of all-possibility], *we* will make a likeness." When God made man [in the eternal *now*] he wrought in the intellective soul his like-work, his ever-abiding like-work. That like-work was so great that it was nothing other than the like-work of God. God's nature necessitates that he must act in the soul. Blessed, blessed be God! As God acts in the soul he loves his act. Where the soul is now wherein God loves his act, there is the soul so great that this act is nothing other than love; the love in turn is nothing other than God. God loves himself and his essence and his isness and his Godhead. In his love [or divine will] wherein God loves himself, therein he loves all creatures—not as creatures, rather creatures as God." Love in God, however, "is the unrestricted *act* [isness] [of his knowledge," is identical with knowledge itself. And continuing, he says: "God knows [66] himself. In the knowledge wherein he knows himself he knows all creatures, not as creatures, rather as God." [67]

When from the *instasis* or inverted standpoint it is said: The meaning of the intellect, which is reflected knowledge, is God, there is no implied affirmation that God is reflected knowledge. God cannot be reflected knowledge since "he is pure, transcendent Knowledge-in-itself." Eckhart reminds us that "it is impossible for God to be formally all things." True, God is not the intellect, is not reflected knowledge—"God is neither this nor that, God is only God." [68] One must, however, say that the intellect, inasmuch as it is, signifies God, has God for its *meaning;* otherwise the intellect would be devoid of any reality. This is simply saying that the Principle of the intellect's isness is God, that he is *meaning* as the Principle of all being and of all intelligibility.

Now the immediate consequence of the intellect's distinct reality is the presence in itself of an inverted and transcendent meaning that is pure Intellect, or Knowledge-in-itself. And transcendence indicates, as noted throughout, not a higher scale of being but that which is "beyond being" and therefore the inversion of universal manifestation. To identify infinite Intellect with the individual intellect is delusion and the source of delusion and of the insane works that men have wrought. It is, as Eckhart says, the *reverse* identification that is made in principial intellection and that makes for true knowledge. As Eckhart has already frequently explained, a failure to understand this pre-eminent truth is a failure to understand the mode of Divine Knowledge.

In the long passage that we have just quoted Eckhart insists that "God's nature necessitates that he must act in the soul." Elsewhere he will say: "To stop God loving me would be to deprive him of his Godhead," and "I am more necessary to God than he is to me." [69] For the faculty of reason these are disturbing statements, if removed from the context of principial knowledge. But in his Latin commentary on the first chapter of Genesis he will put it this way: "Given that God acts by natural necessity, then I say: God acts and produces through his infinite reality. But God's infinite reality is knowledge itself and with him isness is in function of knowledge: therefore he produces in being because he is knowledge itself." [70] In other words, 'necessity' is taken in the order of intelligence rather than in the order of existence.

When we normally think of 'necessity' we think of "what cannot be otherwise," [71] which in this connection asserts necessary being in an exclusive way, since the 'otherwise' excludes all other possibilities. What we are doing, of course, is relating knowledge to being and apprehending it in function of being. For Eckhart, however, there is another and, in principial or inverted mode, a truer formula: "what cannot *not* be thus," [72] which excludes nothing but what is excluded by the 'thus', which may in principle be every *thus* that does hot of itself imply limitation or contradiction. Whereas the first formula may be affirmed only of God as supreme substantial Being, Eckhart's is applicable in principle to "every divine possibility in Godhead," [73] or in unrestricted knowledge itself. For 'possibility' here, as already explained, does not refer to the conjectures of human logic, which are mere reflections of All-possibility from which no existential deduction can be made.

It is in virtue of "divine necessity" in this sense, that is, in God as Knowledge-in-itself, that Eckhart understands the All-inclusive as necessitating its own affirmation, without which it would not be all-inclusive. But affirmation as such, by virtue of its exclusiveness, has a character of negation. He reminds us how "the Son is the affirmation of the Father, but the Father is not the Son, although the Son and the Father are One." [74] Here again Eckhart is with Aquinas, who insists that "distinction" and not "otherness" is the principle of plurality. [75] In other words, the All-inclusive would not be transcendently infinite, would not be All-possibility, unless it also included in an unfathomable way the possibility of its own negation and every mode of its negation.

Transcendent negation, according to Eckhart, in no way

implies "strict contradiction." "God cannot contradict himself," but "his Self-giving is a Self-negating." Hence "there where God works his eternal work in the soul, he negates himself in the soul." "God negates his very being [as supreme Substance] in his haste to disclose the whole abyss of his Godhead and the all-possibility of his unmanifested isness."[76] If, in principle and in a perfectly strict sense, God negates himself in the manifested self, it is because without this divine Self-negation, God would be the manifested self in his affirmation.

In no sense does Eckhart conclude either that there is a *kenosis* of God or that All-possibility implies an ultimate indetermination. He repeatedly insists that "God is not indeterminate, not privation."[77] The Unconditioned is not indeterminate. The transcendent All-possibility is simply that which is not made evident by thought or by word or by anything whatsoever, yet is that by which thought and word as well as everything are made evident. Indeterminancy does not in any way apply to the Principle, but rather to the mere potentiality of nature. Indeterminancy is below being, unconditioned All-possibility is above and beyond it. And if we say that this consideration of God as Knowledge-in-itself makes for a dialectical difficulty in presenting a theory, Eckhart will ask us whether we really have to present a theory! He does not present a theory in the philosophical sense of the term, but only so many springboards to *That* in which and by which all knowledge has its intelligibility. "Since every affirmation is a limitation and hence a negation, then the negation of an affirmation is a negation of a negation and as such divine, infinite affirmation."[78] How frequently we find him using inverse analogy and pointing out the requisite of *negatio negationis*!

All words referring to the principial order, whether solely mental or audible and written, are formalizations of that which is intrinsically without structure or individuality.[79] For this reason the individual word is delusive, not in the sense that many modern semanticists or linguistic analysts insist, but in the sense that the word is of that which is a reflection of the Word of God. The word is necessary for

human understanding and communication, but though it
may enlighten, it is nevertheless true that the word killeth.

The silence of ignorance is hardly distinguishable from
the quantity of misdirected words. But the silence of knowledge is indistinguishable from the Word of God, and that
silence should never be disturbed by words unless it can be
improved by those which signify participatory awareness and
ultimately the glory of the principial mode. In this respect
humor and elliptic utterances play an important role insofar as they divert the rational mind from that overwhelming
seriousness with which it considers its own pre-eminence
and the priority of individuality and ontological cognition.
There is no direct way of affirming that which is beyond
affirmation, and any dialectic leading there must have a
quasi-symbolic value. Whatever it retains that is true, effulgent, and positive is there to indicate the leap beyond itself,
that is, its inversion in strict principial 'mode', assuming that
such an expression is here still appropriate.

Beyond this principial "unknowing knowledge" there is
nothing to be known, inasmuch as all is realized as inverted
and transformed by it. Being the knowledge that transcends
all words, symbols, and distinctions, it nonetheless, by means
of words, symbols, and distinctions, asserts the supreme
Principle as the triunity of Persons. Thus it signifies the
unity and identity of God as containing all actuality and all
possibility. Eckhart endeavors to point out that this is the
pre-eminent and principial meaning of Divine Knowledge,
of which the Holy Trinity is an incommensurable sign. For
situated as it were within the Godhead, this transcendent
knowledge excludes only contradiction and strict nothingness. In Divine Knowledge Principle, Principiate, Recession
are One, or nondual. Thus it is that "divine necessity directly
signifies principial identity in Divine Knowledge" and that
"no possibility is dispensable in All-possibility."[80]

Moreover, and without any confusion with the Holy
Trinity, this inverted mode of knowledge also, by means
of words, symbols, and distinctions, asserts Godhead as a
triunity of aspects constituted in the unmanifested Selfhood: Knowledge, Isness, and Beatitude. "As isness is in

function of knowledge, so beautitude, or divine love, proceeds from the realization of their identity."[81]

But this awareness cannot be acquired by human effort alone. It is imparted by God himself to those who truly will to know. Only the disciplined and regenerated intellect, "who naughts the self and all individuality," can enter that kingdom, where we have been in principle from all eternity.[82] No other light shines there but Divine Knowledge itself, which is the light of the manifested world where all else shines by a reflected light. It is in that peerless light *there* that everything here is enlightened, and the enlightenment of everything here signifies nothing other than its inversion. "But *there* one knows purely and clearly and knowledge is not clouded by anything."[83]

5

The Veils of God

In this exposition of Eckhart's insights into Divine Knowledge the intention is to make it as synthetic as possible. Special effort is exerted to point out distinctive features of various important considerations and also their relationship to Divine Knowledge, which is the common ground of all aspects of the doctrine and the point of departure of their developments. At the same time no opportunity should be neglected to emphasize certain considerations that bear on the doctrine when apprehended as a whole.

It is in this connection that these last two chapters are to be understood, since they deal respectively with degrees of knowledge and with what is necessarily involved if final realization of Divine Knowledge is to occur. For the doctrine not only "represents the ultimate synopsis of all knowledge,"[1] as Eckhart says; it is, in essence, "the principle from which all the rest is derived" as so many specifications. If any aspect of knowledge were not dependent in this way on what Eckhart designates as "pure and detached intellection in divine Intellect itself," it would in fact be lacking in principle and therefore "bereft of all intrinsic quality."

These remarks show how a multitude of participatory ways of understanding can exist together within the principial unity of the unique all-inclusive doctrine without in any way affecting this unity. Since each person brings with him a way of understanding reality that is peculiarly his own, then Eckhart is not incorrect in saying that "there are as many ways of understanding as there are human knowers."[2] But in the same stroke, he points out that this is true only so far as the "just human" starting point is concerned, for once the realm of the human self has been transcended "all these differences necessarily vanish." This is so because

190

they are all situated as it were within various degrees of manifest intelligibility which, in descending order of specifi-
cation, are removed from the supraindividual domain of all-
inclusive principles in the Word wherein differentiation is
out of the question.

When God is considered as manifesting himself in degrees of intelligibility, Eckhart speaks of him as "clothing
himself in a succession of veils," representing so many
realms of manifestation. Now to think of these 'veils' as bodily garments would, of course, be inappropriate, for it is only
the last or outermost veil that pertains to corporeality. It
must also be kept in mind that "God himself cannot be contained within such veils, inasmuch as he in himself is wholly
insusceptible of any restriction and is in no way conditioned
or affected by any condition of being." [3] Since apart from
God there is strictly nothing or contradiction, the veils pertain to participative intelligence and are referred directly to
God only according as he is considered in relation to this or
that realm of intelligibility.

THE FIVE VEILS

Though "God is transcendent isness itself, transcending all
human understanding, he first assumes the veil of truth or
intelligibility . . . an indwelling in his own pure essence." [4]
The initial and innermost veil is simply the "essence of
God," or the possibilities of manifestation that God comprises in his eternal actuality in the principial and undifferentiated order. It is "the realm of blessedness," for it is
by this first veil that God manifests his fullness in actuality.
Comprising all 'structureless manifestation," [5] inasmuch as it
is in no way really distinct from God himself, it is prior to all
contingent being that presupposes it.

With this first veil we are therefore in the structureless
order of truth, goodness, beauty, and unity; the manifestation as such of the undifferentiated triune Godhead itself;
the transparent "quiddity disclosing God's superessential
nudity"—all of which are directly subsisting in all-inclusive
God. It is only when this veil is considered in relation to
structural manifestation, and in sofar as the latter is prin-

cipially contained within it, that this first "concealment" can
be said to designate that by which all structures will be actualized and rendered intelligible in the succeeding realms.

The next veil is the first in the created order and is "constituted by the directly reflected light of the Logos, which is
infinite Intellect itself."[6] "With this veil we are concerned
with suprarational knowledge, the ground of the soul, or
higher intellect";[7] it is knowledge in the distinctive mode,
inasmuch as it implies production. "Though the intellective
soul most truly dwells in God, God is here under this cover-
ing regarded as dwelling in the ground of the soul and
veiled as grace present to the soul."[8]

This is the realm of direct insight whereby "the knowing
being becomes that which he knows and realizes himself
through knowledge," and "whereby detachment of the intellect understands all things in itself without images and
structures and without going outside itself or a transformation of itself."[9] It comprises the faculties of "reason, memory, and will, not as active, but in their elementary roots,"
conceivable but not perceptible in their intellectual activity.[10] That is, this veil arises out of conjunction of the ground
of the intellective soul with the intellectual faculties of cognition proceeding from the determination of things, the
outward development of which constitutes the five senses of
corporeal individuality. This veil designates the first principles in the individual order which are direct reflections of
the ultimate Principle.[11]

The third veil, in which the constituents of the preceding
realm are joined in the operations of the intellect, pertains
to the faculty of distinctive will as active or decisive and to
the faculty of reason as analytical. Whereas the function of
the will as active "devolves on morality and art," the function of the faculty of reason "is to apprehend one thing
under a diversity of concepts, to distinguish those things
which are in nature and in being, and to apprehend somehow the order whereby one thing is prior to another and
one person derived from another."[12] This is "the power in
the soul by means of which it thinks; it forms within itself
the things that are not present, so that I may recognize

these things as well as if I saw them with my own eyes, and even better—I can in fact think of a rose in the winter."[13]

This realm refers exclusively to the individual and structural order, to "the veil of abstractions, concepts, ideas, and all mental images," and "whereby the intellect understands rationally the images and structures of all things with distinctions."[14] Though directly exposed to and linked with sense data, its development depends upon its principle, the higher intellect, and its process arises from the will to know within a determinate individual realm that is specifically human.

The fourth veil comprises the faculties that proceed from the vital principle, that is, the modalities of the life function, the faculties of sensation and motion.[15] These modalities and faculties compose the sensitive elements of the soul under its vital aspect and determination to preserve life. These sense faculties "receive impressions from outside [in corporeal structure], as does the eye."[16] They initiate the knowing process which "by comprehension, questioning, and reflection culminates in reasonable determination."

This realm is "the garment of the outward self, that is, sensitivity;" It is also "the veil of the collective sense, of anger and concupiscence." It is the realm of the pain-pleasure factor, "fear also residing in this sensitive part,"[17] and it must never be confounded with "either the reasoning intellect or the higher intellect." These sensitive elements, of course, already exist principially in the preceding realms of intellectuality as purely receptive faculties, at which stage there could be no question of outward action any more than of perception or experience. Sense experience enters only in this fourth realm and its data promote the rational course of understanding and the well-grounded judgment of concrete existents in the light of principles realized in the higher intellect, thus making up the dynamics of human intellectuality, wherein each determination raises a further question.[18]

It should be clear that these last three veils constitute the compound intellectual structure in relation to the corporeal modality; which also accounts for the heterogeneous nature of the human being. Thus we again meet with the distinction between the basic modes of structural manifestation, the intellectual and the corporeal.

There remains to be considered, then, the outermost veil, which for the human being represents the corporeal realm. It is that "physical modality whereby the souls [as vital principles] of all living things and the souls of men are covered by a corporeal form which, being gross with materiality, is most inferior and most potential to all that is superior and to being." [19] This veil is made up of all the material elements out of which "all living bodies are constituted," those "material elements which are potential to form and intelligibility." Assimilated to it are the combined organic elements received in nutriment, secreting the finer parts that remain in the living body, and excreting the coarser. For instance, "there is the power of digestion, more active by night than by day, whereby man grows and thrives." [20]

As a result of this assimilation engendered by the vital principle, the finer substances become the flesh, bone, blood, the nervous system, and all that makes up the physical and chemical composition. Every organic being contains, in a more or less complete degree of development, these physical, chemical, and sensitive functions, and according to their manner of reproduction they distinguish themselves into various organic species. Man is the highest inasmuch as he alone comprises, intrinsically with his corporeal modality, all three realms of intellectuality: "the sensitive, rational, and higher intellect, being but parts of the one intellective soul [with which man is endowed.]" [21] Moreover, and for this reason, "the wise physician always considers the whole man, for any illness is the consequence of more than one factor." [22]

In these considerations it is, of course, the human knower with whom Eckhart is primarily concerned. Hence, the veils of structural manifestation, that is, the four outer veils, correspond to the condition of the human being, which includes intellectuality and corporeality in one central structure, or integral substance, as already explained. But these conditions must not be confused with that unique state which is special to each human knower and distinguishes him as this or that person. Rather Eckhart is referring to the different realms or modalities to which in a general way any one human being is normally subject. Taken as a whole these modalities can be related to both the corporeal and intellectual realms, the former being confined to the bodily condition and the latter comprising the great indefinite remainder of the human being as a person.

That which transcends the human knower does not strictly belong to the individual being; that is, all that which pertains to the realm of structureless being and, beyond being, the supreme and unconditioned principial state. Metaphysically, however, all the modalities of being are really related to all-inclusive God, inasmuch as it is he alone who is the Principle that constitutes the fundamental reality of all being and all conditions of being, including the human being. After all, every condition of the human being would be unreal and therefore unintelligible if one attempted to separate him from God, "for there is no doubt whatsoever that without God, in whom [the human knower] has his being, he does not exist."[23]

The different realms of being, that is, "all that which is a composite of isness and essence," whatever the nature of any such condition, represent nothing but manifest possibilities in the essence of God. That is why Eckhart is able to speak correctly and consistently of the different conditions in which being veils or distinguishes itself as manifestations of God, and why the human being can be intellectually considered as "in the conditions of the being of God." Though this is perfectly valid in the sense of our present consideration, it must always be understood that "God in himself, in his nudity, is in no way affected by these conditions of being [or veilings] and does not on this account cease to be unconditioned."[24] In the same way God never actually becomes manifested, although he is the transcendent Principle of all modes of manifestation.

If we presently leave aside any consideration of the ultimate supradeterminate state wherein God is completely unveiled in his unmanifested reality, then the conditions of

human intellectuality, proceeding inwardly with each unveiling, are: the condition of sensory knowledge and practical experience, the condition of enlightened comprehension and judgment, and the condition of formless contemplation.[25] Eckhart is here considering the general conditions
of the whole intellective soul, including its rational and vital
powers along with its unitive function. This means that the
outermost veil of gross corporeality is penetrated once experience occurs by means of the intelligence-imbued sensitive
faculties, for they are here assimilative, not to strict corporeality, but to intellectuality.

"These three conditions signify three modes of knowledge. The first is sensory: for instance, the eye sees from afar
things that are external [in respect to the knower]. The second is rational and is much higher. The third signifies a
noble function of the soul, which is so high and noble that it
apprehends God in his own naked isness. This function
["the ground of the soul" or "higher intellect actualized by
the divine spark"] has nothing in common with individualization; out of nothing it makes anything and everything.
It knows nothing of yesterday or the day before, of tomorrow or the day after. For in eternity [the principial standpoint in which its knowledge is situated] there is neither yesterday nor tomorrow; there is an ever-present *now*. . . . It
apprehends God in his wardrobe [unclothed and un-
manifested]. The Scriptures say: "In him, by him, and
through him:"[26] "in him," that is, in the Father; "by him,"
that is, in the Son; "through him," that is, in the Holy
Spirit."[27]

It should also be noted that the posthumous condition of
the intellective soul as well as the condition of 'beatific vision' are not really distinct from pure contemplation. "All
the powers of the soul that work in the body die with the
body, except contemplative knowledge and the will to know
unitively; these alone remain in the soul."[28] Moreover, "the
highest kind of ecstasy occurs when the contemplative intellect realizes God in God himself through his essence."[29]
Pure contemplation, as we shall discover, is a supraindividual state in which intellection inverts likewise into the

structureless order, "the intellective soul withdrawing into the bosom of the Father in the direction which leads to the very Principle of all, where is the throne of God." After all, "God is Intellect-as-such which consists in the knowledge of itself alone. He dwells in himself alone, where nothing has ever affected him, because he is there alone, naked in his [unmanifested] stillness. In his knowledge of himself God knows himself in himself."[30]

PRACTICAL AWARENESS AND ENLIGHTENED AWRENESS

From what Eckhart has just indicated in generic form we find that we are presented with the requisite possibility of differing and expanding degrees of awareness, or stages of unveiling. They are, of course, accomplished by the dynamics of the unlimited and detached will to know, regenerated and sustained as it must be by transcendent act.[31]

The first condition of awareness has knowledge of sensible objects, or corporeal manifestation, for its province. In this condition the self, as manifestation of ultimate Selfhood, becomes aware of the world of sensible beings. It does so by means of all the sense faculties and organs, which are "so many entrance paths of awareness for everything belonging to this domain, together with the common sense." But this "bodily nature itself [comprising these sense faculties] does not distinguish between the thing and the idea, for it does not know the idea, which is only received and known by rationality."[32] We must therefore include as means of awareness in this condition the "thinking power" considered as the faculty that "gives form to sense presentations and associates them one with another."

This state of practical awareness, in which the operation of the organs and faculties in question are exercised, is acknowledged as the first condition of the intellective soul. Moreover, the corporeal veil to which it corresponds occupies the outermost degree in the developing order of manifestation, starting from its unmanifested Principle. It marks the limit of that development, at least in relation to the condition of existence in which human individuality is situated. For it is in this modality that we find the basis and starting point, initially of individual realization in its integrality and self-identity as a knower, and afterwards of all further realization that transcends the individual possibilities and implies further unveilings.

This state of practical awareness, wherein the outer veils are progressively removed insofar as the integrality of the human being is determined by rational act, may be taken as signifying the totality of individual manifestation. Thus it is that the state now under consideration may be related to "the greatest possible [suitable to our capacities] Self-communication of God to man, that is, the Word-made-flesh,"[33] Christ the God-man. This state is related to him and described as constituting his body, conceived by analogy with the body of the individual man, an analogy of the macrocosm and the microcosm.[34]

This state also signifies that which is common to all human beings, comprehended as the specific difference or distinguishing mark of the human species as a rational animal. "I have sensory perception in common with the animals, and life is common to me and the trees. I have being in common with all creatures." "But if I am to be a man [a reflective, determining knower], I cannot be a man in the being of an animal, rather I must be a man in the being of a rational creature." For "man is a rational animal and 'mankind' lives by art and reason, that is to say practically."[35] Moreover, it should be noted that this state is common to all individuals, whatever may be their other modalities in which they are capable of developing themselves in order to actualize, without going beyond the human level, the full range of their respective possibilities.

What we have, then, in this state of practical awareness, is the intellective soul oriented outwardly toward the sensible world. Thus "the sensitive faculties receive impressions from outside" and reason "draws things into itself, splitting off the coarsest [corporeal] elements. Reason is always receiving something from without that is related to time and sense experience."[36] This is the "outward self" who is "served by the five senses and yet the outer self operates by the intellective soul."[37] Here the intellective soul is anchored in the life principle according to which "life is so desirable in itself that one [in this state] desires it for its own sake.. . . Why do you eat? Why do you sleep? In order to live. Why do you wish wealth and honor? You well know. Why do you live? For the sake of living, and yet you do not [in this state of practical awareness] know why you live."[38]

"Merely living is one thing; learning how to live rationally is quite another."[39] To live rationally the human self must acquire knowledge of the proper relationship between ends and means, of social values and reasonable ideals. Moreover, he must acquire the habit of decisiveness, the willingness to be unselfish. The next condition of awareness, then, is one of enlightenment, inasmuch as it refers to knowledge of abstract or "inward mental objects." In this state "the outward faculties, while existing potentially, are as it were withdrawn into the inner faculty which resides in the light of mental structure."[40] Here one is aware that "the body is much more in the soul than the soul in the body . . . that the soul contains the body rather than the body the soul. . . for here all things are clearer and nobler than they are in the outer world."[41] Furthermore, "all creatures enter my reason in order that they may be made rational in me." They are made "luminous to the passive intellect in the light of the active intellect" so that there is comprehended the universal element of the object known as a mental concept or idea which is "understood by the reasoning intellect."[42]

But "whatever the intellect thinks or achieves with its reasoning powers, however bright it is in the soul, it is nevertheless mixed." For here in this enlightened state the self "understands rationally the images and forms of all creatures with distinctions [the first being that between existence and essence]."[43] Since there is no longer any question of sensible qualities, this is the 'world' of intelligible structural manifestation, "the domain of forms." Everything pertaining to this formal realm is intimately connected with the nature of life itself, inseparable as it is from light which gives it meaning. Moreover, this luminosity should be regarded as "the reflection and defraction of the intelligible Light, or of unrestricted Intellect itself," in the extrasensible modalities of abstract structures that are drawn out of the sense data. After all, abstraction means simply the elimination of all that is not necessary for the comprehension of a concrete object.

In this enlightened state "the individual intellect is for itself its own light and it produces concepts and ideas through the action of its own will."[44] Issuing entirely from the individual intellect itself, the world of abstractions, arranged in multiple combinations dependent upon the intellectual structure of the individual himself, are merely so many "secondary and conceptual modifications of [concrete] reality." Indeed, the veils of corporeality and sense perception have here been removed, so much so that "the light of the rational intellect raises a stone above the realm of sense and above all here and now."[45] Though "reason receives from the senses, it strips away the sensitive element and understands abstractly where there is no time."[46]

Be that as it may, there is always something "incomplete and uncoordinated" about these abstract productions insofar as they as such are "essences separated from real existence." For this reason they are very delusive, possessing an apparent or mental existence. But in the concrete world where these productions are constituted, the intellect possesses the act of experimentally determining the actual existence or nonexistence of these essences and therefore of acting wisely.[47] Though this proximate reality is also delusive when compared to ultimate reality itself, and is contingent and transitory like all individual manifestation, nevertheless its relational reality is sufficient for the needs of human life, social enterprise, and rational endeavor.

It is not that the previous practical state is necessarily more effectively realistic than the enlightened state. Indeed there is a sense in which the possibilities of the enlightened state are far more extensive than the practical in that they allow the human being to become liberated in a certain degree from many of the restrictions to which he is subject in the corporeal modality.[48] Moreover, it is by the light of reason that the human knower can, if he so desires, avoid much that is otherwise debilitating in his intersubjective world.

But it is precisely here that we are confronted with the danger of an aberrant condition. Indeed, the luminosity of abstract concepts and ideas may become so attractive to the reasoning intellect that the luminosity can easily be mistaken for reality itself, or as that of which concrete objects are mere projections or copies. As the temptation inherent in the practical state is to absolutize sense experience for its own sake and so adopt a position of radical empiricism, so the even greater danger of the enlightened state is to absolutize mental objects and adopt an idealist position. In both cases there is always present the allurement of limited and specific desires that abort the unlimited will to know and that if extensively or exclusively followed make for a refusal to participate in being as directly apprehended by the higher intellect. The nonparticipation in being is here a stopping to gaze at it as "something out there separated from the knower"; it is an occlusion of the will to know. "Luminosity attracts, but reflected light attracts deceptively."[49]

The indubitable truth, according to Eckhart, is simply that "God in himself is the Light of which all creaturely knowledge is a reflection."[50] In fact all degrees of individual knowledge must be considered as just that—reflections. Pure Reality is God alone, is all-inclusive. It is utterly unattainable by any sensation, experience, concept, or idea, "confined as they are to the consideration of outward or inward objects," the knowledge of which constitutes respectively the practical and enlightened states. Certain nontraditional philosophers, in diverse times and places, have actually restricted themselves to these two states. Thus they condemn themselves to remain enclosed within the limits of structural manifestation and human individuality, presenting at best nothing more than closed systems.

However this may be, the luminous realm should be described as an ideal world by reason of its assimilation to the inward mental faculties. Thus it is to be distinguished from the sensible or practical realm, which is the world of structural corporeality.[51] In the enlightened state, however, we are still only concerned with structural ideas, inasmuch as the possibilities that this state contains do not extend beyond individual existence. The enlightened state is confined to the realm of reason and does not pertain to the higher intellect, or ground of the soul, which is "united with the Logos." There alone the Light that shines, or the Word that speaks, makes for supraindividual and unitive knowledge.

The removal of the veils of corporeality and sense perception does not mean that reality is abolished, for the practical and enlightened states do not stand in opposition to each other. We can be sure that any notion of such an opposition is here meaningless. Everything that is, regardless of the modality in which it may happen to be, has for that very reason a relational degree of reality consonant with its own nature. Insofar as "some individual being consists conceptually"—and this is the proper meaning of a true concept, inasmuch as it has a real foundation in being—it is neither more nor less real on that account than something consisting corporeally. Each possibility necessarily finds its proper place at the level of the universal hierarchy determined for it by its own nature.

But since a concept is the content of an act of conceiving, and since the bare human act of conceiving is limited by the appropriation of the structure of experienced objects, all concepts (and ideas) enjoyed by the rational mind are greatly confined. Though the human knower has an unlimited will to know, he is, as a human knower, incapable of enjoying an unlimited act of comprehension, that is, a concept (or idea) of God or of any structureless manifestation. "God alone [being totally unrestricted in every way] enjoys the idea of himself," for he is the unlimited act of comprehension.[52]

Analogous to this enlightened state is "the reflected light of the moon." The moon "gets its light directly from the sun, but owing to the fact that of all the stars it is the nearest to the earth, it suffers from two drawbacks: being pale and speckled and also being able to lose its light. [53] It is, figuratively speaking, pale because it is indirect light and drawn to individuality; it loses its light because it is transitory and revolves around structure. Illuminating by a reflected light and comprehending only reflection, the intellect at this stage "does not understand all things in truth." Only when the ground of intellect is realized as directly united with the transcendent Light itself does there consist the possibility for that, "since then nothing is concealed from the higher intellect." And Eckhart quotes St. Paul for a further analogy: "The Scriptures say: 'Men ought not to cover their heads, but women should be covered.'[54] The woman, that is the luminous realm, is covered. Man is the higher intellect, that is, bare and uncovered."[55] Regardless of sex, the human knower is endowed with both male and female principles, "both unitive and discursive functions of knowledge."

What Eckhart wants to point out, of course, is that "the intellectual faculties ascend by a process of abstraction. Abstraction, however, comes to a standstill in being, above which is God, the Principle of being. Those things which rank as lower than reason exist in a nobler state in reason than they do in themselves, and the contrary is the case with those things that are of higher order than reason."[56]

In other words, in this enlightened state now under consideration, "all knowledge of things is obscure, dark, and gloomy *until* it is reduced to their principles by intelligence, since it involves the fear that the alternative view may be correct. But the demonstration, or syllogism, that enables us to know without fear and not just as a matter of opinion is derived from the proper principles. . . . Man obtains his knowledge from things *a posteriori* and proceeds to principles by the exercise of reason."[57] Yet here in the knowledge of structure and individuality "nothing shines, nothing is known, nothing effects knowledge, save the quiddity, the concept of the thing itself, its definition or idea."[58] Obviously the veil of luminous concepts and ideas must be peeled away if unitive or principial knowledge of reality is actually to be attained: "Therefore strip yourself of all structures and unite yourself with structureless isness."[59]

Moreover—and this is important—in this state of enlightenment "a light is sometimes uncovered in the intellect and
man *thinks* it is the Son, and yet it is only a reflected light."[60]

THE CONTEMPLATIVE STATE

When the veils of corporeality, sense perception, and structural comprehension have been successively removed; when
the knower is aware of no desire other than the unlimited
will to know and is no longer the subject of any image, concept, or idea, his condition is that of contemplation. In this
"noble state the intellect, in the very ground of the soul
where oneness is effected, becomes [in knowledge] one
with all being, without differentiation and without distinction."[61] By uncreated grace the knower has identified
himself with the synthesizing Principle of unitive knowledge.
He is "filled [by assimilation] with blessedness," actually
enjoys that blessedness, and "the mode of knowledge is pure
awareness itself."[62] From the ground of the soul, but no
longer identified with it since the veil of all structural reality
has been removed, this unitive knowledge is situated within
the eternal Word and, by inversion, the intellect is
assimilated to unconditioned Intellect itself. "Here is the
True Man," "the Christ," "the Son," "the divine Selfhood,"
and the knower truly *is*. For knowledge is now as it were
above and beyond any special condition; it is principial
in act.

That there are degrees of contemplation is clear from the
fact that "as long as there is progression in contemplation it
is not yet pure." "Indeed, so long as we progress *with* grace
it still remains in us as grace and it is small and we can only
know God from afar. But so far as we are *there*, grace is no
longer 'grace,' rather it is the divine Light in itself.... There
within there is no approach."[63] So far as man is *there* in pure
contemplation "he is not this man Henry or this man
Conrad or this man so and so." He is "godly poor" and
"object free," for "*there* is the True Man; in that Man all men
are one Man and that Man is Christ eternal."[64] Insofar as
there is progression in contemplation "there are still rem-
nants of distinctions in the awareness,"[65] distinctions rela-

tional to structureless manifestation and to the complementary principles of isness and essence.

It should be acknowledged, however, that the "mode" of God in participatory contemplation is his essence. Though it is referred to by Eckhart as a veil, it is not really distinct from God, since we are here beyond the realm of real distinctions. If Eckhart refers to this state as blessed, it is because this unitive knowledge comprises all the possibilities of individual manifestation. For it must be understood that unitive knowledge is here completely transcendent to all distinctive knowledge, which is applicable only to individual or structural cognition characterized by the preceding enlightened and practical states.

Thus when contemplation is pure, and no longer directly centered in manifestation, "the term 'I' or 'Selfhood' refers to the Light of Intellect-as-such"[66] inasmuch as this Light strips away all manifest and accidental qualification. Here the contemplation is divested of individuality and self-substantial identity, for "insofar as 'I' signifies individual substance, it nevertheless must be denied."[67] If the Selfhood, or the Son, with which the contemplation is identified, "enjoys this blessedness as his rightful kingdom" it is because this kingdom is nothing other than the fullness of those possibilities actualizable in the divine affirmation of himself.

Being essentially a structureless and supraindividual state, this realm of contemplative knowledge has nothing in common with any psychological condition, as certain modern interpreters of Eckhart have supposed, or as indeed did some of his contemporary critics. Correctly speaking, psychology pertains to nothing more or less than the structural realm of individuality, which includes sense knowledge as potential to comprehension, questioning, and the acts of rational determination and decision.

In making this assimilation the term "psyche" must be understood in its primary sense without confounding it with the diversified and far more specialized meanings attached to it in modern times, whereby it cannot be made to apply even to the whole of the structural realm. For the most part modern psychology deals only with those restricted parts of human individuality where the sensitive and mental faculties are in contact with corporeal manifestation.[68] Considering its methods, which are those of observation and evaluation, psychology is, as a science, incapable of going beyond its objective, which is exclusively the study of mental phenomena and behavioral patterns in direct relation to those particular phenomena. Since its objective is strictly confined to a small portion of the domain of individuality, the contemplative state necessarily and completely transcends its study. In fact the contemplative state is inaccessible to psychology in a twofold way, first because it transcends the realm of discourse and differentiated thought, and second because it transcends structural manifestation and hence all phenomena of any kind.[69]

The contemplative state, says Eckhart, is that of "non-otherness; of not-self," wherein knowledge is integrally concentrated in the fundamental unity of God as the unmanifested Principle. This unmanifested, apprehended as the seed of the manifested, which is only its effect, is identified in this respect with the essence of God. But it is really God's isness as well as his essence, since they are identical in his indistinctness, as Eckhart has explained. If in pure contemplation God is immediately known as beyond the distinction of isness and essence, it is simply because this state of knowledge is no longer situated in any mode of direction toward God. That is, it is no longer oriented in terms of conditioned existence or even of distinctive complementary principles. Actually pure contemplation is situated wholly *within*, transcendent to conditioned existence and therefore without direction and duality in every respect. It is situated "there *in patria*, the unrestricted and hidden [unmanifested) isness of Knowledge itself," or "undifferentiated Godhead." "The last and highest leave-taking [or unveiling] is leaving God for God . . . where God is essentially hidden in himself."[70]

The relational distinction of isness and essence must go; the veil of all structureless manifestation must go. "The soul that loves God loves him under the veil of goodness, but [here in pure contemplation] the contemplative intellect takes away from God the veil of goodness, of being and all determinations."[71] Thus "the intellect is nobler than the will. The will takes God under the veil of goodness. The intellect apprehends God naked, as he is, divested of goodness and being. Goodness [like truth, beauty, and unity, which pertain to his essence as structureless manifestations] is a veil under which God is hidden [and unmanifested]."[72] "Love does not unite, not in any way; what is already united it holds together and keeps bound. . . . But contemplative knowledge altogether peels off unity and takes God unveiled, as he is, pure [unmanifested] isness in himself." Likewise since "God assumes the veil of truth, this too must be cast off."[73]

"The ground of the soul [when realized as directly united to God by transcendent act] is remote from the kingdom of this world [of structural manifestation], since it is now in another world, above the faculties of the soul, above the active intellect and will. Although such faculties enjoy a remarkable eminence [over the lower faculties] . . . God himself, when he enters into them, only does so under the veil of the truth and goodness of structured being. But no creature [or distinctive structure] ever enters the ground of the soul, and there God [who alone dwells therein] must be stripped of every veil." In this state of contemplation "glory shall be revealed, because glory itself is revealed in the blessed state. every veil is removed—this is implied in the word 'glory'—including even the veil of goodness, under which the will receives God, the veil of truth, with which the intellect receives him, and the veil of being itself in general and even isness insofar as it is a distinction. . . . In pure contemplation every veil [or distinction] is removed."[74]

Nonetheless isness and essence are realized in this pure state, and it should be acknowledged that structureless manifestation is also known *within*. For, as already explained, the realm of structureless manifestation, being supraindividual, is necessarily included within the order of Divine Knowledge. Furthermore, it is not to be forgotten that all realms of manifestation are integrally contained within the unmanifested and unconditioned Principle, and hence are known obliquely in this pure state. "One should be aware that those who know God unveiled know also the creatures with him or in him. For Knowledge-in-itself is the Light of the soul."[75]

The "outer self"[76] of which Eckhart speaks pertains to the practical state; the "inner self" pertains to the luminous. But the "innermost Self" is realized in the pure contemplative state and is God, for "therein all creatureliness and differentiation have been transcended." As eternity transcends time and the uncreated the created, so "the innermost Self [or God] transcends both the outer and inner self."[77] Also "when one knows the creatures in themselves that is called 'evening knowledge,' and there one knows the creatures in images that are variously differentiated. But when the creatures are known *in* God that is called and is 'morning knowledge' and in this [principial] mode the creatures are known without any differentiation and stripped of all images [concepts and ideas], and deprived of all likenesses in the One, who is God himself."[78]

"The most insignificant thing known as in God, even a flower as it is in God, is nobler than the entire universe [as known externally]. To know the vilest thing as it is in God is better than angelic knowledge. . . . When creatures are known without God, that is delusive, twilight knowledge; when creatures are known *in* God, that is morning knowledge. But when God is known as pure isness in itself, then that is the unrestricted knowledge of high noon. . . . Opposites must be transcended. What are opposites? Weal and woe, white and black are in opposition and have no place in real isness. . . . The soul knows no opposition when it enters the Light of pure Intellect."[79]

It is therefore important to note that in pure contemplation the distinctive manifested beings, including those of individuality, are not annihilated. Rather they subsist in principial mode, being unified by the fact that they are no longer apprehended according to the mode of contingent and real distinctions. Inasmuch as pure contemplation "is not a mental activity," then "all beings necessarily disclose themselves among the possibilities of the divine Selfhood which is eternally aware in itself of all these possibilities as indistinct." [80]

It is with the divine Selfhood that this pure contemplation is identified. Hence it is without activity, being "actionless act and totally aware of its own immutability in the now of eternity." After all, "grace does not destroy nature, but perfects it. The beatific state does not destroy grace; it perfects it, for beatification is grace made perfect. Therefore there is nothing in God that would permanently destroy anything that has any kind of being [not even corruptible entity as considered from the standpoint of individuality], but he is the perfecter of all things." [81]

Since all the veils of God are now removed, it is then precisely this pure state that alone gives integral meaning to the Christian doctrine of the final "resurrection of the dead and the glorified body." The doctrine as such is a formal theological exposition of a revealed truth known principally in pure contemplation. And the truth is that the "resurrection of the body," or its transposition beyond the condition of individual existence, is the realization of the changeless and eternal possibility of which the body is but a conditioned manifestation in structural modality. [82]

Wholly actuated by God the detached contemplative state is "that wherein one is most immediately united with God, is by grace what God is by nature; wherein one is identified with the exemplar of what he was when he was in God, when there was no difference between him and God, before [metaphysically] God has created the world." [83] It is impossible to suppose that manifested individual beings do not subsist eternally in the Principle. For such a supposition would mean that these objects would be strictly nothing; they would not exist at all, not even in a delusive manner. Moreover, were that the case there could be no entering into the state of contemplation and no return from it to the enlightened or practical states of awareness, because all structural manifestation would be irremediably annihilated for the intellective soul. A return, however, is not only pos-

sible for the soul that is not finally liberated or saved from
the conditioned state of individual existence through the
decomposition of the body, but it does actually occur.

THE ULTIMATE REALIZATION

It is quite clear to Eckhart that a realization of pure contemplation is not reserved only to the final posthumous condition of the soul in the "beatific vision," but is a present
possibility. "God can be known in the same perfection and
blessedness can be in the same mode in this life as in the life
to come." [84]

Eckhart continues: "Detached intellect [in contempla-
tion] originates from the eternal Principle as knowledge
and contains in itself intelligibly that which God contains.
This noble divinity, the detached intellect, principially realizes itself in itself according to the mode of God in its egress
[from Divine Knowledge], and in its innermost meaningful
content it is very God; but according to the [rational] mode
of its proper nature the intellect is creature. But the detached intellect is fully as noble in us now [in pure con-
templation] as in the afterlife [or beatific vision]. Still, the
question may be asked: How then does this life differ from
the life to come? I answer that the detached intellect which
is blessed in precisely the same way as God is, is at present
virtual in us. In this life we know God according to possibility. In the afterlife, when we are quit of the body, possibility
will be transformed into the act of beatitude which is normative to the detached intellect. The transformation will
render the fact of beatitude no more perfect than it is now,
for detached intellect has no accidents or any capacity to receive more than it innately contains. It follows that to be
beatified *there is* to be completely deprived of virtuality and
to realize beatitude only actually, according to the mode of
divinity. As David said: "Lord, in thy Light we shall see Light;
with Divine Knowledge we shall realize the perfection of
Divine Knowledge itself, which alone is our entire blessedness, here in grace and there in perfect beatitude. Hence,
were I wholly that I am I should be God." [85]

In other words, in this life "there can be no lasting persis-

tence in unwavering contemplation." But "when you consequently stand outside it and this nascent knowledge
through identity is withheld, you will think you have been
robbed of eternal bliss and then you will directly want to
return into contemplation in order that this knowledge may
again be realized." [86] Eckhart certainly affirms that though in
pure contemplation, or even in the beatific vision, the possibilities of all manifestation are directly and principially
known to the intellective soul, unmanifested All-possibility
in itself remains forever unknown to the soul as such. Hence
there is always for the soul a certain incompleteness when
compared to all-inclusive knowledge in itself.[87] But to speak
of the "soul as such," since the soul is created and therefore
individual, is not the same as speaking of "divine Intellect-
as-such," which is uncreated and beyond individuality. To
speak of the "soul as such" is, as Eckhart has made clear, to
speak within the formal framework of individual structure,
which of course must be inverted when the indication
is pure Divine Knowledge. The loss of the awareness of
self-identity or "this burial in God" is nothing but "the crossing over into the uncreated order and this crossing is
beyond the order of multitudinous and individualized
knowledge."[88]

It must always be clearly recognized that the term "knowledge" as applied to the contemplative state is not to be understood in the limited sense of structural thought, which is
but a reflection of Divine Knowledge. Rather it is to be understood in the sense of "unknowing knowledge" as the perfect awareness of God considered principially in his relationship with his unique "object," which is his own beatific
essence. Though his beatitude, or essence, is in a certain
sense a veil of his infinite Selfhood, as Eckhart has already
explained, it is not really distinct from his Selfhood, as it
indeed could not be once there is no longer any real distinction.

Despite the indiscriminate meanings attached to the
terms "subject" and "object" by modern philosophers, their
usage should not, when considering the divine Subject, lead
to any obscurity. After all, Divine Knowledge transcends all

opposition and real distinction between subject and object. The contemplative state, constituted as it is in Divine Knowledge, is a realization of "the Knower as subject and the Known as object and Knowledge itself as the relation," and, as Eckhart has explained, divine relations are without real distinctions. "Operative power receives all its isness from its object and receives the isness of the object itself and the object. What then can be disturbing or bitter for such a power if God is its isness, if its isness is God's isness, that is, if its isness is isness in God?"[89] For then "God is the power, the actionless act." Thus "Knowledge, Isness, and Beatitude are identically One, and One is God," the "perfectly Real." God is "the Knower, Known, and Knowledge," which are identical in him and with which the contemplative intellect is identified in principle and as considered beyond all the particular conditions that determine each of God's multiple states of manifestation.

In this state of pure contemplation the Word, or eternal Light, is realized directly by the detached, unitive intellect and no longer in reflection through the mental faculty as occurs in the individual states. The unitive or higher intellect "is the capacity of suprarational and supracreaturely [or supraindividual] knowledge when actualized by uncreated grace." It is the ground of the soul in which the Word dwells as already present, that is, "in truest reality it is the soul already dwelling in the Word." In this respect, therefore, the unitive intellect as purified of real distinctions must, by transposition, be included in the state of contemplation. It comprises in knowledge all that transcends individual structure and existence, including its own, and it does so transcend because "its contemplative act is fully actualized, not by itself or its own light, but by the Word, the Light that is Intellect-as-such."[90]

Of course, "if the spiritual self contemplates God, he also knows and is aware of himself as the one who knows, that is to say he knows that he contemplates and knows God. Now it has appeared to some people[91] and it seems quite credible that the flower and kernel of beatitude lie in that knowledge in which the spiritual self knows that it knows God.

For if I had all joy and knew nothing of it, of what use would it be to me, and what kind of joy would it be to me? Nevertheless, I decidedly say that this is not so. . . . For the first thing on which blessedness depends is that the soul should contemplate God unveiled [beyond any individualized or distinctive condition]. In this state the soul receives its isness and reality from the ground of God and knows nothing of active knowledge nor of love, or of anything at all [since that knowledge 'transcends action, individuality, and real distinction']. It is there wholly and completely silent and undifferentiated in the isness that God is. There the soul knows no-thing [all individual identity having been transcended] but is one with pure isness itself, or God who alone is the Knower. But when the self knows and is aware that he himself is contemplating, knows, and loves God, this is a breaking out [of *pure* contemplation] and a return to the previous stage."[92]

In the ultimate realization, which is after all primal, the divine Intellect is the Knower, essence is the Known, and the contemplative intellection corresponds to Knowledge itself, which is as it were a resultant of the "common act" of the "Subject" and "Object." Thus the divine Intellect is essentially in actioniess act while the unitive intellect is wholly passive and by inverted analogy the latter is realized as indistinct from the former. "There [in pure contemplation] in our passivity we are more perfect than in action. . . . There God alone acts and the soul is passive."[93] There the soul is "in darkness, in the silent desert," without direct awareness of individuality and distinction between subject and object.

"But what is this darkness? . . . It can only be called potential receptivity. . . . Should you however return [to a lower state of awareness] it would not be for reason of any truth; it would be only because of the senses, the world or the devil."[94] In other words, all that can be said of the Word in itself as well as in relation to manifestation can be said of pure contemplation, which is principially identified with the Word. A fall from knowing within the Word simply means that a desire or desires other than the detached and unlimited will to know have intruded. In this respect

Eckhart reminds us that "prior to original sin [the failure in detached willing to know] there was original wholeness [or virtue and excellence], but the Word, our Lord Jesus Christ, not only makes possible the restoration of that original unity, he enhances it in divine glory."[95]

Assuming, then, that all the veils of God have been removed, we can, with Eckhart, say: Beyond the consideration of manifestation, the unitive intellect when in pure contemplation "knows God through God."[96] In that knowledge the soul is not really distinct from God "who knows himself by himself in the soul." For then there is no longer any known reality that is differentiated from the Knower, everything being comprised within its own possibilities.

It is in the knowledge of divine and infinite Selfhood, the truest *I* of the knower, that beatitude resides. "The true Word of eternity is in act only in identity, where individuality [or self] and otherness are deserted and alien."[97] There "the knower is the Son,"[98] the Lord of all manifestations unitively included in their Principle. All being is present in pure contemplative knowledge and all effects are known directly in the principial uncaused cause. Immediately known is the *alpha* of all procession in the multitude of possibilities, and the *omega* of all recession from the multiplicity of beings into unity.[99] All the veils of God are known, but now principially *within* in a reverse order, and as long as pure contemplation is in act, it is in no way affected by them. "When I stood in the Principle, the ground of Godhead, no one asked me where I was going or what I was doing: there was no one to ask me. . . . When I go back into the Principle, the ground of Godhead, no one will ask me whence I came or whither I went. There no one misses me, there God-as-other [or God veiled in manifestation] passes away."[100]

6

The Detachment

We naturally tend to laud the human intellect for its piercing ability to discriminate that which is essential and primary from all that is accidental and sequacious in manifest reality. But for Eckhart it is evident that unless the intellect is always expounded in terms of its double role of discrimination and delusiveness, pseudointellectuality is bound to result. The intellect, as we have discovered, is delusive because of its great luster, which is nothing other than the reflected light of Intellect-as-such, the ineffable radiance by which it is lit.

The luster of this reflected light is indeed an effulgence that can ecstasize the self. It is the substance of the Promethean dream—objective, abstract, ecstatic in its spellbound movement, and though incommensurable with corporeality and the sensitive parts of the soul, it is nevertheless a created light. "He who does not put this reflected light behind him shall not find God." And Eckhart goes on to say: "Even the Light that is truly God, if I gaze at it where it plays upon my soul I would not do justice to it. Must I then gaze at it there where it breaks out? I cannot really see the light that shines upon the wall unless I turn my eyes to where it comes from. But if I gaze at it there where it breaks forth then I am robbed of its effect. Must I then participate in it as it is pending in itself? Yes, and I say more: I must realize it where it is neither contiguous nor breaking forth, nor yet pending in itself [that is, I must not gaze at it at all, and even participation in it must be transcended]; for these are all modes of being. God must be realized as modeless mode [that is, principially] and as the unconditioned, for he is free of modes of being."[1]

It is obvious that intellectuality must affirm the principle

that "the intellect knows all that it is"; and this is true insofar
as the intellect is considered "according to its participation
in the divine Light." But if it would preserve itself from delusion, intellectuality must pre-eminently affirm the principle
that "the intellect is all that it knows"; and this is true insofar as it certifies its principial *instasis* in divine Light, "insofar as it is that Light." Unless the identification of the intellect with pure Intellect-as-such is made in and by transcendent act, or uncreated Light, the intellect can only appear
as inert, flat, having the character of a separate object. "God
is not in us nor are we in God except by the Holy Spirit"; in
fact, "that which is not *in* the Holy Spirit is relatively nothing."[2] Knowledge in itself, the only completely real knowledge, "irradiates all things and is sufficient unto itself."[3] The
I in pure knowledge is that knowledge; it is contemplative;
it is not the who is now thinking or seeking.

"Pure knowledge is contemplation and not, as in pas-
sionate, seeking, penetrating thought, something in action."[4] Moreover, "when the intellect enters the Light (or
'life,' the 'modeless mode') of Intellect-as-such it knows no
antithesis."[5] Its exterior logic, necessary for one to think
and talk about it, derives from and depends on this innermost "unknowing knowledge." Thus intellectuality reveals
that it has both concentric circles and radii, both modes of
analogy and modes of identity, and the former is delusive if
not considered in the unconditioned Principle. Not to affirm this twofold truth is to court the danger of intellec-
tualizing badly. And not to revert to Divine Knowledge is
tantamount to replacing God in practice, if not in theory, by
the operations and acquisitions of the active mind—and
that is to court the danger of idolatry.

But it is not possible for man in his individual, unregenerate condition to understand that the pronouncement "I
am apart from God" is false before he realizes that it is true.
Eckhart is insistent on this point: "Man must accept the
given before he can realize the *gift.*"[6] Man must know God
as other than himself before there is a realization of the primal truth that there ultimately is no otherness.

Even while all this is intellectually understood the fact remains that the presence in man's intellect of this deepest metaphysical certainty is of itself alone ineffective for the ultimate end. Though intellectual certainty concerning the truth of Divine Knowledge is something of God, it is not God, not Divine Knowledge. Though it suffices on the doctrinal level, it is in no way sufficient on the level of pure spirituality. Though man may enjoy it theoretically, it does not yet pervade his whole being. "It must be quickened by that faith which moves mountains, that faith which is an adherence of one's whole being to God."[7] Indeed, rather than abolish faith, it gives it an innermost meaning, and to have faith "is to act as if one were wholly within that which one knows to be true."[8]

Now to "act as if" one were wholly within and identified with divine Selfhood has nothing in common with "acting" or "playing out a part." Rather it implies the forming of an enduring disposition that more and more develops into the actual realization of being there.[9] It means a ceaseless choice of the ultimate "ought" and acting as the divine Self acts, that is, "simply *being* to the full in actionless act as one was when one's proper self did not yet exist, beyond here and now, and strictly nonattached to anything."[10] And "fully *to be* is to love as God loves." However, insofar as one is not there *in patria* one is here "on the way." It is therefore most appropriate to speak of the disposition of detachment requisite if the actual realization of "being *there*" is to be fully consummated, and this disposition is cultivated by forming the habit of making the moral and intellectual demands of detachment upon oneself.[11]

THE PRE-EMINENCE OF DETACHMENT

If the process of detachment is symbolically referred to by Eckhart as the "divine journey," it is obviously not the self that makes this journey. Rather it is "the return of the Word to the Father,"[12] which involves a step-by-step "dispossession of the self," in its inward as well as in its outward condition, until that dispossession is complete. The "return" of the Word to the Father actually signifies "the going away from all that is not undifferentiated Godhead" and is, of course, an exposition that is concessive to intellectuality situated in individual manifestation. For in truth the Word "never goes anywhere," since it is totally without movement and potentiality. The communication of this "journey" applies at once to the realization of pure contemplation in this life, that is, at the moment of death, as well as to the posthumous destination. But the "journey" is undertaken during the entire course of gradual "liberation from all distinctive and individual modes of knowing." It is effected by standing as it were *in* the intelligible Light of divine Intellect and withdrawing back into its source by a detachment from all that is not unconditioned.

To speak of the "divine journey," or more accurately, to speak now of the preparation for that journey, is to concern oneself with human conduct and virtue. This is not the place to consider in any detail Eckhart's philosophy of ethics, which is clearly and consistently Christian in the scholastic mode. It is only important to point out that it is thoroughly grounded in principial knowledge and reducible to "the transcendent identity of the soul with God, the realization of which is effected by the union of the unlimited will to know with divine grace."[13]

This means that morality has a twofold aspect: that conduct which prepares one for the divine journey and that which is necessary for the journey itself, which begins once it is realized that the Word has been heard in the ground of the soul. For "whenever the Word speaks in the soul and the soul answers in the living Word, the soul begins to live in the Son."[14] This, however, cannot occur "unless the soul is first established in right conduct and cleansed of willful sin," right conduct being the habitual exercise of the natural virtues,"[15] and sin being nothing other than "the privation of the good," a "deprivation or falling-off from the good of created nature."[16] But human virtue, since it is necessarily restricted, must therefore be transcended, not from without but within: "You should pass through and transcend all virtues and only receive virtue in the ground of the soul where it is one with the divine Knower."[17]

It is precisely this second aspect of morality that presently concerns us—that which pertains exclusively to the withdrawal back into the order of principial knowledge from which all that issues forth originates. Since the divine Knower is wholly detached, "man should so live that he may be one with the only-begotten Son. . . . Between the only-begotten Son and the soul there is principially no real distinction. . . If I were to behold God as I behold color, I should be in the wrong direction, for this beholding is temporal and everything that is temporal is far from God and foreign to him. When one takes time, if one takes even the smallest segment of it, it is still time and remains in itself. As long as a man has time and place and number and quantity and multiplicity, he is in the wrong direction, and God is separated from him and alienated from him. All creatures as such are nothing in themselves. Hence I have said: forsake Nothing [that is, stop trying to gaze at or behold being] and participate in perfect isness, in which the detached will to know is established. . . . All creatures receive their being without medium from God. Hence the creatures derive from their real nature the fact that they innately desire God more than themselves. If the creature fully realized its naked detachment [as it is in God], it could never turn aside to anything else, but would remain in its naked detachment." [18]

It should now be clear, as has been maintained throughout, that as long as one adopts the position whereby one stops to behold or take a mental gaze at being as though it were "something out there" or "in here," rather than participating in it, knowledge is necessarily restricted. Then the unlimited will to know is aborted, and morality is subjected to a particular perspective. Yet this has been the dilemma of most modern philosophy, and no doubt largely accounts for the extrinsic diversity of its conflicting positions and the subsequent vacuity of its moral views, since they are no more than "views." When we grant preference to the intrusion of desires other than the unlimited will to know we then choose not to culminate our knowing course by determinations and moral decisions rationally grounded *in* being.

We are then "prevented from hearing the eternal Word by three things: the first is corporeality, the second is multiplicity, the third is temporality."[19]

In other words, the failure to let ourselves participate in being[20] contracts our awareness into a separative mode of cognition whereby all things appear as though constituted only in corporeality, multiplicity, and temporality as separated from any ground of isness and as self-sufficient. Then corporeality is separated from spirit, multiplicity from unity, temporality from timelessness[21] In fact "if a man had passed beyond these three things [as so separated] he would be able to hear the eternal Word and be in the right direction for dwelling in eternity, in unity, in spirit, and [ultimately] dwelling in the Godhead. Now our Lord says 'No one hears my word or my doctrine unless he has abandoned self.'[22] . . . In the eternal Word that which hears is identically that which is heard. All that the eternal Father teaches is his isness and his nature and all his Godhead. He reveals this fully to us in his only-begotten Son, and he teaches us that we are the same Son."[23] And "no matter how many sons are born as conceived rationally by the soul, there is nevertheless not more than the unique Son, for the birth takes place beyond time in the day of eternity."[24]

"If one had detached himself completely, in such a way that he had become the only-begotten Son [in principle and inasmuch as being is in function of knowledge],[25] he would be detached as the only-begotten Son is detached. Whatever God manifests and whatever he teaches, he manifests and teaches it all in his only-begotten Son. . . . In order that we may be the only-begotten Son . . . he reveals to us the whole abyss of his Godhead and the all-possibility of his isness and of his knowledge. . . . Such a detached soul dwells in the knowledge and love that God is, and becomes none other than God himself in knowledge and love."[26]

God is totally detached, in fact "God's own nature is purity and unity and these come from detachment." "That God is God is due to his motionless detachment, and it is from this detachment that he derives his purity and his simplicity and his immutability." In this motionless detachment

God has stood forever and does always so stand [for he is without potentiality and apart from God there is strictly nothing]. Know also that when God created the heavens and the earth he might not have been producing anything at all for all that it affected his detachment. . . . Further I say that when the Son in his Godhead willed to be made man and became so and endured martyrdom, God's motionless detachment was affected no more than if he had not been made man."[27]

No theme is more pervasive throughout the Commentaries, Tractates, and Sermons of Eckhart than that of detachment. He wrote three distinct treatises on it; he employed it as the fundamental doctrine in his *Book of Divine Consolation;* he returned to it in almost every sermon and even in his Latin dissertations and exegetical writings. Its ultimate conclusion is spelled out in his special commentaries on Matthew 5:3,[28] for to be "poor in spirit" is to be as "totally detached as we are in the Principle" and "eternally poor as we were when we were not so and so."[29]

The detachment of which Eckhart speaks is not to be confused with a lack of interest. Nor does it imply that man is confronted with obstacles that have to be eluded in order that liberation from the restrictions of individuality and the self may be attained. The body cannot constitute an obstacle to liberation any more than multiplicity and temporality or any other type of contingency. Nothing can enter into opposition with all-inclusive God, in the presence of whom all particular things are as if they were not.

Though "detachment is to be extolled above any love," honored "above humility" and "more than mercy," these virtues are all included in detachment, which is their root and without which they are not divine in operation.[30] Without detachment love is "a going out to some other," humility is "an abasing of oneself before an other," and "mercy means nothing else but a man's going forth of self by reason of his fellow-creature's lack." But in Principle there is no other, "for you must know that when a free intellect is really detached it takes God as its Self and were it to remain structureless and free from contingency it would take on the very knowledge that God is. . . . He who is detached into eternity is no longer affected by any transitory 'other' nor is he aware of any particular corruptibility; the world as such [which is the entire realm of individuality or otherness] is for him dead, he having no desire for any differentiated aught, for there all differentiation is naught. . . Know, then, that the intellect that is unmoved by any contingency, affection or sorrow, honor or disgrace, is really detached." Detachment is then compared by Eckhart to the hinge of a door: "When the door opens or closes the outer boards move to and fro, but the hinge remains immovable in one place and it is not changed at all as a result. So it is here, if you only knew how to act rightly."[31]

POVERTY OF SPIRIT

The doctrine of detachment is finally summed up in Eckhart's commentary on "the poor in spirit," the keynote of which is: "A poor man is he who wants nothing, knows nothing, has nothing."[32]

First, in asking what is meant by "a man who *wants* nothing," he draws attention to those who furnish an incomplete explanation: "Those who speak of a poor man who wants nothing as meaning that he never follows his own will but is bent on performing the will of God . . . their intention is good and we commend them for it . . . but . . . as long as a man has something toward which his will is directed, as long as it is *his* will to do the will of God, he has not the poverty of which I speak. . . . If he is truly poor he is as free from his created wants as he was when he was not yet 'somebody'. . . . When I stood in the Principle I had no God and I belonged to my truest Self; I willed not, I wanted not, for I was without destination, knowing what I was in divine truth; then I simply willed what I was and no other. What I willed, that I was; what I was, that I willed. But when I stepped out of this freedom to take on a created nature, then I also possessed a 'God'; for prior to creatures God was not 'God' [as other]: he was what he was. Even as creatures became and as created nature began, this God-as-other was not God-in-himself, but God-in-creatures. Now we maintain that God merely as God-as-other is not the ultimate end of creation, nor has this 'God' even as great a plenitude of isness as the smallest creature has in God-in-himself. That is why we pray that we may become empty of 'God,' thus knowing in truth and enjoying eternity."[33]

Continuing, Eckhart says: "A poor man is one who *knows* nothing . . . to him must be applied all that pertained to him when he was neither for himself nor for contingent reality, nor for 'God.' He is so poor and empty of every mode of active knowing that no conception or idea of God is alive in him. For while he stood in the eternal, actionless mode of God, there was no other; what was there in act was the Self. And so we say this man is as free from his own individualized knowledge as he was when he was not his proper self; he lets God be in act as he will. . . . In this sense he is so detached and free that he does not know, is even unaware, that God is the act. . . . Being poor in spirit means being poor of all distinctive knowledge, simply as one knows no-thing, neither 'God,' nor creatures, nor himself in any individualized mode. Here there is no question of desiring to know or being aware of the manifestation of God."[34]

"Third, the poor man *has* nothing." After extolling the value of voluntary external poverty Eckhart maintains that "one should also be detached from all things and activities inwardly as well as outwardly, so that one becomes a proper place in which God may act." But above this is still the ultimate state of detachment that is the essence of the whole doctrine, for even the inward self must be transcended. The "inner self" is in no way "absorbed" on the attainment of final liberation or "salvation from individuality," although it may appear so from the standpoint of universal manifestation. But from that standpoint what appears as an absorption is really an inversion or transformation. Regardless of appearances or mental cognition, "the Holy Spirit is actually the Transformer."[35] For when considered from the standpoint of reality *in divinis* the soul is "blown up beyond all limit," since it has effectively realized the fullness of its intellective possibilities.

"Granting a man stands detached from all things, from

creatures, from himself, from 'God,' yet remains so constituted that God finds in him room in which to act, then we
say; as long as this is so he is not poor in innermost poverty.
God does not intend in his act that man should have within
him a place in which he might act. Poverty of spirit means
above all dispossession of 'God,' of all individuality and of
self, so that if God wills to act in the soul, he himself must
be the 'place' in which he will act. And how gladly he wants
this! Finding a man so completely poor, then God is his own
work as well as his own workshop, since God is in himself
the working." To be strictly poor in spirit is to be totally without this or that spirit, but principially identified with pure
Spirit or Intellect-as-such. "It is here in this poverty of spirit
that there is regained that eternal state of being what has
been, what now is, and what shall be forever."[36]

This strict detachment is the actual realization that only
the Principle itself is totally and necessarily real, that everything else is derivative and ultimately superfluous. The realization is effective only if the soul finally becomes strictly
detached by renouncing all otherness and the very self. By
"following Christ into this poverty," the soul dispossesses
itself of its "God". Then true God himself is the sole act, the
single *I*, the only Self, in the simplicity and detachment of
his own nature.[37] Indeed it is precisely in nonpossessive simplicity and detachment that God superabounds. Since nothing excludes God, he cannot possess; "he is without property" and "his compassion is without passion."[38] Thus the
inversion into that divine detachment where there is no
doubt, no effort, no desire; where there is no awareness of
the soul *having* any being, but only perfect awareness or
"unknowing knowledge." Dispossessed of all *having*, the soul
is wholly in God and, as Aquinas has also reminded us, "that
which is in God is God,"[39]—a constantly repeated truth in
Eckhart's teaching.

Such a doctrine takes us beyond what is formally understood by detachment or spiritual poverty—that detachment
from all that hinders the soul from perfectly possessing
its own being, or from considering its being as dependent
on God. It is at this point that all formal as well as normative

religious understandings stop short. Inasmuch as these understandings always refer to extensions of the human individuality, the states of which they give access must necessarily preserve some connection with manifested being, even
when they reach beyond it to distinctive isness. They are
therefore not the same as this purely transcendent state to
which there is no access except by way of transcendent act
itself. The realization of Divine Knowledge is constituted in
that act, and that act in itself precludes any un-binding or
re-binding, that is any "religion." For "in principle nothing
has ever been disunited."[40] This statement is especially applicable to the religious "mystical states'. And as to the posthumous states, there is precisely the same difference between "immortality," in the religious sense, and principial
liberation as there is between "mystical experience" and
realization in Divine Knowledge.

If we follow Eckhart and reflect on immortality correctly,
then we shall not regard it essentially as an extension of the
possibilities of the individualized order. In terms of detached intellection "immortality" does not primarily consist
in an indefinite prolongation of life under conditions that
are to a certain degree transformed but that always remain
more or less similar to those of manifested existence. In
order to be fully effective "immortality can only be attained
beyond all conditioned states [individual or otherwise], and
in such mode that, being strictly detached from any possible
mode of succession, is identical with eternity itself."[41] Immortality, which is akin to the state of pure contemplation
and detachment, essentially means that there is no longer a
need to pass through further conditioned states of any kind
or to pass through other dispensations or manifestations.

In the case where liberation or detachment is about to be
obtained directly from the human state, the true goal, as
Eckhart has explained, is no longer the being of God but
the undifferentiated Godhead itself. "The objective of
detachment is neither this nor that. . . . It must aim at pure
no-thing (non-otherness, the not-self) in which there is
all-possibility."[42] That is to say, it must aim at the "unqualified and undifferentiated Principle in its total infinitude and

suprabeing." Comprising the possibilities of both manifestation and nonmanifestation, therefore, the superessential
Principle is beyond both while including both. Suprabeing,
like the unmanifested, can be metaphysically understood in
a total sense whereby it is identified with the infinite Principle. In any case a correlation between suprabeing and
being, or between the unmanifested and the manifested,
can only be a purely intellectual relation. From the standpoint of pure detachment in Divine Knowledge, the disproportion between the two terms does not permit of any real
comparison between them.

The transcendent identity therefore is the finality of the
detached and liberated knower, that is, of the knower who
is freed from the conditions of individual existence as well
as from all other limiting conditions, which may be considered as so many attachments. When the knower who was
previously in the human state is thus detached and therefore saved from himself, the divine Self is fully realized in its
own undifferentiated nature and is then an omnipresent
awareness. Here there is no stopping to consider what was
one's *own* being in the state of individual manifestation;
there is only complete dispossession in the *now*.[43] Eckhart
does not say that we necessarily *are* more by having less;
rather it is the man who intentionally has *nothing*, not even
an inner self he can call his own, who is truly detached and
therefore one with God *in* God.[44]

For Eckhart the individual self, in both its outward and
inner orientations, designates *that* in the intellective soul
which tends toward ownership, toward having, toward affirming even its own dependent existence, not to mention
its imagined autonomous existence. To the degree that the
soul merely gazes at reality and thus tends toward corporeality, multiplicity, and temporality as such, it is greatly
bound in self-centeredness. Even to the degree that it insists
on having this self, this being, or refuses to at-one itself with
"divine Not-self," that is, with the all-inclusive Word—to that
degree is the soul united to something other than God. And
to that same degree "the innermost Self, the New Man, the
divine Person is not revealed."[45] It is the self that con-

structs an economy of "self and other," that above all advocates experience, mystical or otherwise, that stops short with a "God" who is less than God-in-himself. In short, it is the self that ignores *isness* and in its place puts *having*.

Conversely, "becoming poor in spirit is letting God be God,"[46] and it is here that Eckhart introduces Aquinas's principle of "infallible necessity."[47] In other words, "if a man has become detached from himself and all things, then God necessarily fills him," for "God must give himself up." The very isness that God is would be restricted if he did not give himself completely to a soul prepared to receive him completely, since God is also responsible for the preparation.

"It is in spiritual poverty, detachment, simplicity, that the oneness between man and God is found. And this oneness is through grace, for it is grace that draws man away from earthly things [or structural manifestation] and rids him of all things conditioned by mutability and corruptibility. I would have you know that to be detached from manifested things is to be full of God, and to be full of manifested things is to be empty of God."[48] True, but Eckhart does not counsel detachment so that God can fill *us* and act in *us*, thereby bestowing an enrichment on our *selves,* for "to be full of God is to realize nothing other than God." The "infallible necessity" actually means that "the detachment necessitates the liberation and transposition of the intellective soul into the Divine Knowledge which God is."[49]

THE NOTHINGNESS OF THE HUMAN SELF

Meister Eckhart illustrates the transposition into Divine Knowledge by referring to the Eucharist, and quotes what Christ said to St. Augustine: "I shall not be changed into thee as food of thy flesh, but thou shalt be changed into Me."[50] We may be familiar with that which makes possible the transposition of the individual human subject in itself to the human subjectivity in Christ.[51] But that which further makes possible the subjective transposition to divine subjectivity in God transcends any point of view available to the human knower as such.

Though this ultimate standpoint of knowledge, situated

as it is within God, never denies structures from without, it does transcend them within. And to be wholly within is to be "beyond individuality, beyond comparatives, beyond dualities, participating in the eternal communion of the Father and the Son." [52] It is inconceivable that the rational being which is not-real in itself should not be realized by God and determined by him to be transposed in his all-possibility. [53] Yet that transposition explains why the human self must forgo "God as other" and the consideration of itself as a co-traveler in "the return of the Son to the Father," even the consideration of itself "as being realized by God." For the ultimate term of that knowing which is intrinsically divine is beyond any consequent determination. "It is the naked supra-being of the Godhead." [54] Such realization does not actually "take place" in the soul; it has always been, only now the detachment from all that is not this realization is complete.

Analogous to detachment, or spiritual poverty, are such terms as "silence," "emptiness," "nudity"; and like them detachment is profoundly intelligible. It is not strict nothingness, because no contradiction is involved; nor is it confined to our sphere of structural manifestation. Detachment, silence, emptiness, nudity are not made; rather they are realized only when possessiveness, noise, objects, coverings are withdrawn. Because these latter manifestations are relatively limited to the former, meditation on the nonpossessive, unutterable, unfathomable Reality of all realities is given a support by these terms. Still, even this support must finally be disowned, give way to unattached isness, since the root of these manifestations is the infinite Principle, which is in no way affected by any manifestation, structured or structureless. [55]

The detachment signifies, as Eckhart has explained, the actual realization of Divine Knowledge and not just its intellectual affirmation. It is situated there within, that is, *in patria* rather than *in via*, which accounts for its expositions as being largely reducible to the destruction of error. However, our rightly asserted antipathy to modern subjectivist views has made much of Eckhart's language appear as a hindrance to our understanding of truth in the principial mode in which he expounds it. No doubt for this reason a lack of discernment has caused some of his interpreters to turn detached intellectuality, in the name of which he speaks; into a psychological and subjectivist extravaganza, and others to brand it with labels such as monism, pantheism, and immanentism. As if the unmanifested Selfhood, the principial divine *I*, were not transcendent!

It is too easily forgotten that transcendence is not to be confused with either philosophical absolutism or its opposite relativism, or with unicity or complexity.[58] It is fundamentally ungraspable, since it is not the object of any cognition. There is no ontological 'proof' of the divine Selfhood and no existential or empirical path that leads there. But there is, in truth, no other reality than the divine *I* and there is not anything that ultimately has any other reality. "All creatures as such are a mere nothing. I do not say that they are small or just partially something; they are a mere nothing. . . . If God turned away for an instant they as such would be annihilated."[57]

The link between the finite and the Infinite, or between individual manifestation and unmanifested God, is that the finite is in its principle Infinite, while the finite as such is not. In other words, "Knowledge-in-itself [the Principle] is, in effect, the ground of universal order, of distinctive knowledge, and of experience."[58] There is obviously no commensurable proof to be drawn from lower levels of reality, but what is proved is the lack of ultimate reality in anything other than unmanifested and undifferentiated God.

Furthermore, it is made clear in Eckhart's teaching that what one is called upon to do is not to adapt or even reconcile points of view, but to verify them wholly in the Principle, the key maxim being: "When in doubt turn within." This can only be in the divine Self in whom there is no other. There need be no anxiety about the agreement of truth with unconditioned Truth. Christ, he says, has already seen to that, but *we* can't have it on the surface or in any individualized mode.

Detachment is the "means" of getting within, and regardless of the degree of inwardness it is still in Christ the Word.
"St. John says: 'Blessed are the dead that have died in God.'
It appears odd that it should be possible to die in him who
himself said that he is the life. But reflect: the soul breaking
through its eternal exemplar is plunged into the profound
no-thingness or [nonmanifestation] of its eternal exemplar.
This [detachment] is a spiritual death. . . . When the soul
realizes that its eternal exemplar has been objectivized into
otherness, which is a negation of identity, the soul puts its
own self to death to its eternal exemplar, and thus breaks
through its eternal exemplar and abides in the nonduality
of the unmanifested divine Godhead. These are the blessed
detached who are detached in God. No one can be
detached and beatified in the Godhead who is not dead to
self and to 'God,' that is, in the eternal exemplar, as I have
just explained. . . . Christ rose out of God into Godhead [the
undifferentiated Trinity, though in actuality triune God and
Godhead are identical], into the unity of the Principle. That
is to say, in Christ all intellective souls, being dead to their
exemplar, rise from that divine death to be blessed with the
joys above it, namely the fullness of the Godhead wherein
there is beatitude."[59]

Eckhart reminds us that as long as the soul is considered
as being situated in structural manifestation "the presence
of God to self, of first cause to its effects, is understood as
nearness, as of he and I," and the beatified life as "loving
and being loved as between two."[60] But if, as he counsels, we
advert to the reality into which that relationship of love
immerses us, what is now realized *in* that reality is neither
near nor far, active nor passive, but an unqualified and undifferentiated unity. What is now realized in pure detachment is what can be given to no diversified other and what
no diversified other can receive. It is an eternal and infinite
I-ness, the Principle without which nothing is. In this reality
itself "God must be very *I* and *I* very God, so that he and *I*
are one *I*, one *is* and in this isness working one eternal
work."[61] "God's isness is my life. If my life is God's isness,
then God's isness is my isness and God's mode is my mode,

neither more nor less. . . . In the Book of Wisdom we read that 'the just live eternally, and their reward is in God'— identically so!" [62]

"In, the eternal exemplar the soul is God and there the soul has equality with the Father, for the eternal exemplar, which is the Son in the Godhead, is in all respects equal with the Father. . . . But where there is still equality there is no identity, for 'equal' indicates a negation of identity. . . . I am not equal with my proper self; I am here [in structural manifestation] identically my proper self. Hence the Son in the Godhead, inasmuch as he is the Son, is equal with the Father, but as such he is not identical with the Father. Identity is where Father and Son are *one,* that is, in the unmanifested and undifferentiated unity of the divine Principle. In this unity the Father knows no Son, nor does the Son know any Father, for *there* there is neither Father nor Son nor Holy Spirit [as differentiated]. When the soul is within the Son, its eternal exemplar and wherein it is equal with the Father, and then breaks through the eternal exemplar, it, in the Son, transcends equality, and identity with the three Persons is realized in the unity of the nondual Principle." [63]

Yet in this detachment in the Principle, the "effects" of its trinitarian affirmation and the manifestation of itself in intelligible being, and hence ourselves as distinct, are also known through their proper relations. Why? Because that "unknowing knowledge" manifests and necessarily so, the unfolding of God's all-inclusive aspects in actuality through his affirmation of himself in his eternal act. [64] "For David says: 'Lord, in thy Light we shall see Light.' That is, in the Light of the undifferentiated Principle the divine essence shall be known and also the whole perfection of that essence as manifested in the variety of the Persons by their multiplicity and distinction in the unity of their Principle. . . . Thus there shall be the transposition from manifested light into the unmanifested effulgence of the divine Principle and the soul shall be as it is [in the detached realization of Divine Knowledge]; that is, it shall be that which it is in principle." [65] The beatitude of the detachment "is to realize

all as it is and all profusion that is possibly to be desired; to
know it all at once and whole in the undivided Intellect and
that in God, unfolded in its perfection, in its flower, where
it first bursts forth in the Principle; and to know all where
God himself knows. Now that is the beatitude of detachment.[66]

If the detachment is altogether equivalent to a death and
resurrection in Christ, it is because the divine exemplar actually signifies this essential metaphysical principle: "It is
impossible for isness to be differentiated from isness; for
nothing can be differentiated from isness except strict nothingness."[67] In truth we are apart from God insofar as we *are*
not. "That which is considered apart from God or as something only in itself, neither is nor is of God."[68] It is always in
this sense that Eckhart speaks of the unreality and nothingness of the human self.

If, when Eckhart refers to "the human self as such" and
means that which is outside God, then precisely to that
extent he is not deluded in calling the self a "nothing," a
"naught." And we understand what he means when he says
that the realization of this nothingness, not just a theoretical consent to it, is a spiritual death. "What must a man
be to know God? He must be dead. But dying to this world
[of structure and individuality] is not to die to God."[69]
"Withdrawn from time sunrise is sunset, going up is going
down, and thus isness is always in principle." But "some people fondly think that they have attained realization within
the Holy Trinity who have never got beyond themselves";
they think they are detached in will and thought, but "they
are loath to be detached from self."[70]

On the other hand, if Eckhart refers to the intellective
soul as that which is already and eternally *in* God, then precisely to that extent he is not deluded in saying that man's
"truest *I* is God." For from this standpoint, if a further
reminder is needed, "God is pure *instasis,* standing in himself, in whom there is neither this nor that, for whatever is
in God is God."[71] "In God there can be nothing alien, nothing other. Heaven affords us an example: it can never
receive others as other. Thus whatever comes to God is in-

verted; however insignificant it is, when brought to God it turns from its self, from all nothingness. . . . Now reflect and marvel! If God inverts and transposes insignificant things into himself, just think what he does with the intellective soul which he has dignified with the direct image of himself." [72]

THE TRANSPOSITION BY TRANSCENDENT ACT

An essential point previously noted must now be considered in more detail if we are to understand the way in which the detachment is effected.

Eckhart is never unmindful of the perennial principle that the relation of subject, whether of the rational intellect to the ratiocination that takes place in it, or of prime matter to the structure of material things, or of substance to accidental determinations, is a relation of potentiality to act. Transcendence, in other words, is only in virtue of what already is in act at a higher degree of knowing and isness. And divine transcendence is only in virtue of what eternally is in act at the incommensurable *instasis* of the unrestricted actuality of Divine Knowledge. A leap beyond structure by way of potentiality is, of course, unintelligible—a fact rarely considered in modern philosophy. It can only be by way of *act* and, as Aquinas says, so far as we are knowing subjects it is effectively in virtue of the actuality of God. [73] Transcendence, then, necessitates in us the raising up of the subjective principle to an unrestricted order of receptivity of knowing and isness.

Some interpreters of Eckhart, ignorant of the essentials of metaphysics, understand his doctrine as implying a withdrawal into the indeterminancy of the potential principle. This, however, he clearly denies, and instead insists repeatedly that "nature cannot transcend nature," [74] as we have noted several times. With Aquinas he clearly insists that there is no transcending of the human self by way of potentiality, only by way of act. [75] In order to attain detachment and "ascend to Intellect in itself," it is requisite, says Eckhart, "to withdraw from all accidental determinations and from every ratiocination of the mind." Only thus is there ef-

fected a realization of God as divine Selfhood, the unrestricted act of knowledge itself—and hence the truth signified in the statements "I am that Son and not other" or
"my truest I is God." In other words, "we must go back into
the *Grund, der grundlos ist.*"[78]

It is clear, then, that this withdrawal from particular actualization must be a "recession into an axial eternal act."
And there should be no doubt as to what *act* that must be if
there is to be a realization of the detachment necessary in
order that pure contemplation may be attained. It cannot
be the individuality or substantial being of the soul. Though
that is an enduring act and affords the possibility of transcendence in the intimacy of God's presence in the soul,
thus denoting a possible "mystical condition" that is genu-
inely religious, it nevertheless does not afford a transcendence of real distinction. But going beyond real distinction
is the very nature of knowledge *in divinis,* of pure contemplation. Eckhart is fully aware of the passivity that is at
the root of action. He is also aware that the "axial eternal
act" can be neither an act understood as action nor an act
understood by the common analogy of action. "When
detachment attains its supreme perfection it becomes inac-
tive, unknowing knowledge through Divine Knowledge."[77]
Transcendence, which is the very essence of detachment,
can only be by way of *act* as known in the order of inversion
and thus "by way of unrestricted isness in primal act, that is,
by God himself."[78] Grace is essentially "the uncreated act" of
God, that is, the Holy Spirit itself. Or, to put it another way,
"grace is the indwelling of the soul in God."[79]

It must be remembered that the principial notion of
grace inverts the order in which the connection of created
grace and uncreated grace are understood. In the transcendence to the principial order Eckhart grants priority, as
it were, to uncreated over created grace. He understands
first God's immediate Self-giving and secondarily the manifested and therefore relational reality by which that Self-
giving of unmanifested pure act is distinct.[80] Hence he considers the obediential potency—the detachment, the "pure
virginity"[81]—of the intellect's essence with regard to un-

manifested act, instead of considering it with regard to the manifested quality that is sanctifying grace.[82] Indeed, since both created and uncreated grace, which intervene in the supernaturalization of the intellect's essence, focus upon the same obediential potency, there should be no difficulty in understanding the intellect as directly actuated by God with whom uncreated grace is identical.

Thus God is the *act* of the intellect's essence, or to speak formally, its "like-work," its "quasi-form." He is principially the actual Knower, which means no more than that he terminates the relation of the intellect's direct union with the unmanifested and undifferentiated Selfhood. This union is the immediate link of the intellect with pure Intellect, because the "Light of God" is not an intermediary but that which gives reality to the intellect's oneness with divine Intellect.[83] From the standpoint of structural manifestation, or of the soul *in via,* this union signifies a real distinction; *in patria,* that standpoint situated within the Principle, it signifies only an intellectual relation.

"There is a distinction between being by grace and being grace itself. . . . Grace is nothing other than the flowing Light of God proceeding immediately into the soul; it is a supernatural informing principle of the soul, which gives it a supernatural nature. This is what I meant when I said that the soul was unable of itself to transcend its own individual activity; this [transcendence] is possible only in the act of uncreated grace, which transposes the soul above activity. . . . So long as the soul is in the process of being transposed beyond itself into the nonindividuality of itself and beyond its own activity, it is 'by grace'; the soul 'is grace' when this transcendent flight is effected, so far as it now stands in pure detachment alone, aware of nothing but of being according to the mode of God's knowledge. . . . For to be grace itself [that is, to actually realize transcendent identity or nondistinction] the soul must be detached from all activity, inward as well as outward, as [uncreated] grace is detached, which [being the act or isness that God is] knows no activity. . . . Grace detaches the soul from its own activity; it detaches the soul from its own individuality. In

this supernatural transposition the soul transcends its natural light which is creature [and which, being reflected light,
pertains to structural manifestation] and stands within in
immediate oneness with God."[84]

If the soul is finally to become detached from its own activity it must cease to seek. "The intellect as seeker penetrates beyond discursive thinking. It goes looking about,
seeking, casting its net here and there, acquiring and losing.
But above this intellect the seeker is Intellect, which does
not seek but rests in the pure and unconditioned isness of
its own divine Light. And I say that it is in this Light that all
the powers of the soul are transposed."[85] The human mind
is like a child in a room the door of which is made to open
inwards, and who habitually pushes the door in order to
open it. The more it pushes the less the door can open, but
if it stops pushing for an instant the door will open by
itself.[86] "Now intellect the seeker must recede into Intellect
which does not seek,"[87] that is, into its Principle. "The more
one seeks God the less one finds God," and "he who seeks
or aims at any individualization [general or particular],
seeks and aims at nothing [in comparison with the All-
inclusive]."[88]

"'I sought him and I found him not. . . . I sought him all
night through,' says the soul in the *Book of Love*.[89] There is
no night without light; it is only veiled. Though veiled the
sun is shining in the night, but by day it shines eclipsing all
other lights. That which we seek in creatures is all night. My
meaning is really this: all that we seek in creatures [or in
structural and individualized manifestation] is no more than
a shadow [though a real shadow or reflection]. . . . All that is
not the principial Light is darkness and night. That is why
she did not find God. 'I rose and sought him all about and I
hunted through the broadways and alleys. . . . Then when I
passed a little by I found him whom I sought.' This *little*, this
insignificance that hindered her from finding him—this has
often been the point of my teaching. He to whom all
transient things are not insignificant, little and as nothing,
that man shall not find God. . . . When you consider God
as an objective light or a being or a boon—whatever you

know about him, that God is not. Understand, one must transcend this 'little,' discard the adventitious and realize God as One [without an other]. . . . Anything individualized, anything that may come to your knowing, *that* God is not, because he is neither this nor that. Whoever says that God is this or that, believe him not. The Light that is God shines in darkness. God is the true Light: to realize it one must be blind and stand in God detached from every 'what' . . . . When the soul stands in the One of nonduality, and is set therein by the complete discarding of its own self, then God is realized as it were in a naught [as unmanifested]. . . . The soul that is detached from things comes home to stay in the undifferentiated pure Light. It *has* no love, is without anxiety and fear, for knowledge is the basis, the foundation of being, and love is meaningless unless in knowledge. When the soul is blind and can apprehend no other, then it realizes only God, and necessarily so. . . .God is all-inclusive."[90]

While Eckhart's "method" of detachment is not explicitly founded on the formal concept of grace, it nevertheless does of necessity lead to the *lumen Dei*. But grace and method are not incompatible agents; they are merely two converse sides of the one single reality. Moreover, "do not *worry* whether God acts with nature or above nature. Both nature and grace are his. . . . Once a man very much wanted to direct a stream into his garden, and he said: 'If only I could have the water, I should not care through what kind of channel it flowed to me, whether it was iron, wood, bone, or rusty metal, as long as I got the water.'"[91]

The method of detachment is also the "gift," is in itself already the freely given grace by the fact of its revelation. As such it is necessarily efficacious in its mode of withdrawal from all active willing, knowing, and having, from all that is not uncreated act. What, after all, is the "gift' if not the Principle inversely signified in the ground, or isness, of the "given"? The soul's "I" reflects God's *I*; nevertheless, the soul's "I" signifies nothing other than an inverse principle by comparison with the divine *I*.

All formal doctrines of grace stop short of this aspect of

inversion and, by their very nature, do not consider the aspect of identity. Indeed it is not within their province to combine aspects of nondual Reality in a simple and structural apprehension. But without the ground of Divine Knowledge, which is constituted in identity, religion and theology are meaningless. And for Eckhart, who speaks in the name of Divine Knowledge, the inversion is already effective and "the detached unknowing *I*, which knows no otherness, signifies God's actionless act."[92] After all, as Aquinas reminds us, "divine isness is unqualified pure act and therefore unqualified by any activity or otherness."[93]

"The true *I*," says Eckhart, "indicates God's isness, that God simply is. All things are in God; out of him, without him, is nothing. All individualities or creatures as such are insignificant, and as mere nothing they are incommensurable with God. What they are in Truth, that they are in God, for only God is the Truth. *I* means the actuality of Divine Knowledge inasmuch as it is the sign of the All-inclusive. It affirms that God alone truly is. Again, *I*, means that God is inseparable from all manifestation, that he is more in things than they are in themselves. And we should be inseparate from things, not as depending on the self, but as completely detached from self. . . . So far as you are nothing to your self so far are you not other from all things; and so far as you are not other from all things so far are you God [in principial knowledge], for God's Godhead consists in non-otherness. Thus the man who realizes non-otherness realizes Godhead as it is in God himself. . . . Now God is all-possibility[94]: God made you [that is, in manifestation you are] like himself, a reflection of his Selfhood. But *like* implies something different and individual. Now between God and the soul there is no diversity nor any individual relationship, and hence in truest reality the soul is not to be considered 'like' God, rather [in principle] it is identical with him and one with God's Self. . . .

"More than this I know not and cannot know, so on this point my teaching must stop. But on the way I was thinking that one ought to be totally detached in one's intention, having no individuality, indeed nothing in mind but the Godhead in itself—not happiness nor this nor that, but only God and his Godhead in itself. If one intends otherness in any way, it is a delusion of Godhead; therefore apprehend Godhead as unmanifested in itself." [95]

"As truly as the Father in his unconditioned nature begets his Son innately, so truly he begets him in the ground of the intellect, and this is the innermost world. Here is God's Principle my Principle and my Principle God's Principle. . . . From this innermost Principle you should enact all your works without why. I say further: As long as you enact your works for the sake of the heavenly kingdom, or for God's sake, or for the sake of your own eternal happiness, in other words from without, then truly all is not fulfilled in you. It may be tolerable and good, but it is not the best . . . . For he who seeks God according to some distinctive structure lays hold of the structure and misses God who is concealed in the structure. But he who seeks God without structure apprehends him as he is in himself." [96]

"When discoursing about God I often shudder at how totally detached the intellective soul must be to attain that identity [in God]. But one must never regard this as impossible. It is not impossible to the soul established in God's grace. In fact nothing is easier for the soul established in God's grace than to leave off all things." [97]

REQUISITE SUPPORTS

Action, no matter how well intended, cannot under any condition liberate from action; it can only bear fruit within its own sphere, which is that of human individuality. Thus it is not through action that it is possible to become detached from and so transcend individuality. But as long as there is a trace of active willing, active knowing, and the having of self, the method of detachment essentially requires distinctive supports, without which it quickly becomes nothing more than a means of autonomous indifference and thoroughly delusive.

Eckhart is emphatic on this point and necessarily so in the name of pure metaphysics. To the extent that a man denies God's unique communication to man in the Revelation and

Christ's Church,[98] to the extent that he knowingly refuses to partake of the sacraments,[99] to the extent that he refuses to acknowledge and love God in his neighbor,[100] to that extent is he separated from Truth. "To be one with Truth is to be all that one *knows.*"[101]

So long as man is bound by the cords of existence there is always the ethical imperative of selflessness. There is also always something of faith in his intellection, otherwise there would be nothing separating him from that which is known. And as long as man is so bound, then: "Let us know only Jesus Christ who alone is our light, our support and way to the Father."[102] Furthermore, "the Body of Christ is the Church, which is built up by the unity of the Body from the many faithful," and "as God's will is in Christ so it is in the whole Church."[103] As to the sacraments: "Sacrament means a sign . . . they all point us to the underlying truth . . . the union of the soul with God." And "all these signs are requisite supports as long as we are in sight of but not yet one with what we know." "We must not however stop at the enjoyment of the sign, but go on to the underlying reality."[104]

Eckhart asserts that the primary function of the Church, "the Body of Christ," is the preservation and transmission of the traditional doctrine, which is "the spirit of Christ." The discharging of this function is the fundamental reason for the Church's existence and for its establishment by Christ. The real reason for the existence of every human knower finally rests on the divine basis of the doctrine. Hence no human knower can hope to find apart from it those eternal principles that alone confer more than "just human meaning" and the incentive to emerge from the enclosures that that individualized meaning entails. As the function of a teacher is in fact a true "spiritual parenthood," so the function of the Church is to make possible a "second birth" for all disposed to receive the teaching. But inasmuch as this "second birth" is a symbol essentially "signifying our primal origin and generation *in* God," then the teacher must before all else function as "the unfailing, requisite support and reminder of this essential truth."[105]

Those who would extract Eckhart's teaching from the

Christian faith or pretend to reduce his insistence on participation in the Church and its sacraments and rites to mere psychological theraputics should be ignored. Either they are dishonest regarding what he says—if they have studied all his genuine works—or, for some reason, are incapable of understanding all that is intrinsic to the method of detachment that he expounds. Intrinsically the Church is "the union of the soul with God, the marriage of human and divine nature." "Not in vain did God entrust the key to St. Peter, for 'Peter' signifies 'knowledge.' For knowledge has the key and opens and penetrates and breaks through and finds God unveiled."[106]

"While the rites [of the Church] are not to be cultivated at the cost of the underlying reality, for the reality itself is inside and not in the outward display, they point us to the one and only Truth."[107] The rites are compared with the sails of a ship, which help a man to reach his destination more easily, and without which he would have to rely on oars. Some who with valid reason are prevented from participating in the rites may indeed acquire true detachment and knowledge of God, yet "only by maintaining their attention perpetually concentrated and fixed on the Word, in which consists the one and only-indispensable preparation."[108] In the sacraments, which are "informed by the Word," the outward forms are properly speaking "supportive pointers" and these eminently contingent means produce a result that is of quite a different order from their own. It is by reason of its very nature and of the human conditions determining it that the intellective soul requires such "supports" as a continuing and perennial point of departure for a realization that transcends them.

As long as the intellect is in any way bound by the cords of existence it requires that continuing point of departure. The intellect requires it because the disproportion between the means and the end corresponds to no more than the disproportion that pertains between the individual state, taken as the starting point for that realization, and the unconditioned state that is its term. Speaking *sub specie aeternitatis,* therefore, the essential principle of the efficacy of the

Church (and its sacramental rites) is that everything that is
contingent insofar as it is a manifestation ceases to be so
when realized as an eternal and immutable possibility. Everything that participates in positive being must be redis-
covered in the "unknowing knowledge" and detachment of
nonmanifested God. It is this which allows of a transposition, or inversion, of the soul into the All-inclusive, by the
detachment from restricted, and therefore negative, conditions that are inherent in all structural manifestation.[109]

Knowledge does not have to become something other
than what it is in order to save; it has only to become consonant with its true, detached nature. But will must deny itself—in willing particulars, in willing to conceive and to
possess anything in individual manifestation—if the soul is
to be brought back to its original source and Principle.
"God does not compel the will; rather he establishes it in
freedom so that it may choose to will nothing other than all-
inclusive God himself and liberation itself. Then the intellective spirit is incapable of willing other than as God wills:
this is not its nonfreedom but its principial freedom. Some
people say: 'If I have God and the love of God then I am
free to do everything according to my own will!'[110] They
understand falsely. So long as you are capable of doing your
own will or doing anything against God and against his pre-
cepts, you have no true love of God, though you may
deceive the world that you have it. The soul established in
God's will and in the love of God is fully willing to do all that
conforms with God, leaving undone all that contradicts
him."[111]

Pure knowledge is not at liberty to err, but will is quite
free to assert its independence and do ill. It is only when will
conforms to its primordial movement that it is effecting its
true act in willing to know without restriction. Thus it is that
knowledge can save only on the condition that it fosters
decisiveness to opt for the ultimate imperative—
selflessness—and solicits by faith all that one truly is in principle. When it does this it engenders love; it produces an
immediate reintegration of the will in God and an awareness of God in the "other."[112]

Eckhart has much to say about love; some of his passages on divine love are the most sublime ever written. Yet it all boils down to this: "Love is simply the will reintegrated into principial Truth." [113] "Here in love there are not two, but one and unity; in love I am more in God than I am in myself."[114] "The soul established in God's knowledge and in God's love is nothing other than that which God is. If you love your true Self you love all men as your true Self. So long as you love anyone less than your true Self, you have not attained to true love; you still do not love all men as your true Self, all selves in one Self: and this Self is God-Man [Christ the incarnate Word]."[115]

As previously noted, "love keeps bound that which is eternally united in Knowledge, that is, in Godhead." To be sure "some people want to see God with their eyes [or know him individually as an object] as they see a cow, and to love him as they love their cow—for the milk and cheese and profit it beings them. This is how it is with people who love God for the sake of outward gain or inward consolation. They do not rightly love God when they love him for their own advantage. Indeed, I tell you in truth, any object [or idea] that you hold in your mind, however good [even objective or subjective being, for transcendence is neither by way of extroversion nor introversion], will remain a barrier between you and the innermost transcendent Truth."[116]

If a person wills to know with pure knowledge, his whole being must be brought into Godhead, and if this implies detachment and poverty of spirit, it also implies undifferentiated love. If love is supremely necessary, it is because it is not possible for a person to realize in pure knowledge the certainty that that knowledge enjoys unless the whole being is integrated in this realization. The innermost Self of pure knowledge is not realized without including the impartable "other" of being. The intellective center is not truly known in principle without involving the volitive circumference.

If the person blessed with principial knowledge does not intrude upon or abuse an "other," it is because the "other," whether it be a flower, a worm, or a human, is of God, his truest Self. Liberation, or salvation, then, is only effective [either in this life or posthumously] insofar as it essentially constitutes "unknowing knowledge" as it were in Godhead. Conversely, that knowledge, to be "unknowing," presupposes of necessity the realization of what has already been termed the transcendent identity, or nonduality, which includes the reintegration of the will in undifferentiated love. Thus the detachment, liberation, undifferentiated love, and knowledge are but one and the same. And if Eckhart says that knowledge is the means of liberation, it must be added that in this case "the means and the end are inseparable, for knowledge, unlike action, carries its own fruit within itself."[117]

"Now we cannot love God without first knowing him, but the essential point of God is in the Principle, equally transcendent to and immanent in all creatures, and the only way of getting within it is for the natural intellect to be withdrawn into a light infinitely more intense than itself. Supposing, for example, that my eye were a light and strong enough to endure the sunlight in its glory and unite with it, then its innermost state would be due not to itself alone but pre-eminently to the sunlight. So the intellect. The intellect is a light and if it is turned completely away from all things and is wholly in the Light of God, then, since God is eternally flowing with grace, my intellect is illumined and united with love and therein knows and loves God as he is in himself. Here we have an explanation of how God is flowing out into all rational beings in his light of grace and how we with our intellect apprehending this glorious light are transposed out of ourselves and to there within the Light of God himself. . . . To enter there we shall have to ascend by way of natural light into the light of grace and therein be inverted into the Light that is the Son in himself. There in the Son all is loved by the Father with his love, the Holy Spirit, which has its eternal source in him, and having issued forth in his eternal birth, namely the Son [the Word], is carried back to the Father as the knowledge and love of both. Thus identified with the Son, by the Holy Spirit, the Father with the Son shall be known and loved [in the unmanifested and undifferentiated Principle, the Godhead] and all that is impartably 'other' in and by him." [118]

"To my outward self all creatures are known as creatures, for instance, as wine, bread, or meat. But to my inner self all individuality is not known as creatures, rather as gifts of God. To my innermost Self, however, they are known not as gifts of God, but as eternally not other." [119]

Notes

Unless otherwise noted all references to Meister Eckhart designate, by abbreviation and number of page, the following publications:

DW—*Meister Eckhart. Die deutschen Werke,* ed. by Josef Quint, et al. Kohlhammer edition, vols. I—V, except IV which is in preparation. Stuttgart, 1938 ff.

LW—*Meister Eckhart. Die lateinischen Werke,* ed. by E. Benz, J. Koch, et al. Kohlhammer edition, vols. I—V. Stuttgart, 1938 ff.

Q—*Meister Eckhart. Deutsche Predigten and Tractate,* ed. and trans. by Josef Quint. Munich, 1955. Reliance on Quint is requisite for a correct understanding of some of the Mittelhochdeutsch texts. This work is here used in conjunction with DW and Pf, and especially in reference to some German Sermons not yet published in DW.

RS—*Eckharts Rechtfertigungsschrift* (Defense treatise in Latin). Gabriel Théry: *Édition critique des pièces relatives au procès d'Eckhart contenues dans le manuscrit 33b de la bibliothèque de Soest.* Archives d'histoire doctrinale et littéraire du moyen âge, 1926-29. (Designated by Section and Article.) For this Trial Document see LW V and the edition by A. Daniels in Beiträge zur Geschichte des Philosophie des Mittelalters, 23, 1923.

Pf—*Meister Eckhart,* ed. by Franz Pfeiffer. *Deutsche Mystiker des 14 Jahrhunderts.* Bd. II, 1857 and 1924. Under the direction of Quint my use of these *Mittelhochdeutsch* texts has been carefully selective as to their reliability and referred to inasmuch as they remain as yet unpublished in DW IV.

For an Eckhart bibliography the reader may initially consult James M. Clark's *Meister Eckhart,* London, 1957, p. 259 ff. and his *Meister Eckhart, Selected Writings,* London, 1958, p. 258 ff.

Foreword

1. The two volume translations by Bernard McGinn , Edmund Colledge, and Frank Tobin, published by the Paulist Press, and M O'C Walshe's three-volume translation for Element Books, relied upon the monumental scholarship of the great German Eckhart scholars Josef Quint and Josef Koch.

2. *"The writings of Adi Da Samraj are the most doctrinally thorough, the most philosophically sophisticated, the most culturally challenging, and the most creatively original literature on radical nonduality currently available in the English language."*
—Jeffrey J. Kripal, J. Newton Rayzor Professor
of Religious Studies, Rice University

3. Bernard McGinn, *The Flowering of Mysticism: Men and Women in the New Mysticism—1200-1350* (New York: Crossroad,1998), p. x

4. Jeanne Ancelet-Hustache, *Master Eckhart and the Rhineland Mystics* (New York,: Harper Torchbooks, 1957, p. 6

5. C. F. Kelley, *Meister Eckhart on Divine Knowledge* (Berkeley: DharmaCafé, 2009), p. 15

6. Quoted in Bernard McGinn, *The Mystical Thought of Meister Eckhart: The Man From Whom God Hid Nothing* (New York: Crossroad, 2001), p. 143

7. *Self-Realization of Noble Wisdom: The Lankavatara Sutra*, compiled by Dwight Goddard (Clearlake, CA: The Dawn Horse Press, 1983), p. 103

8. Adi Da Samraj, *The Knee Of Listening: The Divine Ordeal Of The Avataric Incarnation Of Conscious Light* (Middletown, CA: The Dawn Horse Press, 2004), p. 571

9. Christopher Dawson, *Medieval Essays* (New York: Sheed and Ward, 1954), p. 109

10. Kelley, *Meister Eckhart on Divine Knowledge* ,p. 110

Introduction

1. We should understand that the word "divine" is directly derived from *divinitas*, the fundamental meaning of which is "Godhead" or "that which is most excellent as the supreme Principle." Divine Knowledge, then, is knowledge in Godhead, *in divinis*, as Eckhart explains.

2. The word *Mystik* in German has the meaning of mystical theology, of higher intellection or sublime spirituality, whereas *Mystizismus* means merely an escapade in pseudoanalogies and images and is common to that emotional and impulsive faculty which is really beneath reason and not above it. Even so Eckhart can be designated *a Mystiker* only if that term has been purified of all notions of knowledge, including the *unio*

mystica of any experienced or determined mystical state, which are external to that which is as it were wholly in Godhead.
LW IV, 9; cf. 103, 299.

3. Cf. Vladimir Lossky, *Théologie negative et connaissance de Dieu chez Maître*

4. *Eckhart* (Paris, 1960). While pointing out certain aspects of Eckhart's
teaching that pertain to the order of mystical theology, enticing as that
order was to Lossky's personal involvement in Eastern Orthodox theology,
he nevertheless tended to subordinate all of Eckhart's teaching to that
order of direction toward God and thus failed to acknowledge the purely
transcendent order of knowledge *in principio,* which is the essential standpoint of the doctrine of Divine Knowledge that Eckhart expounds. To
understand Eckhart we must transcend the dialectic between cataphatic
and apophatic theology, both of which are constituted not as it were *in*
God but in the finite human knower when apprehending God as objectively other, either positively or negatively. It is the transcendence of this
dialectic that alone grounds the wholly supranatural and supradeterminate consideration of Divine Knowledge and distinguishes it from any
particular "religious" mode. When our concern is only genuine mysticism,
which is focused not on knowledge *in* God but on the realization of God
in us and on our desire for or love of God, we can do no better than turn
to the writings of St. John of the Cross and St. Francois de Sales. See my
Spirit of Love—Based on the Teachings of St. Francois de Sales (New York and
London, 1951).

5. F. Vetter, Ed., *Die Predigten Taulers* (Berlin, 1910), Ser. XV. p. 69.

6. LW III, 131, 233, 278. In this sense "pure metaphysics", or "detached
intellection," is *not* to be regarded as a branch of philosophy. It is perhaps
more approximated by what B.C. Butler calls "metachronics" than by what
Aristotle designates as metaphysics. What Eckhart discerns from Holy
Scripture is that the after-history or end of time underpins and is "prior"
to history, that the entire order of time, the past and the future, is fully
consummated by the incarnation of the Word of God in Jesus Christ (LW
III, 403). But the incarnate Word is more than the culmination of history.
Pure metaphysics, situated as it is *within* the Word, and therefore wholly
unrestricted, not only culminates, underpins, and is therefore "prior" to
history, time, and physics (i.e. natural phenomena), but also the entire
order of mind, individuality, and universal being, that is, *Totius Naturae,* the
meaning of which is to be found in its Principle (the Word) and of which
the totality of Nature is a manifestation. In his studies of Eckhart J. Koch
uses the term *Transzendentalien-Metaphysik* to designate the Meister's pivotal
consideration. See e.g. *Sinn and Struktur der Schriftauslegungen* in R. Öchslin, ed., *Meister Eckhart der Prediger* (Freiburg, 1960). This *Festschrift* in com-
memoration of the seven hundred-year anniversary of Eckhart's birth contains some insightful contributions to Eckhartian studies. See especially
those by J. Koch, H. Fischer, R. Öchslin, and B. Dietsche.

7. This is also to say, as Eckhart does, that "Holy Church is inseparable

from Christ, as body is inseparable from soul" (LW IV, 45; III, 298). Man's perennial access to Jesus Christ is "through the Church" and Eckhart believed, with well-grounded reason, that it is only through the Church, to which the inspired recorders of the life and words of the God-Man belonged, that it can be known that he actually was and is who he is. Though "the speaking of God to man" was not and is not wholly restricted to the historical Jesus Christ, but "has always been in act" [yet "received only according to the receptivity of the receiver," in diverse times and places], "all divine communication is fully consummated and finalized [metaphysically speaking] in Christ," in the sense that "the speaking of God to man [regardless of time and place] is always the speaking of Christ, true God and true man" (LW III, 427).

8. See Josef Quint, *Meister Eckhart* (Munich, 1955); James M. Clark, *The Great German Mystics* (London 1949); James M. Clark, *Meister Eckhart* (London, 1957); J. Koch, *Kritischen Studien zum Leben Meister Eckharts,* I and II, in *Archivum Fratrum Praedicatorum* 29 and 30 (1960).

9. LW III, 4.

10. Vetter, *Predigten Taulers,* p. 69; Suso's *Leben,* ch. XXXIII, K. Bihlmeyer, *Heinrich Seuse: Deutsche Schriften* (Stuttgart, 1907). See also my edition of *The Book of the Poor in Spirit —A Guide to the Rhineland Mystics* (New York, and London, 1954), Introduction. It is true that some of the Meister's statements that were condemned by John XXII are theologically unsound if taken in isolation, as indeed they were by the Cologne censors and Avignon judges. They nevertheless disclose a valid meaning when considered in their proper context. Suso warmly defends Eckhart against these charges in his *Leben* (last four chapters) and *Büchlein der Wahrheit,* esp. ch. VI (v. Bihlmeyer, p. 352 ff.). And if it is asked whether Eckhart intended to be heterodox, to initiate a distinctive "German theology" or promote what came to be acknowledged as the *Devotio Moderna* (with its debasement of man's intellectual quest as exemplified by Gerard Groote and the authors of the *Theologia Germanica* and the *Imitation of Christ)* the answer is surely negative.

11. Matt. 9:12; Mark 2:17; Luke 5:31.

12. DW V, 61.

13. Q 17 ff. See also *Meister Eckhart der Prediger.*

PART I: PREPARATORY CONSIDERATIONS
Chapter 1: Difficulties and Misconceptions

1. LW I, 152.

2. Worth consulting as a documented critique of certain Eckhart scholars is I. Degenhardt, *Studien zum Wandel des Eckhartbildes* (Leiden, 1967). For the benefit of the reader unfamiliar with Eckhart studies, it should be pointed out that practically all previous attempts to expound the Meister's teaching—from those of Lasson, Jundt, and Delacroix, etc.,

of the last century to those of Karrer, Dempf, and Lossky, etc., in this—should be studied with a degree of caution. Beneficial as most of these works are, it must now be acknowledged that their authors, in their concern to relate the Meister's teaching to a particular human situation, either failed to consider the doctrine of Divine Knowledge in principle, or greatly distorted it by reducing it to some external mode of understanding or attainment. Much of this is understandable since in most cases they were working with unreliable and largely incomplete texts. In any case, what has been presented by these and other scholars has not been Eckhart's essential teaching on Divine Knowledge, but a teaching confined at best to the human limits of mystical theology in the light of a peripatetic ontology. As to the great contribution to Eckhartian research made by H.S. Denifle, it must be stated that he went too far against some earlier studies with his method of destructive criticism. Both professors Quint and Koch were right in saying, at the Medieval Conference at Cologne in 1958, that our understanding of Eckhart must begin completely anew by a consideration of his teaching from the standpoint of *principial* knowledge (see below, note 4).

3. DW II, 504-5.

4. The principial mode of knowledge is the consideration of all things and all manifestation as it were from *within* the Godhead, the unconditioned Principle, or *tamquam in principio infinito*. It is the consideration of all reality from the standpoint of the full actualization of the *intellectus possibilis*, a consideration made feasible by the communication of the eternal Word of God. (LW II, 247 ff; v. Eckhart's *In Ecclesiasticus*, ed. by H. Denifle in his *Archiv. für Litteratur in Kirchengeschichte des Mittelalters*, II, *p.* 588.

5. DW I, 35-40.

6. DW I, 90; 113-14.

7. LW V, 40.

8. See Gabriel Théry, *Archives d'histoire doctrinale et littéraire du moyen âge* (Paris, 1926–29), 323–24; LW IV, 5 ff.

9. LW III, 12.

10. James Clark, *Meister Eckhart* (London, 1957), p. 99.

11. See O. Karrer, *Meister Eckhart,* (Munich, 1926), p. 56.

12. *De mystica Theologia,* 2 and 3.

13. *De divinis Nominibus,* 2,1.

14. *De mystica Theologia,* 3; 2.

15. Ibid., 1.

16. *De divinis Nominibus,* 13, 3.

17. *De mystica Theologia,* 5.

18. *De divinis Nominibus,* 5,1; 2,11; 4;35.

19. LW V, 92.

20. *De libero Arbitrio,* 11, 5, *8; De civitate Dei,* 11, 28; *De Trinitate,* 5, 2, 3; *Tractatus in Joannis Evangelium,* 99, 4.

21. *De Genesi ad litteram, 8,* 26, *48; De Trinitate, 15,* 7, 13.

22. *De Ideis, 2.*

23. *Summa Theologica* I, q10, al; *a4; Commentarium I Sententiarum xix,* qll, a2.

24. LW III, 181.

25. "Isness" (Eckhart's *istigkeit*) is by far the best English term available to convey the meaning of the Latin *esse* ("to be" as noun), thus running less danger of confusing it with *ens* (being) which designates "existence-essence," or that which derives from *esse* as from its principle. Only since the sixteenth century has the term "existence" been commonly used for *esse,* and this unfortunate usage has led to much confusion by actually distorting and restricting the metaphysical significance of *esse.*

26. "As long as the intellect fails to find the actual truth of things, does not touch the bottom and find their principle, it remains in a condition of quest and expectation, it never attains rest, but works unceasingly to find their primal source. It spends perhaps a year or more in research on some natural fact, discovering what it is, only to work as long again stripping off what it is not. All this time it has nothing to go by, it makes no determination at all in the absence of knowledge of the principle of truth. Intellect in this life never rests. However much God manifests himself in things, it is nothing to what he is in pure Intellect" (Pf. 20–21).

27. DW I, 120—23.

28. LW III, 208.

29. *Opuscula* xvi; *De Trinitate* q6, al.

30. *Summa Theologica* I, q79, a8; a9.

31. Ibid., I, q35, al; q5, a2; q85, a2, ad 1.

32. Ibid., I, q12, a2, ad3.

33. Ibid., I, q79, a2, ad2; q18, a4, adl; q27, a3, ad2; q79, a3; *De Veritate,* q2, ad4; *Compendium Theologiae* 37, 41.

34. *Summa Theologica I,* q18, a4; *Compendium Theologiae* 131; *De anima* 15.

35. *Summa Theologica* I, ql, a6, ad3; *De Div. Nom. ii,* 4.

36. *Summa Theologica* I, q79, a4; III *Contra Gentes* 54.

37. *Compendium Theologiae* 104; III *Contra Gentes, 40; Compendium Theologiae,* 106.

38. II *Contra Gentes,* 4.

39. *Perihermenias,* 1, 14; *De Veritate,* q2, al.

40. I Cor. 3: 1–2; *Summa Theologica,* Prologue, I, ql and q2.

41. DW I, 164—65.

42. 42. LW IV, 431; DW V, 207.

43. LW I, 297.

44. For Eckhart "act" (or *in actu*) has nothing in common with "action" but means actuality or isness. Hence Pure Act means unconditioned isness itself in contrast to the restricted isness, or "act of being," which all manifest beings have. Cf. Aquinas, *De Potentia,* ql, a2. LW IV, 350; Q 332.

46. LW II, 239; V, 49, 96; II, 22–27.

47. Q 420–21—Pf 7; LW III, 318.

48. LW III, 297.

49. LW IV, 454; DW I, 51–52.

50. LW III, 287.

51. LW I, 153.

52. LW I, 154.

53. DW II, 467: "It amazes me that Holy Scripture is so completely full and the masters say that the Scriptures are not to be taken merely as they stand. The common and gross meaning in them must be translated to a higher plane, but to do this one needs symbols. . . . There is none so simple-minded that he cannot find meaning there according to his measure; there is none so wise that when he tries to fathom them will find that they are beyond his depth and containing more to be found. All that we here on earth hear from the Scriptures and all that man may tell us about them has a primary, hidden meaning. For all that we here understand of them is unlike the primary meaning they have in God, as though they did not exist."

54. LW III, 419 ff.

55. Q 427—Pf 12; DW II, 100; DW II, 304 ff.

56. LW III, 3–4; see RS III, 1.

57. LW IV, 356.

58. LW V, 91–92.

59. LW IV, 265; v. Aquinas, *Summa Theologica* I, q28, al.

60. LW V, 45 ff; DW III, 379: "If there were in God that which we could affirm as nobler than another, it is Knowledge. For in Knowledge God is purely open to himself; in Knowledge God proceeds in himself; in Knowledge God manifests himself in all things; in Knowledge God creates all things. Were God not primal Knowledge, there would be no Trinity, there would be no creatures."

61. LW III, 7; 115–17.

62. LW I, 154.

63. LW III, 116; LW III, 44: "Each and every thing, whether produced by nature or by art, has its isness or the fact that it *is* directly from God alone."

64. DW II, 87; III, 112.

65. LW V, 39; DW II, 316.

66. See my *Book of the Poor in Spirit*, Introduction.

67. As Hans Hof, in his *Scintilla Animae* (Lund, 1952), p. 152 ff., correctly points out, there is nothing in common between Hegel's "antithetical dialectic and Eckhart's analogical dialectic," nor between Hegel's Absolute Idea and the Godhead of which Eckhart speaks. An example of trying to turn Eckhart into a "philosophical existentialist" is Joachim Kopper's *Die Metaphysik Meister Eckharts* (Saarbrücken, 1955).

For example: Evelyn Underhill, *Mysticism* (London, 1911); W. R. Inge, *The Philosophy of Plotinus* (London, 1918) and *Christian Mysticism*

(London, 1899); Rufus Jones, *The Flowering of Mysticism* (New York, 1939); Aldous Huxley, *The Perennial Philosophy* (New York, 1944); G. della Volpe, *Eckhart o della filosofia mistica* (Rome, 1952); O. Bolza, *Meister Eckhart als Mystiker* (Lübeck, 1933); R. van Marle, *De mystische leer von Meister Eckhart* (Haarlem, 1916); Carl Jung, *Psychological Types* (London, 1938); R. Otto, *West-Östliche Mystik* (Gotha, 1926).

69. E.g. Shizuteru Ueda, *Die Geburt in der Seele and der Durchbruch zur Gottheit* (Gütersloh, 1965); D. T. Suzuki, *Mysticism—Christian and Buddhist* (London, 1957); A. K. Coomaraswamy, *Hinduism and Buddhism* (New York, 1942).

70. LW II, 487.

71. LW IV, 146: "If I call God *a* Being, it would be just as erroneous as to call the sun pale or black."

72. IV *Contra Gentes*, 65; Eckhart, LW IV, 278–79.

73. DW I, 13; 199; DW III, 191; DW I, 12–13.

74. LW III, 123; II, 78, IV, 301.

75. LW I, 37; DW V, 222–23.

76. LW IV, 176; Q 432.

Chapter 2: The Reality of the Divine Self

1. LW II, 371; v. Aquinas, III *Contra Gentes*, 38.

2. LW III, 348.

3. DW I, 52 ff; LW II, 353; DW III, 173 ff; LW III, 117. The "detached and unlimited will to know" is that intellective desire or spiritual appetite innate and immediate in the human soul. Preceding all other desires, it is essentially unrestricted and remains dynamic unless aborted by a determinate interest in something less than unrestricted knowledge itself.

4. DW I, 365–66; LW III, 206: "The intellect, which possesses nothing, has the entire range of isness for its object, since it has the same isness as its object, the realm of isness." See LW II, 331; LW III, 265–66; Aquinas, I *Commentarium I Sententiarum* d19, q5, a1.

5. *adequatio intellectus et rei*. Cf. Aquinas, *De Trinitate*, q5, a3; *I Commentarium I Sententiarum* XIX, q15, a1, ad7.

6. LW IV, 263.

7. LW I, 177.

8. LW I, 178.

9. DW I, 94.

10. LW IV, 114; LW III, n. 675.

11. DW I, 365; LW II, 62.

12. DW I, 55; LW III, 21; Aquinas, *Summa Theologica* I, q16, a3. On "participative knowing" see LW III, 52.

13. LW III, 199.

14. LW II, 24.

15. Exodus 3:14; John 1:1.

16. LW II, 27. Here Eckhart is in complete agreement with Aquinas, *Summa Theologica* I, q2, al, ad 1.

17. DW I, 55. Eckhart repeatedly states this fact: v. DW I, 331, 123; Q 433—Pf 25; DW V, 204; Q 295; Pf 21, etc.

18. LW II, 25 ff.

19. DW V, 50; LW IV, 280; DW I, 69–70.

20. LW I, 156–59; LW IV, 267–68; LW V, 93.

21. LW IV, 269.

22. LW I, 158; LW IV, 267–68: "In inquiring about anything I always ask whether or not there is intellect or intellection in it. If there is not, it is clear that a thing which lacks intellect is not God or the primal source of all things, which are so clearly directed toward definite ends. If, on the other hand, it has intellect in it, I then inquire whether or not there is any being in it apart from intellect. If there is not, I have now established that it is one and unconditioned, and furthermore that it is uncreatable, primal, and so on, and hence that it is God. But if it has some being other than intellection, then it is compounded and not simply one. It is perfectly clear, therefore, that God alone *is*, in the truest sense of the word, that he is pure Intellect or Intellection, and that he alone is pure Intelligence. Therefore God alone brings things into being through Intellect, because in him alone isness is unrestricted Knowledge."

23. This "demonstration" is not set forth in any distinct article as such, but it clearly unfolds itself throughout several of his writings, particularly in the following from which the substance of the argument and our quotations (through p. 68) are taken: DW I, 34, 49 ff, 102–4, 151 ff, 249–53, 376 ff; DW II, 167, 219, 306, 323; DW III, 57, 169–79, 293; F. Jostes, *Meister Eckhart and seine Jünger, Ungedrukte Texte* (Freiburg, 1895), No. 10 (Reliable), 77; Pf 185; LW I, 502; LW III, 19–20, 24, 25, 28, 36, 43; LW IV, 115, 198–200, 265–67; LW V, 47.

24. DW I, 146.

25. LW II, 24; Pfeiffer, *Zeitschrift für deutsches Altertum* (Berlin, 1866 etc.) Bd 8 (2); v. DW III, Pred. no. 71.

26. Cf. Aquinas, *De Ente et Essentia, V; De Potentia*, q7, a3.

27. DW I, 185, 187.

28. LW III, 32; *v. In Genesis* II, n. 45.

29. DW III, 179.

30. Exodus 3 : 14.

31. LW II, 26.

32. LW II, 24; LW I, 157.

33. DW V, 43; LW I, 50. Though in agreement with Avicenna on several points, Eckhart, like Aquinas, rejects him on this question, for Avicenna claimed that God necessarily creates or is compelled by his nature to manifest certain possibilities. But Augustine had previously rejected certain Neo-Platonists on the same question. See *Avicennae Metaphysices Compendium*, trans. Cerame (Rome, 1926), p. 126 ff; Aquinas, Summa

Theologica I, q19, al, 2 and 3; I *Contra Gentes*, 80–83; *De Veritate*, q23, a4; Augustine, *Patrologia Latina* (Migne) 40, col. 30.

34. Aquinas, *Summa Theologica* I, q25, a6, ad3.

35. LW I, 220, 272.

36. DW I, 80, 185; DW III, 161. Commenting on "All things are made by Him" in St. John's Gospel, Eckhart says: "He [St. John] does not deny that there are other causes of things (finite or natural causes), but he means that the effect does not have its *isness* from any other causes, but from God alone" (LW III, 43; see RS III, 6).

37. LW IV, 264; DW I, 66—67; DW II, 94—96; LW III, 119 and n. 549; Aquinas, *Summa Theologica* I, q8, al.

38. DW III, 171—72. This does not mean that, in the causal order, God is the only cause. God is the cause of the isness of all manifest beings (v. note 36), which are in him because he is their ultimate principle and end. Yet there is subjected causality within manifestation itself insofar as individual selves are agents, for "every agent acts inasmuch as it is in act." Eckhart states that many people falsely or crudely think that since all creatures are dependent on the Principle, or God, for their own isness, they are therefore without causal power of their own. Or they mistakenly think that God's all-possibility implies two *equal* acts of causality, God and creatures. The first conclusion eliminates free will; the second is pantheistic. But Eckhart, with Aquinas, rejects both: v. LW IV, 29—31; Aquinas, *De Potentia*, q2, al. See also LW III, 43.

39. Referred to as *accidie*, which Aquinas says "is a contraction of the mind" (XI *de Malo*, 3, ad4); and "every sin happens because of some lack of knowledge" (IV *Contra Gentes*, 70).

40. LW III, 43—44, 78; LW II, 38 ff, 336 ff.

41. In this sense "what God knows he knows entirely within himself. Therefore God does not directly know us insofar as we are in sin [or willful contracted awareness, the primary sin]. Hence God knows us in the same measure as we are in him, that is, to the extent that we are without sin [i.e. without that from which wrong decisions and wrong actions are fostered]." (DW I, 78; see RS IX, 28).

42. DW I, 53, 54, 99: "God issues everything forth alike, and as flowing from God all things are equivalent in him; angels, man, and all creatures flow from God alike in their first issuing forth. To consider things in their primal flowing out is to consider them all alike. . . . A flea considered as it is in God is nobler in God than the highest angel in itself. All things are the same in God and are God himself."

43. Jostes, *Eckhart and seine Jünger*, No. 10.

44. *Summa Theologica* I, q85, a2; *De coelesti Hierarchia*, 2, 5.

45. LW IV, 192. This theme of a hierarchical universe of superiors and inferiors is emphasized throughout: v. LW III, 18, n. 531; LW IV, 143, 100, 188; LW I, 154, 229; LW II, 360, etc.

46. LW II, 364.

47. LW II, 120; LW III, 189—90: "It should be understood that in

creating all things God instructs and enjoins, advises and commands them
. . . to participate in him and conform themselves to him, to turn and hurry
back to him as the primal source of their entire isness, in accord with the
words of Ecclesiastes (1 : 7): 'Unto the place from whence the rivers come,
thither they return again.' . . . Moreover, the Principle and the end, the
good and the end, are identical. Therefore, just as everything created follows and pursues its end, so likewise it follows and returns to its Principle."

48. DW I, 386; cf. DW I, 233.

49. LW II, 37.

50. LW II, 378. Even "the damned have a natural desire for being, which
they have immediately from God, and consequently for God himself." (LW
III, 189; cf. DW I, 105).

51. DW I, 239.

52. LW V, 117.

53. DW III, 265: "God's Godhead consists in the full communication of
himself to whatever is receptive of him; were he not to communicate himself he would not be God."

54. DW I, 377.

55. LW IV, 377; v. DW III, 39; LW V, 197.

56. Q 415—Pf 3.

57. LW III, 321.

58. DW I, 40.

59. *De Veritate,* q4, a2.

60. LW I, 329.

61. *Posterior Analytics,* 100b-17.

62. Ibid., 99b-25.

63. LW V, 45; LW III, 27.

64. Aquinas, *Summa Theologica* I, q17, a2 and 3.

65. LW IV, 240, 454.

66. Speaking of the "possible intellect" as distinguished from the "active
intellect' and the "passive intellect," Eckhart says that "before this is begun
by the intellect and completed by God [that is, 'the intellect becoming passive so that God himself may undertake the work of the active intellect']
the intellect has a knowledge of it, a possible understanding of all it may
know and as it were fully actualized. This is the meaning of the "possible
intellect" [*mügeliche vernunft*], but it is greatly neglected and so nothing
comes of it" (Pf 14; see entire discourse). Unfortunately certain scholars
have translated *mügeliche vernunft* as "potential intellect," thus distorting
Eckhart's meaning (v. LW III, 585) and also Aquinas's, which he follows.
(*v. Summa Theologica* I, q79, a2 and 7.)

67. DW II, 305.

68. LW IV, 325.

69. DW III, 485 ff. This discourse on Martha and Mary clarifies
Eckhart's teaching on the *vita activa* and the *vita contemplativa.* These complementary ways are inseparable, the former resulting directly from the lat-

ter, and yet neither has anything in common with the life of the "activist" who is "engrossed *in* things rather than *in* God." See also Quint's note 23 on p. 495 and RS III, 12.

70. Ibid. 489; v. DW II, 165; DW V, 368; LW IV, 287.

71. DW I, 122.

PART II: THE DOCTRINE
Chapter 1: God and the Human Self

1. LW III, 34; DW I, 135 (v. note 2); also v. LW III, 10, 16, 17; DW III, 179, 174, etc.

2. The actual reality of God is not here in question, for in pure metaphysical knowledge it is already known. This question was dealt with, according to Eckhart, when we considered the human self in its relative unregenerate condition in Ch. 2 of Part I.

3. DW II, 420; LW III, 194 ff. See also Eckhart's *Von dem Schauen Gottes*, W. Preger, *Geschichte der deutschen Mystik im Mittelalter* (1874), I, p. 484 ff. Discussions with Prof. Quint in 1958 assured me that this discourse is reliably attributable to Eckhart.

4. LW III, 200.

5. LW I, 187; LW IV, 263; DW III, 226.

6. LW III, 27.

7. LW III, 61: *Principium semper afficit principiatum, sed principiatum nullo sui afficit suum principium.*

8. DW III, 150.

9. LW II, 27; LW III, 181; LW IV, 9; DW III, 339; DW I, 358.

10. See LW III, 135—39.

11. LW III, 5 ff. As Aquinas also makes clear: *Summa Theologica* I, q33, al.

12. LW III, 17.

13. LW I, 50; v. LW I, 189, where Eckhart speaks "against those who say that God creates and produces things from natural necessity."

14. *esse in se.*

15. *ens.*

16. LW I, 176—77; LW III, 174; v. Aquinas, *Summa Theologica* I—II, q4, a5, ad2. See also DW V, 115; LW III, 27. Aquinas: "Within God there is no real distinction of his absolute *esse*, which is his nature [*intellectus*], supremely single and simple, but only of relations within him" (*Summa Theologica* I, q78, a3; q28, al, ad4).

17. P. Strauch, *Paradisus anime intelligentis* in *Deutsche Texte des Mittelalters*, xxx (Berlin, 1919) (Q 272-73). This distinction is not real but only intellectual because what is here involved is not an acknowledgment of two diverse transcendent principles but simply a transposition of considering the one unique Principle as ultimate, indistinct Subject in itself. Eckhart makes clear that the "isness which God is," or "the unrestricted

isness of Divine Knowledge itself" is identically his Godhead (LW IV, 263 ff).

18. LW I, 197: *Creatio autem est collatio esse.* Cf. LW I, 160; III, 47.

19. LW I, 159 ff, 39; LW IV, 208.

20. DW I, 358; LW II, 27; LW III, 181; LW IV, 9, 60, 79, 206; a metaphysical truth constantly emphasized by Eckhart.

21. LW III, 41 ff.

22. LW I, 157–60, 376; LW III, 6.

23. LW III, 37.

24. Out of *nihilum antecedens*, not out of *nihilum absolutism.* Cf. Aquinas, *De Potentia*, q3, a4.

25. DW II, 468–69.

26. LW III, 304; DW V, 30; LW II, 43; LW III, 16.

27. "Where there is intellect, which is spiritual [i.e. noncorporeal and nonmaterial], there is personality, for personality means completeness, and infinite personality is pure Intellect or pure Spirit" (LW II, 487; v. LW III, 284 ff). See Aquinas: *Commentarium I Sententiarum xxiii,* q1, a2, ad4.

28. LW II, 386.

29. LW I, 212 ff.

30. One might also add the type of opposition posed between "religion" vs. "science," or "theology" vs. "philosophy." The recognition of these as distinctions only and not as separations or opposites is the recognition of a supreme Principle in which they have their common source.

31. LW IV, 270.

32. LW III, 162–63.

33. LW III, 39.

34. *ens.*

35. *esse.*

36. LW III, 43, 7–8; DW I, 56; LW IV, 22.

37. DW I, 270–71; cf. DW V, 60 and LW III, 19.

38. *Summa Theologica* I, q13, a7, q28, a1; LW II, 45.

39. Aquinas also reminds us that infinite *esse (in se)* transcends real distinctions in that each divine perfection, known to us analogously by the distinct perfection of creatures, is, *in Deo,* the divine essence itself *(Summa Theologica* I, q4, a2, q12, a4, ad1).

40. DW I, 123; v. DW I, 55, 330; DW II, 303–4; Q 433—Pf 25, etc.

41. LW I, 562.

42. DW I, 146; DW I 330: "Whatever one says that God is, he is not—not this, not that; what one does not say of him, he is rather than what one says he is."

43. What is here involved is simply the consideration of God in himself in his unmanifested and undifferentiated Godhead and the consideration of God-as-other and for us, inasmuch as we are in manifestation. See LW II, 421.

44. LW I, 171 ff.

45. DW I, 287 ff; Aquinas, II *Contra Gentes*, 56, 57; *Summa Theologica* I, q74, al, q84, a2.

46. DW I, 55; LW III, 21, 158; Aquinas, *Summa Theologica* I, q5, a2, q16, a3, q85, a2, ad1. We are not here concerned with the inorganic which does not directly pertain to the human integrality, nor should it be inferred that the human being is other than one integral structure; thus it is specifically determined as intellect-body, that is, a "rational being" (LW IV, 200; LW III, 10 ff).

47. DW III, 384, 161, cf. Pf 107.

48. LW IV, 194.

49. Q 273—Pf 180–81—Strauch, no. 26.

50. LW I, 637.

51. LW II, 478.

52. DW III, 225; DW I, 69.

53. See LW I, 319; II, 20, 44, 58, 67; III, 43, 89; DW I, 147, 319.

54. *ens in se, per se.*

55. Aquinas, *De Veritate*, q 1, a3.

56. DW I, 146; v. LW I, 176; LW II, *In Sapientiae*, n. 260.

57. LW III, 28, 201.

58. That a very remarkable mystical movement developed throughout the Rhineland after the death of Eckhart is undoubtedly true. Tauler, Suso, Ruysbroeck, and their immediate disciples were directly and greatly influenced by Eckhart. But if they refrained from teaching publicly the "pure metaphysics" which their master taught, it was because of the decline in intellectuality in the schools and the climate of "caution" created by the condemnation of some statements attributed to Eckhart in the famous Bull *In Agro Dominico*, in 1329. See my *Book of the Poor in Spirit—A Guide to the Rhineland Mystics*, Introduction.

59. LW III, 406.

60. Jostes, No. 34; v. DW III, 196.

61. LW II, 76–77; LW III, 175; LW I, 44.

62. LW II, 501.

63. DW I, 132; LW II, 263.

64. Q 360—Pf 71 ff ; v. A. Spamer, *Texte aus der deutschen Mystik des 14 und 15 Jahrhunderts* (Jena: 1912), B.I.

65. Q 430—Pf 15; Q 433—Pf 25; Q 360—Pf 71.

66. LW II, 50; v. LW I, 418.

67. *Von dem Schauen Gottes*, 485; LW II, 487.

68. LW III, 443.

69. DW I, 363.

70. LW II, 77; DW I, 361 (v. note 4), 363; LW III, 175: *Unde deus non est pars aliqua universi, sed aliquid extra aut potium prius et superius universo. Et propter hoc ipsi nulla privatio aut negatio convenit, sed propria est sibi, et sibi soli, negatio negationes, quae est medulla et apex purissimae affirmationis.*

71. LW III, 167, 55, 36; DW I : 52; Aquinas, *Summa Theologica* 1, q41, a5.

1. Q 433—Pf 25.

2. LW III, 18; Pf 105; v. Aquinas, *De Potentia,* q8, a1. Moreover, the human intellect knows itself, not directly, but only through its activities (*Summa Theologica* I, q87, a1).

3. LW III, 8—9; v. Aquinas, *De Potentia,* q3, a1; *Compendium Theologiae,* 41.

4. That is, *in liner vermügenheit.* When Eckhart speaks of "divine power" or "all-mighty" he means "all-possibility"; v. LW II, 38.

5. DW I, 15-19.

6. Q 431—Pf 15.

7. LW III, 29-32.

8. DW I, 92-3.

9. This is why Aquinas insists on the term "principle" in this consideration, "since 'cause' is a far narrower term than 'principle' we should not presume to employ it, especially as 'principle' . . . signifies God or origin in God" *(Contra Errores Graecorum,* 1). *Cause* is a positive, ontological source on which an individual reality depends; *principle* is that from which anything or any manifestation originates and terminates in any way whatsoever.

10. DW II, 11; LW III, 133.

11. LW I, 156 ff.

12. Cajetan, *Commentarium In Summa* I, xxxv—1.

13. DW I, 56-57; LW II, 24-26.

14. DW III, 387.

15. LW IV, 28; cf. LW IV, 26, 72, 91; LW III, n. 481. See Alanus de Insulis, *Regulae Theologicae* IX, P L 210, 628: *Quidquid est in deo, dens est.*

16. DW I, 50; v. LW III, 134; LW IV, 26.

17. Pf 533; v. DW II, 264.

18. LW III, 18.

19. DW I, 210; DW I, 78: "God's eye is turned only toward himself. What he sees he sees wholly within himself." See RS IX, 19. Obviously "eye" and "seeing" are to be understood symbolically as meaning "intellect" and "knowing" (note previous sentence on p. 78 of DW I), a symbolism that is universally acknowledged, not only in the Old and New Testaments, but by Upanishadic authors and even by Plato, particularly in his famous allegory of the cave.

20. LW III, 40-41: "If you wish to know whether all your inner and outer activity is divine or not, and whether it is the operation of God within you and is done by him, then consider if the direct end of your intention is wholly God and as it were in God. If it is, the action is divine because the principle and the end are identical, namely God" (Cf. RS IX, 56).

21. Luke 14 : 10.

22. Eph. 4 : 6.

23. DW I, 359, 366.

24. DW II, 56.

25. Rom. 13: 11-14.

26. LW IV, 437–38.

27. DW III, 265.

28. DW II, 252–53; LW III, 13, 23; LW IV, 269: "Identity is unity."

29. LW IV, 94. Also Q 436: "Know that to find him [God] is not in your power but in his." DW III, 425–26: "The soul makes headway and transcends itself, never by its own act or by its own light, but solely by God's act and the light that he has given it." LW IV, 94: "This grace is in the very isness of the soul and disposes it to one actuality, one life, one working within God."

30. LW III, 245: *Plenitudo temporis est, ubi nullum tempos est.* DW I, 177: "The fullness of time is when there is no more time. He who in time has his intellect established in eternity and in whom all temporality is as dead, in him is 'the fullness of time.'" DW I, 423: "Time is fulfilled when it is ended, that is, in eternity. Time ends when there is no before and after, when all that *is* is present and when all that ever was and shall be is directly known in principle."

31. DW I, 157–58.

32. Psalms 61 : 62 (A.V. 62 : 11).

33. DW II, 98.

34. LW IV, 8.

35. LW III, 24–25: "For the Logos is certainly *in* the primal Intellect, is that Intellect properly speaking; and it is 'with God', that is to say in every intellectual being that is his image or God's offspring."

36. DW III, 142; LW III, 199; RS IX, 59.

37. DW I, 143.

38. DW II, 95; LW IV, 411.

39. LW III, 41.

40. Here Eckhart rejects the doctrine of certain medieval Islamic masters who claimed that God created a First Intelligence who then proceeded to create a second intelligence, etc.

41. LW IV, 7; Q 271; Aquinas, *De Divinis Nominibus,* 2, 2.

42. LW IV, 14.

43. LW IV, 59–60.

44. DW III, 215.

45. DW I, 173.

46. LW IV, 93.

47. LW IV, 114–15, 137–38.

48. "Just as", "as it were"—"I always have in mind this little word *quasi,* which means *gleichwie (als)* . . . it is this that I have considered uppermost in all my discourses" (Q 199; cf. DW I, 154; LW II, 233). That is, from the standpoint of our just human mode of knowledge, the principial standpoint is always an "as it were," *quasi* or *gleichwie* state of consideration, implying inverse analogy, and therefore never to be confused with any individualized mode or mode of ontological "substantiality."

49. DW II, 419; v. DW III, 21–26.

50. The distinction implied in the ground *of* the soul is simply the distinction of the soul's isness from its essence and operations that are wholly dependent upon the former and without which they would not be. See LW IV, 266—67; Aquinas, *Commentarium* I *Sententiarum*, viii, q5, a2.

51. This in no way contradicts the Incarnation which, for the seeking intellect, is a consideration of God's act from the standpoint of manifestation (v. DW *I, Predigt.* No. 5b). Christ the God-Man, the Word-made-flesh, is actualized in time and history by the all-possibility of God, who effects a unique union whereby human nature substantially assumes the Person of the Word. But this unique union is neither accidental nor essential, but a hypostatic and personal union: the human and divine essences are united not in one nature but in one Person. Though essence and person are not really distinct in God, they are according to our human way of apprehension, which means that in the Incarnation the essence of God does not become the essence of individuality. The union in the Incarnation is only in Person, meaning that there are two essences, or natures, in one complete isness (LW III, 36 ff; DW I, 86—87; v. Augustine, *De Unitate Trinitatis*, 15; Aquinas, *De unione Verbi Incarnati, 1*).

52. DW III, 215.

53. DW II, 306.

54. DW I, 364—65.

55. DW I, 284.

56. LW V, 61.

57. That is, an intellect without a body, without ever having a body, an incorporeal substance, or an "angel." See Aquinas, *De Veritate*, q 10, a6.

58. LW IV, 436.

59. DW I, 368—69; v. RS IV, 7 and III, 10.

60. LW IV, 264, 278; LW II, 155. This is the case with every series, whether of time, space, number, relations, or comparatives. See DW I, 148; LW IV, 112; LW II, 366—67; etc.

61. LW IV, 58.

62. DW I, 177.

63. John 1 : 1.

64. DW I, 109—10; RS IX, 39.

65. That is, *in patria, in divinis,* in Divine Knowledge, as Eckhart notes, but never *in via*. Moreover, Eckhart understands "the fullness of time" (v. note 30) metaphysically as "beyond time": "God sends his Son in the fullness of time, that is, to the soul when it has transcended time, when the soul is free from time and place" (DW I, 74).

66. DW I, 72—73; v. LW IV, 356. This statement, and others like it that are principial in context, transcends Augustine's doctrine of eternal and divine ideas which all require inversion because there is no diversity in God. Eckhart will at times speak in reference to the doctrine of divine ideas, but this is nothing more than a concession to knowledge *in via*. The doctrine of exemplarism certainly points most nobly to principial knowledge but it is still restricted by being grounded in a subtle form of indi-

vidualization which, of course, is absent in the principial mode, constituted as it is in the identity of all-possibility with all-inclusive, indistinguishable God.

67. LW I, 187.

68. LW III, 156; LW IV, 429.

69. Q 421–22—Pf 8; Pf 253; DW I, 87; Pf 237; LW II, 476; for as Aquinas
notes: "the truth of all things is infinitely greater in the Word than in created reality" *(De Veritate,* q4, a6).

70. DW I, 312–17.

71. John 15 : 15.

72. DW V, 415 ff., the Tractate *Von Abgescheidenheit.* See also Augustine,
De Trinitate, XII, 4.

73. DW II, 84. Eckhart prefaces these words by saying: "I am amazed
how some priests, even those with pretensions to eminence and learning,
let themselves be misled by these words ["All I have heard from my Father
I have made known to you"] and understand them to mean that God com-
municates to us only the basic mimimum requisite for our happiness. That
is not what I understand and that surely is not the truth." In other words,
the communicated truth lies in the word *all,* i.e. the totality of Divine
Knowledge or Godhead. See RS IX, 9.

74. RS IV, 1.

75. LW V, 92; Q 437.

76. Cf. Aquinas, *De Veritate,* q4, a6.

77. DW I, 329; LW III, 353.

78. LW III, 64; LW II, 38.

79. LW IV, 270.

80. LW IV, 263–64.

81. DW II, 82.

82. DW II, 211; DW I, 332; Pf 79; see RS IX, 3 and M. H. Laurent,
Autor du procès de Maître Eckhart, Divus Thomas (Piacenza, 1936) pp. 344-
46.

83. DW V, 31–43; LW IV, 276.

84. DW II, 416–20.

85. *Leben* here means "Principle."

86. DW III, 315–17.

87. DW III, 321-24.

88. The dilemma of Cartesian and most modern philosophy.

89. DW II, 214. That is, the insisting on the priority of knowledge in
terms of individuality or mentalism and the ignoring of the true priority
of principial knowledge in terms of the All-inclusive.

90. DW II, 53–54, 211; Pf 480; C. Greith, *Die deutsche Mystik im Pre-
digerorden* (Freiburg, 1861), p. 102.

91. DW I, 333; v. note on *synderesis* by Quint on p. 334. Cf. Aquinas,
Summa Theologica I, q76, a12.

92. DW I, 348.

93. DW I, 197; LW III, 417; v. RS IV, 6.

94. DW II, 88.

95. DW I, 198; v. RS IX, 8.

96. DW I, 220.

97. DW III, 320-21.

98. DW II, 237.

99. DW I, 171—72; v. V, 269.

100. DW I, 161; v. 288; LW II, 364; Aquinas, *Summa Theologica* I, q8, al, ad2.

101. LW IV, 22; Pf 253; Strauch no. 26—Pf 180—81; DW III, 447; DW II, 68.

102. DW III, 187.

Chapter 3: The Primal Distinction

1. LW III, 468.

2. LW II, 419.

3. LW I, 461.

4. LW III, 304. See Part II, Ch. 1, note 26.

5. LW IV, 270.

6. LW III, 43; LW II, 144.

7. LW III, 190; v. LW III, 5 ff.

8. LW II, 50, 27 ff.

9. LW IV, 267-68.

10. LW IV, 266-67.

11. LW II, 24; LW I, 159 and note 1; v. RS III, 11.

12. DW III, 119.

13. LW III, 18, 192; Aquinas, *Summa Theologica* I, a47, a2 and 3; I—II, q93, a3.

14. LW I, 473; Aquinas, *Summa Theologica* II—II, q52, a3.

15. LW III, 392.

16. LW III, 36.

17. DW I, 199.

18. LW IV, 269.

19. LW IV, 10.

20. DW V, 115.

21. DW V, 202.

22. Gal. 3 : 20.

23. LW IV, 264 ff. We should remember that the designation *esse* (isness or act of being) did not come into its full significance until Aquinas expounded it in its metaphysical depth.

24. DW II, 86—87.

25. LW II, 64—65; IV, 99; I, 69; v. RS I, 15.

26. LW IV, 9-10.

27. DW II, 101; v. V, 40.

28. LW I, 518.

29. LW IV, 267.

30. LW I, 45. Cf. RS IX, *14: Humilis homo et deus non sent duo,* etc.

31. Essentially so because "monotheism" as expounded in formal theology is wholly dependent on negative theology, as previously explained.

32. *Summa Theologica* III, a73, a2; I, qll, al, qll, a3, q3, a7, *Compendium Theologiae* 24.

33. LW II, 342; RS II, 3. Efficacious or efficient cause, fully dependent on the notion of God as *Ipsum esse,* is that by which its *act* produces and imparts something of itself to that of the effect. It is essentially the pre-eminent cause in Christian metaphysics and is not found among the four causes of Aristotle. See Aquinas, *In Metaphysica V,* lect. 1, n. 751.

34. LW III, 199; Augustine, *De moribus Ecclesiae,* II, 2, 2.

35. LW IV, 191-92.

36. LW I, 154; Aquinas, III *Contra Gentes, 47.*

37. LW IV, 95.

38. DW V, 115.

39. LW III, 175.

40. LW I, 397.

41. LW IV, 9, 98-99, 299, 321, 368.

42. DW I, 380-81.

43. DW I, 381-82.

44. LW III, 199.

45. LW III, 6-7.

46. LW IV, 279; v. LW II, 123.

47. LW II, 37; Aquinas: *"Esse* [isness] itself is the most perfect reality. Therefore *esse is* the actuality of all beings—through *essentia*—even of forms [as contained potentially in essence]" *(Summa Theologica* I, q4, al, ad3).

48. *Scotus Erigena, De Divisione Naturae* I and III.

49. LW IV, 279; LW III, 99; LW I, 47.

50. DW I, 316; Pf 57; v. *In Genesis* II, n. 271.

51. DW II, 279.

52. LW II, 447.

53. "Pure intellects," that is, "pure intellectual structures without corporeality," or "angelic beings," whose composite structure is simply intellect and isness, are never to be confused with intellective souls, which in order to be, require having or having had a body to animate. Nor are they to be confused with Pure Intellect, or God, who is noncomposite in every respect. See LW III, 413; Aquinas, *Summa Theologica* I, q75, a7, ad3.

54. DW II, 78.

55. Pf 250—Greith, p. 99 ff.

56. DW II, 189. This, of course, is the only way a human being can be regarded by a computer or by mere logical analysis disoriented from being and isness, inasmuch as "human personality" is the subsistence proper to an intellectual being and which makes that person to be uncommunicated or unshared by the being of another.

57. Q 439—Pf 30.
58. LW IV, 279; LW III, 174; LW II, 42; Pf 133.
59. LW II, 25.
60. LW I, 47.
61. DW III, 365—66.
62. LW I, 162-64.
63. LW I, 190.
64. DW II, 261—62.
65. LW III, 9.
66. LW III, 181.
67. RS III, 8.
68. See Denifle, p. 460.
69. DW V, 418; v. Isadorus, *Sententiae*, I, 8.
70. Quoted by Eckhart in his *Von Abgescheidenheit*, DW V, 417; Augustine, *De Trinitate*, 26.
71. LW I, 50—51.
72. Psalms 61:12.
73. LW III, 179.
74. DW I, 34; v. also DW I, 166, 171; LW IV, 160.
75. DW V, 60.
76. LW III, n. 429.
77. Gen. 1:2.
78. See Eckhart's commentary on this theme: LW I, 218—29.
79. Ibid; v. also LW III, 421.
80. LW I, 462; DW II, 94; DW V, 203.

Chapter 4: The Inversion

1. Stressing this point Eckhart once said: "If anyone has understood this sermon, I wish him well. If no one had been here I should have had to speak it to this almsbox" (Q 273—Pf 181—Strauch, No. 26). Thus implying that detached intellection, being constituted wholly in Divine Knowledge, is neither dependent on its being understood by anyone nor subject to popularization, but is to be perennially expounded by those who do—inwardly for their own understanding and fulfillment, outwardly for the diffusion of the doctrine to those capable of receiving it.
2. DW V, 288; Aquinas, *Summa Theologica* I, q1, al, ad2.
3. Aquinas, *Summa Theologica* I—II, q109, al, ad 1—from St. Ambrose's gloss on I Cor. 12:3.
4. LW V, 83; DW II, 317.
5. LW III, 436.
6. DW I, 288—89.
7. DW I, 73; DW II, 492, 66.
8. *Summa Theologica* I, q54, al.
9. DW III, 293; LW III, 175—76.
10. See Aquinas, *De Veritate*, q2, a3, ad13. To drive this point home it

is worth quoting one of Eckhart's more elliptic and provocative statements, humorously designed to shock one out of satisfaction in the supposed priority of formal, rational knowledge: "If I say God is good, it is not true; I am good, God is not good. I say further: I am better than God, for what is good can become better; what is better can become best. But God is not good; hence he cannot be better and since he cannot be better, he cannot be best. For God transcends all three: good, better, and best, inasmuch as he transcends all comparatives [and every series]" (DW III, 441; v. DW I, 148; LW IV, 31). It was with statements like this that Eckhart's ecclesiastical censors in Cologne and Avignon could not cope. See RS IX, 54 and Denzinger, 229.

11. LW I, 162—64; LW III, 83.

12. DW I, 69-70.13.

DW III, 384; DW II, 81: "To abandon all things here in restricted reality, in that they are changeable, is to regain them in God where they are truly real [and not differentiated). Everything that is here dead or naught is life and aught there, and all that is here material is there in God spirit and is God." See RS IX, 13.

14. DW I, 363–64; v. Aquinas, *Quodlibet X*, ql. al, ad3; *Commentarium I Sententiarum xxiv*, ql, a3, adl.

15. LW III, 274; v. DW I, 52: "What *here* is distant is *there* [in God) immediate, for there all is present [without otherness). What occurs on the first day and the last day is there present."

16. DW II, 255—5.6; LW IV, 314; DW II, 468.

17. DW II, 473; v. DW I, 212.

18. LW II, 58—60.

19. Pf 182; v. LW III, 390.

20. LW IV, 111.

21. DW II, 470; LW IV, 111; 367; 269 and note 1; DW I, 297.

22. DW I, 385—86: RS IX, 1: *radix similitudinis est unum ipsum*. See DWV, 30.

23. *In Genesis II*, n. 113.

24. Aquinas, *Summa Theologica* I, q14, a4; Aristotle, *De Anima* III, 8, 431b, 21.

25. DW I, 48—49

26. DW I, 153; *v. In Genesis* II, n. 83; LW IV, 370.

27. DW I, 129.

28. DW I, 314-15.

29. DW III, 229.

30. DW I, 122.

31. LW V, 49; LW IV, 111 ff.

32. LW V, 40.

33. DW I, 150; v. 129.

34. In other words, "All that which is except Knowledge-in-itself" is determinate and as it were from without the Godhead and therefore distinctive. "Such determinations as the intellect makes of God are gotten of

its own understanding. . . . In Knowledge-in-itself, however, God remains beyond all such determinations because he is unconditioned and without activity in his hidden stillness. He is without the determinations applied to him" (DW III, 381–82).

35. LW IV, 270.

36. LW V, 45; v. LW III, 61.

37. LW IV, 112.

38. LW III, 32; LW I, 189, 195; LW III, 27, 32.

39. LW V, 45.

40. DW III, 229.

41. DW III, 177.

42. DW III, 171.

43. Q 425—Pf 10–11; DW III, 320.

44. DW II, 24-25. We have used the term "knowledge" for *Warheit*, since in the context it is knowledge *in se* that is meant in the scriptural passage and thus it should not be confused with "truth" the transcendental.

45. Q 430—Pf 15.

46. Q 433—Pf 25.

47. DW I, 136.

48. Aquinas, *Summa Theologica* I, q8, al, ad2.

49. This theme is frequently stated by Eckhart and is quoted in the Bull. See Denifle II, p. 636 ff. no. 23; Q 453; Otto Karrer, *Meister Eckhart* (Munich, 1926), p. 273 ff. The Bull of John XXII *In Agro Dominico)* of March 27, 1329, is also in *Denziger*, 1948, pp. 227–29; J. M. Clark, *Meister Eckhart* p. 253 ff. and Q 449 ff.

50. Psalms 101:28 (A.V. 102:27).

51. I Cor. 6:17.

52. LW IV, 269.

53. An example used frequently by Eckhart in both the German and Latin works.

54. John 1:5.

55. LW III, 13–19.

56. DW I, 56–57.

57. DW I, 56. See RS IX, 1 and IX, 50.

58. LW III, 519–20.

59. DW II, 33.

60. LW III, 484.

61. We must not forget that it is only in relation to our own individual apprehension that isness and essence constitute two complementary aspects of the ultimate Principle. Insofar as it can be said that God manifests himself, it is the aspect analogous to essence; insofar as it can be said that he is unmanifested, it is the aspect analogous to pure isness; and the latter, of course, answers more profoundly than the former to God in his immutable reality and unfathomable intelligence.

62. LW I, 593.

63. LW I, 529.

64. DW III, 148.

65. LW II, 466.

66. The word *schmeckt (smacket)* means "knows" in this context—"tastes," of course, not being strictly applicable.

67. Q 271–72; Pf 179–80—Strauch, No. 26.

68. LW III, 63; RS III, 5; DW III, 148; LW V, 47.

69. DW II, 469; DW III, 97; DW II, 97.

70. LW I, 194–95; v. LW V, 37, 40; Aquinas, *Summa Theologica* I, 19, a4, ad2. Eckhart's statement here does not contradict what he says in note 13, ch. 1, Part II, for God's perfect freedom is grounded in the all-inclusive Knowledge that he is.

71. *Non posse aliter se habere.*

72. *Non posse sic non se habere.* See LW I, 156–58; LW II, 37; LW III, 278–79; Aquinas, *Metaphysica* IX, 9.

73. LW II, 40 ff. See his entire commentary on *Omnipotens nomen eius* of Exodus 15:3.

74. LW III, 133; LW II, 61.

75. Aquinas, *De Trinitate*, q4, a 1: *quia divisio non requirit utrumque condivisorum esse, cum divisio sit per affirmationem et negationem.*

76. *Von dem Schauen Gottes*, p. 484 ff. See DW I, 363: "He is One and negates all otherness, for apart from God is nothing. All creatures are in God and in his Godhead, and that means plenitude [*vüllede*]:"

77. LW III, 174; LW IV, 10.

78. LW III, 175; LW V, 48; LW II, 77.

79. See Part II, Ch. 1, note 37.

80. LW II, 477.

81. DW II, 376; *v. Von dem Schauen Gottes*, p. 484.82.

82. DW III, 143–44: "God's kingdom is God's Self in all its fullness (that is, as the All-inclusive and All-possibility). God's kingdom is no little thing: consider all the worlds that God could create, that is still not God's kingdom. The soul conscious of God's fullness and aware of how near God's kingdom really is requires no sermon or instruction; that soul is instructed by that awareness and affirmed by eternal life."

83. DW I, 51.

Chapter 5: The Veils of God

1. LW III, 422.

2. LW IV, 352.

3. LW II, 514; DW V, 41. As with other essential themes, "the veils of God" is central in Eckhart's teaching, though here also he refrains from formulating it in one particular treatise—unless it is one of those forever lost; rather it is drawn upon throughout his commentaries.

4. DW I, 56.

5. LW IV, 114; DW V, 431.

6. LW I, 512.

7. LW IV, 189; LW III, 72.

8. LW I, 522.

9. DW I, 250.

10. Eckhart on occasion includes "memory" along with reason and will as faculties of the human soul (v. LW IV, 6), thus following Augustine *(De Trinitate,* X, 12, 19). But these faculties "are not operative in the ground of the soul," though the unlimited desire to know is there in its dynamic root, and these faculties are known only through their differing activities. Cf. Aquinas, *Summa Theologica* I, q87, al.

11. LW III, 433; LW III, 26. That is, principles e.g. "being is being," "causality," etc. See also Aquinas, *Summa Theologica* I, q88, a3, ad1.

12. LW III, 27.

13. DW I, 151.

14. DW I, 249.

15. LW IV, 125; LW III, 205—6; DW I, 105: "Even those who are in eternal pain in hell would not want to lose their lives, neither the fiends nor fragmented souls, since their life [in this case, isness] is so noble and issues forth directly from God."

16. DW I, 364. Considering sight as but one of the sense faculties: "The intellective soul also has a power in the eye, by reason of which the eye is so weak and delicate that it does not apprehend things in their true simplicity as they are in themselves. They must first be sifted and refined in the air and in the light. This is because the eye has the intellect to direct it" (DW I, 151; v. Pf 132 and RS I, 4).

17. DW V, 419; DW I, 231, also note 4; DW III, 445; LW IV, 65.

18. See Aquinas, *Summa Theologica* I, q16, a2.

19. LW IV, 407.

20. DW I, 151.

21. The "higher intellect" being direct insight or immediate intellectual knowledge in the ground of the soul. See DW I, 182, 32; LW III, n. 318; v. note 7. Also v. Aquinas, *Summa Theologica* I, q85, al.

22. DW V, 202; see DW I, 144—45; LW II, 97—98; *In Johannem* n. 609.

23. LW IV, 280. Eckhart quoting from Augustine, *De Trinitate* XIV, 12.

24. LW IV, 431.

25. See also Aquinas, *Summa Theologica* I, q85, al.

26. Rom. 11:36.

27. DW I, 182—84.

28. DW I, 163; v. Aquinas, *Summa Theologica* I, q77, a8; I—II, q67, al, ad 3.

29. LW IV, 202; Aquinas, *De Veritate,* q13, a2.

30. DW I, 150; v. LW V, 40, 42, 43.

31. That is, by the *act* [isness] of God, as Eckhart has previously explained, "inasmuch as potentiality as such can never by itself attain to actuality" (LW IV, 382).

32. LW III, 24.

33. LW IV, 368; DW I, 377: "The most suitable good that God ever communicated to man was to become man himself." DW I, 86–87: "God not only became man, he assumed human nature. . . . (Christ) was a messenger from God to us, bringing us our blessedness." Obviously God simply *is*, never *becomes* anything, "there being no becoming *in* God," but according to our human intellection "the divine became human while remaining divine." See LW III, 381.

34. LW IV, 365. Eckhart warns against false understandings re: the Body of Christ—v. LW IV, 43.

35. DW I, 66, 62; LW III, 52; DW II, 96; LW III, 10; v. Aristotle, *Metaphysics* I, 980b.

36. DW I, 364–65.

37. DW V, 419.

38. DW I, 105–6.

39. DW I, 80.

40. LW III, 474.

41. DW I, 288–90.

42. Q 272—Pf 180—Strauch, No. 26.

43. DW I, 292, 249.

44. LW IV, 419.

45. LW IV, 115.

46. DW I, 364–65; LW II, 62; cf. *In Genesis* II, n. 113.

47. LW III, 52; v. Aquinas, *De Trinitate*, q5, a3; *Commentarium* I *Sententiarum* xix, q1, a7.

48. This is particularly true in the abstract sciences, such as mathematics, as Eckhart frequently notes.

49. LW IV, 341.

50. LW III, 125.

51. This term "ideal world" (LW III, 331) is not to be confused with Augustine's "intelligible realm" or "world of eternal ideas," since his "ideas" are possibilities in the divine essence that pertain to structureless manifestation, in spite of the individualized and overimaginative expressions in which he, like many neo-Platonists and Plato himself, frequently clothed his thought.

52. LW IV, 382–83.

53. DW I, 155–56.

54. I Cor. 11: 6–7.

55. DW I, 184; v. LW III, 72. This analogy of intellectual function is not to be understood as an antiwoman tendency in Eckhart, for elsewhere he says: "When God created man, he created woman from the side of man in order that she should be equal to him in nature." Moreover, "In the Godhead [though not here in manifestation] man and woman, father and mother are the same" (DW I, 106–7; LW III, 165).

56. LW IV, 197.

57. LW III, 17.

58. LW III, 11.

59. DW V, 430.

60. DW II, 264.

61. LW II, 429.

62. LW IV, 278.

63. DW III, 196.

64. Jostes, XXXIV.

65. In *pure* contemplation "the soul enters the union of the Holy Trinity. It is further blessed by becoming one with the naked [unmanifested] Godhead where the Trinity of God is the Self-determination. In the unmanifested Godhead there is no activity. The soul is not perfectly beautified until it casts itself into the desolate Godhead where neither structure nor activity exists and there in undifferentiation loses itself: as self the soul vanishes and has no more to do with things than it had when it was not" (Pf 241-42).

66. LW IV, 198; v. LW IV, 93; LW I, 232; LW III, 117-19.

67. LW IV, 199.

68. By "modern psychology" we mean to include the as yet quasi-science of ESP, "psychic research" and even all forms of "spiritism" and "psychic-metaphysics" (!) which likewise pertain exclusively to the order of nature and the realm of individual and structural manifestation. They in no sense whatsoever pertain to the truly supernatural, to pure metaphysics or detached intellection, or to what Eckhart understands as Divine Knowledge. It should, however, be acknowledged that the psychological insights of Carl Jung and some of his followers at least keep certain doors open that afford a possibility of transcendence of the purely natural order of manifest individuality and an eminent appreciation of the contemplative state.

69. This includes the phenomena of all "spiritual visions or hearings or feelings clothed in form" (LW IV, 327) and all mystical experiences as such, and explains why Eckhart, in the name of detached intellection, is not essentially interested in them, even though some of these "occurences" may, under certain strict conditions, have validity in their own defined and restricted state. See DW V, 226.

70. DW I, 196-97.

71. DW I, 152; *v. In Genesis II,* n. 80; *In Johannem.* n. 568.

72. DW I, 155; v. RS IX, 5.

73. DW I, 122, 56; v. also LW V, 60; LW II, 213-14.

74. LW IV, 114-15.

75. DW V, 116. And he adds that "all men naturally desire knowledge." Cf. Aristotle, *Metaphysics* 1. *1.*

76. Eckhart uses the term *mensch* which here, as in several other instances, means "self" or "individuality." See Q 272.

77. LW IV, 138.

78. DW V, 116.

79. DW I, 132 ff. Cf. DW V, 112, where Eckhart considers the highest stage of spirituality.

80. LW III, 357.

81. DW V, 289.

82. See Pf 183; LW III, 426. There is here no contradiction of the formal explanation of this revealed "mystery" given by Aquinas when he states that since "the soul lasts forever, so it must be conjoined again with the body," for "it is contrary to the nature of the soul to be without the body." It is not that the same particles of matter that were possessed at the moment of death will be reassumed spiritually in the resurrection, but it can be said formally that the glorified body will have the qualities of "impassibility, clarity, and subtlety" and "whatever belongs to the integrity of the human nature of those who have part in the resurrection will rise again." (*Summa Theologica* III, q80; III *Contra Gentes*, 79). See Spamer, *Eckhart Texte*, B. 2: "Now it is the Christian faith that this actual body will rise at the last day. Then things shall also rise, not as themselves as such but in him who has inverted them into himself."

83. DW V, 400—1; v. V, 114.

84. *Von dem Schauen Gottes*, 484 ff; DWV, 118.

85. Ibid. Note that Eckhart does not say "were I wholly *what* I am," etc., but pointedly "were I wholly *that I* am"; thus, the truth that *whatness* is preceded by *isness* which is in function of knowledge. Thus also indicating: "were I wholly that I *am* [i.e. God who identified himself as 'I am who I am.' I]," etc.

86. DW V, 434—35. It is quite possible that this quotation, which is at the very end of the Tractate *Von Abgescheidenheit* (v. also Pfeiffer's text), actually comes from Eckhart's student Suso.

87. See LW IV, 85—86.

88. Pf 249.

89. LW III, 231; Pf 241—42: "In the unmanifested Godhead there is no action."

90. *Von dem Schauen Gottes*. See LW III, 415.

91. See Aquinas, *Summa Theologiae* I—II, q3.

92. DW V, 116—17.

93. Q 430—31—Pf 15.

94. Q 434—Pf 26.

95. LW III, 477.

96. DW I, 18.

97. Q 434—Pf 26.

98. DW V, 42.

99. (LW III, 34 ff. See DW V, 201, 204—05, 228.

100. Q 273—Pf 181—Strauch, No. 26.

Chapter 6: The Detachment

1. DW III, 230—31.

2. LW IV, 26; cf. IV, 24.

3. LW III, 76; 179.

4. LW II, 65; v. LW III, 186.

5. DW I, 136.

6. LW III, 421.

7. LW III, 130-31. St. Paul's dictum is another example of the necessary "inversion" to which Eckhart has repeatedly referred, for the "mountains" signify the entire order of "otherness" which, when removed by knowledge *in principio* and charity, or divine Love (the Holy Spirit), leaves nothing but the "silent undifferentiated desert."

8. LW IV, 374. "That which one knows to be true" is, of course, the Word, identified as it is in every respect with unmanifested Godhead; and this knowledge is of grace. See LW IV, 378 ff.

9. LW IV, 237.

10. LW III, 396.

11. Eckhart is in full agreement with Aquinas on this point, both maintaining that true moral and intellectual development only occurs when man forms the habit of making demands upon himself, demands instituted by natural law which is a direct reflection of divine authority *(Summa Theologica* I—II, q49, a2).

12. John 16:7 and 28. See DW V, 430—31.

13. LW III, 376. "In the moral sphere the beginning [or principle] of all our intentions and actions must be God [this 'beginning' being the ethical imperative of 'not-self']." "Virtue and everything good depend on good will." "The will is unimpaired and good when it is entirely free from self-seeking, and when it has abandoned itself and is formed and transformed into the will of God." (LW III, 41; DW V, 216, 221).

14. DW I, 305; v. LW IV, 316; DW II, 321—22.

15. LW IV, 170 and 96.

16. LW IV, 186.

17. DW I, 276; LW I, 247.

18. DW I, 168—70.

19. DW I, 193; v. 178.

20. As previously noted, the participation in being is a participation in God, for "the ground of being is isness and isness is God" (see LW I, 38).

21. DW I, 193.

22. Luke 14:26.

23. DW I, 193—94.

24. DW I, 167.

25. DW I, 130: "Being is God's circle, the circle of the Knowledge that he is."

26. DW I, 193—94.

27. DW V, 403, 412; 413—14.

28. See especially *Von Abgescheidenheit* (DW V, 400 ff); *Predigt* 12 (DW I, 192 ff); *Predigt* 52 (DW II, 486 ff).

29. DW II, 523.

30. DW V, 404—10.

31. DW V, 413—22.

32. DW II, 486 ff

33. DW II, 492—94. Cf. V, 195 and 297.

34. DW II, 494—98.

35. LW III, 285.

36. DW II, 488—91.

37. See Suso's defence and clarification of this purely metaphysical truth against would-be "subjectivists" or so-called "Free-Spirits," in Bihl-meyer, p. 354.

38. LW IV, 171, 129.

39. *Summa Theologica I*, q27, a3, ad2.

40. LW IV, 360.

41. LW II, 496.

42. DW V, 423—24.

43. LW IV, 78.

44. DW V, 432.

45. LW IV, 242; v. DW I, *Predigt* nos. 6 and 8. Even the desire for the "great mystical experience" contains an element of self-will. See DW V, 226-27.

46. DW V, 35, 432.

47. *Summa Theologica* I—II, q12, a3; LW IV, 377.

48. DW V, 412—13.

49. DW V, 429; v. LW III, 461.

50. *Confessions* VII, 10, 16; DW I, 110—11 and note 1.

51. LW III, 298.

52. LW III, 304.

53. LW IV, 208.

54. LW I, 163.

55. LW I, 181; LW II, 20.

56. It is important to note here the subtle distinction between "unity" and "unicity"; the latter embraces multiplicity and hence can be referred to as the opposite of complexity, whereas "unity," which is "identity" (LW IV, 269), is the principle of multiplicity and, as previously explained, nothing can stand in opposition to the Principle.

57. DW I, 69-70. See RS IV, 15 and IX, 43.

58. LW V, 50.

59. *Von dem Schauen Gottes*, 488.

60. LW IV, 100; cf. DW II, 67—69.

61. DW III, 447; DW II, 265—66.

62. DW I, 106 and 115.

63. *Von dem Schauen Gottes*, 486—87.

64. LW III, 75 ff.

65. *Von dem Schauen Gottes*, 488; v. LW IV, 371.

66. Pf 106.

67. Aquinas, *De Trinitate*, q4,a1.

68. LW IV, 24.

69. Pf 106—7.

70. Pf 242

71. DW I, 55.

72. DW I, 56; v. LW IV, 28, 110.

73. III *Contra Gentes*, 53.

74. Pf 182; DW I, 13–14 and 298; LW IV, 143 and 315.

75. *Summa Theologica* I, q12, a5.

76. Q 343; DW II, 309; v. DW I, 164 and LW III, 244.

77. DW V, 428.

78. LW IV, 226, 452; LW III, 244; v. LW III, 45 and DW I, 164-65. Also *"Das Verspüren* is not in your power, but only in his, i.e. God's act" (Q 436—Pf 28).

79. DW II, 326.

80. LW IV, 94–95; LW III, 274.

81. DW I, 26 ff; Q 434—Pf 26.

82. LW IV, 97; 235–37, 243, 449.

83. LW IV, 167.

84. *Von dem Schauen Gottes*, 485.

85. DW III, 215–16. See Aquinas, *Commentarium* III *Sententiarum* xxvii, ql, al.

86. Cf. Q 436—Pf 27–28.

87. DW III, 216.

88. DW I, 253; 185.

89. Canticle of Canticles 3:2–4.

90. DW III, 219–25.

91. DW V, 306–8.

92. LW IV, 387.

93. *Summa Theologica* I, q3, a3.

94. *mac unde kan got*.

95. DW III, 339–44.

96. DW I, 90–92.

97. DW III, 266–67.

98. LW III, 295–98.

99. Pf 239.

100. DW II, 107.

101. LW IV, 207.

102. Pf 241; v. LW III, 118–19.

103. LW IV, 45; LW V, 118.

104. Pf 239 ff; DW V, 263–64.

105. LW V, 342; LW IV, 278.

106. DW I, 52.

107. Pf 239.

108. DW II, 416. "Preparation," i.e. "way to the Father."

109. Eckhart does not outline or counsel any particular "method" or "exercise" for attaining contemplation. As to particular means of attaining detachment, such as prayer, fasting, meditation, alms-giving, devotions, penance, etc: "Do not restrict yourself to any particular means, for God is

not in any *one* kind of devotion" (DW I, 82). "Not all men can follow one way" (DW V, 252).

110. That is, those who misunderstand or abuse, for instance, St. Augustine's famous dictum: *Ama Deum, et fac quod vis* ("Love God, and do what you will").

111. DW II, 78—79; v. DW II, 11—12.

112. LW III, 242. See RS IX, 16.

113. LW IV, 60 ff.

114. DW I, 80; V, 30.

115. DW I, 194—95; cf. RS IX, 42.

116. DW I, 274; v. DW III, 193-94 and RS IV, 11.

117. LW III, 425; DW V, 40—42.

118. DW III, 298—301.

119. Q 272—Pf 180—Strauch, No. 26. In other words, and as indicated throughout, the *deneget semetispum* of Mark 8:34 designates far more than an ethical injunction. What these words mean is understood by Eckhart when he says that "the self must completely go" and "the negation of self is, in the same stroke, the negation of all otherness." After all, "the kingdom of God is for none but the totally dead to self (Cf. DW III, 628, 630; LW IV, 179; Pf. 600).

Index

abstraction, 200, 203

accidie, 255n*39*. *See also* awareness, contraction of

action, 82, 239, 244, 256n*69*, 260n*20*

activists, 82, 256n*69*

Adi Da Samraj:

"Divine Ignorance," xii; Jeffrey Kripal on, 2n*246*; Meister Eckhart compared to, xiii; as non-dual Realizer, xii; "positive disillusionment," xvi; "the great path of return," xiii, xv; "the illusion of relatedness," xvi; *The Knee of Listening*, 6n*246*

Alanus de Insules, 28, 260n*15*

Albert the Great, Saint, 27, 29

all-inclusive, the, 52, 109, 117; order of, 78, 93, 96-97, 101-02, 106, 166; and individuality, 88; is God, 91, 179

all-possibility, 31, 52, 142; content of pure knowledge, 47, 110; designated of God, 90, 91, 140, 183, 238; content of unlimited will to know, 100; convertible with the Infinite, 109; beyond distinction, 153, 164; not indetermination, 187

Ambrose, Saint, 29

analogy, 11, 127, 169; knowledge of God by, 46-47, 51, 92; proportionate, 98, 169; of attribution, 169, 170; its term is unity, 172, 267n*22*

—inverse, 117, 118, 127. *See also* inversion

Ancelet-Hustache, Jeanne, xv

angels, 170, 172, 262n*57*, 265n*53*

Anselm, St., 29

apophatic mysticism, xvii, xviii

Aquinas. *See* Thomas Aquinas, Saint

Aristotle, 57, 248n*6*, 265n*33*; E. indebted to, 28; on intellect, 79, 172; on categories, 106; on First Cause, 130; on infinite, 178

Augustine, Saint, 38, 48, 53, 78; influence on E., 28, 29; on knowledge of God, 31; on time and eternity, 32-33, 161; teachings of, 39; on essence, 152; on the Eucharist, 227; Pseudo-Dionysius and, xvii; rejects necessity of creation, 254n*33*; on divine ideas, 262n*66*, 271n*51*; on memory,

270n*10*; on love of God, 277n*110*; spirituality, xiii

Avencebron, 29

Averroes, 29

avicenna, 29, 254n*33*

awakening, 45, 81

awareness, 197, 204; contraction of, 72, 89, 119, 131, 163, 220

beatitude, 210, 212, 214, 230, 272n*65*; of God, 47, 188; and beatific vision, 196; perfects grace, 209

Beghards, 40

Beguins, xiv, xvii

Being, 57, 58, 106, 274n*25*; object of intellect, 56–57; participation in, 58, 274n*20*; God transcends, 106, 117, 173, 174–75, 203; in function of knowledge, 173. *See also* Isness belief, 10, 59. *See also* faith

Bernard of Clairvaux, Saint, 3, 29

body, 194, 221; and soul, 137, 140, 199; glorified, 209, 273n*82*. *See also* corporeality

Boehme, Jakob, xi

Boethius, 28

The Book of the Poor in Spirit by a Friend of God (translated by Kelley), xix

breaking-through, the, xvi

Butler, B. C., 248n*6*

Cajetan (Thomas de Vio), 49, 117

cataphatic mysticism, xvii, xviii

categories, 106

causality, 51, 255n*36* and n*38*, 265n33. *See also* efficacious cause

Christ, 7, 9, 50, 130, 227; God's communication in, 10, 76, 198, 249n*7*; the God-man, 45, 198, 262n*51*; God's Self-revelation, 54; faith in, 76; reveals himself in the soul, 114–15; putting on, 120; indispensable, 128; the Reminder, 131, 132; doctrine of, 165; is Truth, 165; the True Man, 204; following, 224; and truth, 229; death in, 230, 232; and the Church, 240–41, 249n*7*. *See also* Word, the, incarnate

Christianity, 23, 50, 54

279

About North Atlantic Books

North Atlantic Books (NAB) is an independent, nonprofit publisher committed to a bold exploration of the relationships between mind, body, spirit, and nature. Founded in 1974, NAB aims to nurture a holistic view of the arts, sciences, humanities, and healing. To make a donation or to learn more about our books, authors, events, and newsletter, please visit www.northatlanticbooks.com.

North Atlantic Books is the publishing arm of the Society for the Study of Native Arts and Sciences, a 501(c)(3) nonprofit educational organization that promotes cross-cultural perspectives linking scientific, social, and artistic fields. To learn how you can support us, please visit our website.